HOMES AND LIBRARIES OF THE PRESIDENTS

For Donald, Lynne, and Amy

HOMES AND LIBRARIES

OF THE

PRESIDENTS

AN INTERPRETIVE GUIDE
(THIRD EDITION)

by

William G. Clotworthy

The McDonald & Woodward Publishing Company

Blacksburg, Virginia

The McDonald & Woodward Publishing Company
Blacksburg, Virginia, and Granville, Ohio

HOMES AND LIBRARIES OF THE PRESIDENTS: AN INTERPRETIVE GUIDE
(THIRD EDITION)
A McDonald & Woodward Guide to the American Landscape

© 1994, 2003, 2008 by The McDonald & Woodward Publishing Company

Printed in United States of America
by McNaughton & Gunn, Inc., Saline, Michigan

First printing, first edition: May 1995
First printing, second edition: March 2003
First printing, third edition: March 2008

14 13 12 11 10 09 08   10 9 8 7 6 5 4 3 2 1

Library of Congress Cataloging-in-Publication Data

Clotworthy, William G., 1926-
  Homes and libraries of the presidents : an interpretive guide / by William G.
Clotworthy. — 3rd ed.
    p. cm. — (A McDonald & Woodward guide to the American landscape)
  Includes bibliographical references and index.
  ISBN 0-939923-34-3 (alk. paper)
    1. Presidents—United States—Homes and haunts—Guidebooks. 2. Presi-
dents—United States—Museums—Guidebooks. 3. Presidential libraries—
United States—Guidebooks. 4. Presidents—United States—Biography. 5.
United States—Guidebooks. I. Title.
  E176.1.C66 2007
  973.099—dc22

                                                    2007027033

Contents

Contents

Contents

Section III
Additional Information about Presidential Sites

Ann Pamela Cunningham
(Photograph courtesy Mount Vernon Ladies' Association)

Dedication

This book is dedicated to Miss Ann Pamela Cunningham (1816–1875), founder and first Regent of the Mount Vernon Ladies' Association. Her vision, tireless effort, and personal dedication inspired thousands of private citizens to organize and contribute to the purchase, restoration, renovation, and maintenance of homes and other places associated with America's great leaders, thereby preserving forever an important part of our national heritage.

Preface

In 1991, I retired from NBC-TV after an exciting forty-two-year career in broadcasting and advertising, but I was unprepared for inactivity. I tried freelance writing and almost immediately sold two magazine articles based on my experiences in the television industry. At about the same time, mudslinging between two political candidates piqued my interest to the extent that I prepared an article on presidential campaign insults. That article did not sell, but while doing the research for it, I became interested in a slightly higher level of presidential history and compiled a little directory of presidents and sites that commemorate them. I proposed this piece of work to a number of history and travel publishers. The single positive reply came from McDonald & Woodward — but they were not interested in the directory. They wanted a real book! *That* was a daunting prospect. In high school and college, I'd had a passing interest in American history (that is to say, I was interested in *passing* American history), but I was hardly a serious student. I'd had trouble writing the second page of a book report and was now faced with the prospect of writing a volume of nearly four hundred pages.

But I began, not without trepidation, a venture that has since taken over much of my life. Early on, I found myself spending great amounts of time not only in the library, but also on the road — visiting the nearly one hundred sites that I described in the first edition of *Homes and Libraries of the Presidents*. That book, which emphasized the residences of presidents, museums devoted to specific presidents, and libraries that housed their official papers — the *crème de la crème* of presidential sites — was published in 1995. The list of presidential sites, however, kept expanding, and so did ideas about what to do with this list. Forging ahead with my newfound calling, I produced a second edition of *Homes and Libraries of the Presidents* (2003) and two other books on the subject.

Presidential Sites: A Directory of Places associated with Presidents of the United States (1998) is an annotated compilation of more than one thousand extant places that are related to our presidents. *In the Footsteps of George Washington: A Guide to Sites Commemorating Our First President* (2002) identifies and describes more than three hundred sites associated with that unique Virginian who figured so prominently in our transition from a collection of British colonies to a sovereign state.

Almost fifteen years have passed since I started my quest to locate and experience the places that shaped, and that commemorate, our American presidents. We have a different president now and soon will have another; additional homes, libraries, and museums of presidents have been opened to the public; and significant changes have occurred at many of the older sites. In this third edition of *Homes and Libraries of the Presidents*, I have added several sites that have opened to the public since the second edition was published, including President Lincoln's Cottage at the Soldiers' Home in Washington, DC; Theodore Roosevelt's cabin retreat, called Pine Knot, in Keene, Virginia; the Ronald Reagan Museum at Eureka College in Eureka, Illinois; the Clinton House Museum in Fayetteville, Arkansas; and the George W. Bush Childhood Home in Midland, Texas. Of particular importance, however, are the Abraham Lincoln Presidential Library and Museum in Springfield, Illinois, and The Clinton Presidential Center in Little Rock, Arkansas — both of which have opened to great acclaim during the past few years. And, continuing the tradition, as this book goes to press we have learned that the George W. Bush Presidential Library will be located at SMU in Dallas, Texas, with the prospect of being opened to the public in about five years.

Additional changes have been made, or are being made, at other sites. In 2006, Mount Vernon dedicated the Ford Orientation Center and the Donald W. Reynolds Museum and Education Center that promise to add a new dimension to that already important historic facility by utilizing new technology to provide insight into the personal life of George Washington. James Madison's Montpelier has undertaken a dramatic historic restoration project by stripping away the additions and modifications made to Montpelier over several decades in order to present the mansion as it actually appeared during the Madison residency. President Wilson's Boyhood Home in Columbia, South Carolina, began, in 2006, a three-year restoration and improvement program. The Saxton McKinley

House in Canton, Ohio, has been converted to the headquarters and showcase of the National First Ladies' Library which has developed an online library of the first ladies who, in addition to their own histories, often have been particularly important if sometimes overlooked collaborators in American presidential history. Other facilities continue to upgrade their physical plants, add to their museum collections, and otherwise improve their ability to entertain and edify the visiting public.

In particular, new themes and new technologies are emerging in the interpretive programs at both older and newer sites as presidential history, and the presidency itself, assumes a more prominent role in popular culture. Contributing to this growing popular interest has been the increasing accessibility of recent presidents, especially Bill Clinton and George H. W. Bush, and the increasing presence of presidential history and historians in the popular media. C-Span produced a marvelous series on presidential homes in which their cameras visited the sites and interviews were conducted with knowledgeable park rangers, curators, and others. The History Channel televised a number of biographical programs on the presidents and the public hunger for presidential history has resulted in the publication and success of major books by eminent historians. David McCullough's *Truman*, *John Adams,* and *1776* have become best sellers, as did *Team of Rivals: The Political Genius of Abraham Lincoln* by Doris Kearns Goodwin. Ulysses S. Grant, Lyndon B. Johnson, Ronald Reagan, Thomas Jefferson, and others continue to be fertile subjects for the biographer.

In my view, the most important change in the social fabric of our nation which partly piqued our interest in presidents is the internet. Abundant bits of useful, and sometimes not so useful, information are easily available online and this has led to increased interest in our nation's history and, thus, its presidents. There are many web sites devoted to presidents and each of the homes in this book has information available through a web site. Many sites also provide virtual tours online, enabling web site visitors to explore the interior of the home without leaving their own. Reading and absorbing the information on the web sites and in books enhances and deepens one's understanding of, and appreciation for, the forty-two men who have led our nation to its preeminence in the world — yet the experience of actually visiting one or more of the sites that commemorate these men cannot be equaled by the use of internet resources and readers are urged to visit these sites in person. I know that I get a thrill each time I visit a presidential site and realize, for example, that I am in a log cabin birthplace of a man who became President of the United States; that I am standing where George Washington lived or fought or governed; that I am where Abraham Lincoln studied or where he wrote the Emancipation Proclamation; that I am admiring the place where Franklin Roosevelt grew to manhood or where he traveled to seek relief from the agony of polio. These are emotional feelings not available on the internet or television or found in a book. They are to be experienced and enjoyed only on the spot.

Another striking change over the past decade is the improvement in on-site and often hands-on educational programs for all age groups, programs that range from biographical displays to archealogical and environmental studies. All of the National Park Service sites and most of the other major presidential facilities increasingly cooperate with local and regional schools and colleges to provide such programs.

Unchanged through all of this, however, is my respect for, and appreciation of, the forty-two distinguished Americans that this book honors and whose haunts and legacies I have been privileged to search out and explore. Likewise, I hope that this book may assist many of you to find and experience places that celebrate our American presidents.

During the period of time that I have studied presidential sites, I have had many wonderful experiences while visiting these locations. The host personnel, whether park rangers, museum curators, teenaged volunteers, or senior-citizen docents, are friendly, knowledgeable, and anxious to enhance every visitor's enjoyment of their facilities. Dedicated to the preservation and maintenance of presidential homes and related sites, these sometimes unrecognized and unappreciated legions are, in effect, protecting and perpetuating the legacies associated with the properties they maintain, study, and interpret. It has been my privilege to meet and benefit from these fine stewards of our history, and I thank and salute them.

My thanks also goes to those who have been of direct assistance in the preparation of this book — the publisher Jerry McDonald, whose vision and gentle (and sometimes not-so-gentle) prodding made the experience pleasurable and whose continued friendship is so important to me; Kathie Dickenson, editor of the first edition, and Judy Moore, editor of the second edition (the foundation upon which this third edition is based), whose valiant attempts to turn an organizer into a writer have almost succeeded; Karl Decker, the king of punctuation; and Tina Stoll, gallant interpreter of scribbles and scrawls, secretary *par excellence*.

Several individuals and organizations generously provided photographs for use in this book. The photograph of the Jimmy Carter Library and Museum on the front cover was provided by The Carter Center. The color plates, identified by plate number and location on the page, are used through the courtesy of, and are credited to, the following: 1 top: Mount Vernon Ladies' Association; 1 bottom: National Park Service; 2: Thomas Jefferson's Poplar Forest, Les Schofer, photographer; 3 top: Montpelier Foundation; 3 middle: Philip Beaurline, Ash Lawn-Highland; 3 bottom: Ladies' Hermitage Association; 4 top: New York State Department of Economic Development; 4 middle: Berkeley Plantation; 4 bottom: Bradley Olmar, Sherwood Forest; 5 top: James K. Polk Ancestral Home; 5 middle: Rix Jennings, Fillmore House Museum; 5 bottom: William G. Clotworthy; 6 top: James Buchanan Foundation; 6 middle: Mordecai Historic Park; 6 bottom: William G. Clotworthy; 7 top: National Park Service; 7 middle: Rutherford B. Hayes Presidential Center; 7 bottom: Ted Podolak, James A. Garfield National Historic Site; 8 top: Vermont Division for Historic Preservation; 8 middle: New Jersey Department of Environmental Protection; 8 bottom: President Benjamin Harrison Home; 9 top: McKinley Memorial Library; 9 middle: National Park Service; 9 bottom: William Howard Taft National Historic Site; 10 top: Woodrow Wilson House Museum, National Trust for Historic Preservation; 10 middle: President Harding's Home; 10 bottom: Vermont Division for Historic Preservation, President Calvin Coolidge State Historic Site; 11 top: Herbert Hoover Presidential Library and Museum; 11 bottom: Roosevelt Campobello International Park Commission; 12 top: National Park Service; 12 bottom: Richard Frear, National Park Service; 13 top: National Park Service; 13 middle: Jerry N. McDonald; 13 bottom: Richard Nixon Presidential Library and Museum; 14 top: Gerald R. Ford Presidential Museum; 14 bottom: The Carter Center; 15 top: William G. Clotworthy; 15 bottom: Brian Blake, George Bush Presidential Library and Museum; 16 top: William J. Clinton Foundation; 16 bottom: George W. Bush Childhood Home. Credits for black-and-white images are given as parts of the captions for those images.

Scope and Purpose

Homes and Libraries of the Presidents is primarily a traveler's guide to almost one hundred presidential homes, libraries, and museums in the United States — and one in Canada — that are open to the public. As such, it is designed to assist visitors to experience and appreciate the many places important to our history and national heritage by providing basic information about the sites' historical significance and interpretive facilities, as well as about access, admission fees, dining facilities, tours, web sites, and facilities for the disabled. Easy-to-read maps have been provided to show the location of the various sites.

The book also attempts to put each presidential life and home into personal and historical context — the colonial gentry lifestyle of Thomas Jefferson at Monticello; the hardscrabble farm life of Abraham Lincoln; the all-American, small-town background of Ronald Reagan — by describing not only the places and the era in which these presidents lived, but their families, communities and education, the fundamental environments, and experiences that helped to shape the forty-two men who have become President of the United States. Thus the book is intended to open windows onto the deeper understanding of the accomplished but different men who have led our nation through more than two centuries to its position of leadership in today's world.

The book is divided into three sections. Section I presents an overview of the historical significance of presidential homes, libraries, and museums; it delineates the history of restoration and preservation efforts directed toward presidential homes and other related structures, and it eulogizes the singular woman who, in the mid-nineteenth century, organized the first great restoration of a president's home, George Washington's Mount Vernon. This section further pays tribute to the local, state, and national historic preservation organizations that have resurrected, restored, reconstructed, or replicated the many presidential buildings and that continue to maintain these

American treasures, efforts that enable us to visit, observe, learn, and honor the distinguished Americans who have lived in them. The first section also traces the role of the federal government, carried out by the National Park Service and the National Archives and Records Administration, in administering and maintaining humble cabins, splendid mansions, ordinary houses, and great modern libraries.

Section II contains a short anecdotal biography of each president, followed by a description of the home, museum, or library with which he is associated; a map showing the location of the site; visitor information; and sources of additional information.

Section III provides brief information about other sites associated with presidents and sources of additional information about the lives, homes, museums, libraries, and other aspects of presidential history. Included in this section are lists of presidential birthplaces, burial sites, and selected historical societies, along with a bibliography of recommended readings dealing with the presidents and structures that commemorate them.

While every effort has been made to ensure the accuracy of the information in the book, visiting hours, phone numbers, admission fees, and facilities for the disabled are subject to change. When planning a visit to any of the sites identified in this book, it would be prudent to call or write the facility, or consult its web site, in advance to obtain the most up-to-date information.

∽

This book is not a text on architecture. Nevertheless, there are references to eras and styles of architecture that should be defined, if only to identify some of the basic design elements of architectural styles and to delineate time frames of architectural popularity.

The earliest American homes, those dating from about 1625 to 1700, are called Colonial. Utilitarian in design, their construction was influenced by weather conditions, availability of building material and familiarity with construction methods rather than by artistry. The materials and geometric details of Colonial structures varied from region to region. New England Colonial homes, for example, were characterized by a box-like look — two stories of small rooms built around a central chimney, tiny casement windows, a steeply pitched roof, and an exterior siding of clapboard or shingles. In the Virginia Colony, Colonial more often describes brick houses of a story or story and a half, with two end chimneys and a sloped roof. The southern houses usually featured more extensive decorative touches than the northern houses.

The eighteenth century brought the Georgian style of domestic architecture from England. This style was named for the four kings George who ruled from 1714 to 1830. At that time, England was becoming urbanized, and its architecture was beginning to reflect a balanced view of life, with the accent on towns and neighborhoods. Georgian styling was marked by symmetry in both the interior floor plan and the exterior façade, a gabled roof, and a central chimney. The period was noteworthy, too, for the introduction of landscape gardening as part of overall home design, its purpose being to display the house and grounds in aesthetic harmony. The Georgian style was in no small measure influenced by the Palladian style, a product of the sixteenth-century Italian designer Andrea Palladio, who recognized connections between nature and architecture and consequently linked his buildings with the countryside.

In the latter part of the eighteenth century, Thomas Jefferson returned from a European diplomatic assignment and brought back ideas about neo-classic building designs influenced by the architecture of ancient Greece and Rome. The style was free, open, columned, and symmetrical; the columns were not merely decorative, but intrinsic to the geometry of the design and the practicality of construction.

At the same time, America was beginning to develop its own unique style of domestic architecture that came to be called Federal, in honor of the newly federated republic. The Federal style paralleled the Georgian but used more delicate classical elements to define entrances and practical gambrel roofs with dormer windows to minimize heat loss. The style was sometimes called Adam Federal, after the brothers Adam, Scottish-English architects known in the United States primarily for elements of interior design — low-relief plaster decorations on ceilings, elaborate door trim, decorated cornices, and slender end chimneys.

Other styles followed, including Greek Revival (ca. 1825–1860), which combined Greek and Roman forms of low-pitched pediments, simple moldings, rounded arches, and shallow domes; Gothic Revival (ca. 1830–1880) that borrowed ideas from castles and vaulted churches in the use of arched windows and expensive carved woodwork; Italianate (ca. 1840–1880), characterized by multiple stories, a low-pitched roof, cupolas, towers, decorative window treatments, and narrow doors; and Folk Victorian, with an overall simplicity of form and decorative treatment in porch and gable trim.

A few other terms that appear throughout the text may seem interchangeable, but they in fact have important differentiating nuances of meaning:

Restoration, according to decorating expert Martha Stewart, means "putting things back the way they were," not to be confused with *renovation,* or "making something new again. . . . Making an old house more livable for today," as when indoor plumbing or air conditioning is added. *Replication* is copying or reproducing, as when a house that has been destroyed by fire or time, is rebuilt. *Redecorate,* according to language maven William Safire, means to "redo the style of interior furnishings, lying somewhere between the old-fashioned *refurbish* and *spruce up.*"

Section I

Preserving Presidential Sites

An Introduction to the Preservation of Presidential Sites

History is but the prologue to the future.

— John F. Kennedy

All too often the study of history, which most of us recall from high school, leaves in our minds a mixture of dates and events; we really learn little about people. Yet George Washington, John Adams, Thomas Jefferson, and the presidents who followed were people with emotions, aspirations, experiences, strengths, frailties, foibles, and problems not unlike those with which the rest of us live every day.

Those high school textbooks may have recounted accomplishments of our presidents in the halls of congress, on the battlefield, or in the White House, but visits to their homes may help us complete a picture of the whole man, for they, just like the rest of us, experienced disappointment and satisfaction, economic hardship and success, tragedy, and joy.

Some of the houses in which our presidents once lived have been razed, some have been destroyed by fire, and others continue to serve as private residences (figures 1 and 2). Many, however, have been preserved or restored as places of historical significance and opened to public visitation. The houses and other buildings that commemorate past presidents are numerous and diverse.

Some of these structures, such as Washington's Mount Vernon, have been restored to their former grandeur. Others, such as Coolidge's Plymouth Notch, are maintained in their original simplicity. Some are rough log cabins while others are imposing mansions filled with priceless antiques and fine furniture. There are estates designed and built by the owners, and there are ordinary houses bequeathed by parents or in-laws. Some are on farms, and others are in large cities. Some reflect inherited wealth whereas others reflect occupancy by members of the working middle class, but all display

Figure 1. The birthplace of James Monroe, in Westmoreland County, Virginia, is representative of the many buildings affiliated with American presidents that have been lost. Figure courtesy of James Monroe Museum.

something of the personality of the men and their families who lived in them. The dignified Monticello, reflecting the genius of Thomas Jefferson, and the simple one-room cabin where Abraham Lincoln lived and studied, represent extremes. Both, perhaps, touch us deeply, but do so in profoundly different ways.

As we walk about Sagamore Hill, we may still sense the joy of Teddy Roosevelt romping with his children over its spacious grounds. But we might feel a different emotion as we visit the tiny tailor shop where Andrew Johnson toiled with needle and thread while his wife or local men sat with him all day long, teaching the poorly educated young man to read and write.

Summer twilight in Canton, Ohio, would find William McKinley on the porch of his modest frame home, relaxing with an after-dinner cigar. Smoking indoors would bother his invalid wife, a courageous lady he tended with life-long solicitude. And as we stand on the verandah of The Hermitage, set amidst the fragrant pines of Tennessee, we may visualize tough "Old Hickory," Andrew Jackson, with his beloved wife Rachel, rocking in their chairs and puffing on their pipes as they shared a rare and tender moment, far from the cares of the day.

Figure 2. Greenway, birthplace of John Tyler, at Charles City, Virginia, is representative of those buildings affiliated with American presidents that are privately owned and not open for public visitation. Photograph courtesy of Virginia Department of Historic Resources.

The ramps built at Hyde Park to accommodate Franklin Roosevelt's wheelchair are poignant reminders that, while some men became president by overcoming disadvantages of birth, poverty, or educational opportunity, Roosevelt adjusted to a severe physical disability in the process of becoming one of the greatest leaders this nation and the world have ever known.

America's heritage is embodied in the forty-two men who have served as chief executive, but who came from different places and diverse backgrounds. Each of these leaders gave part of himself to our national character. Each added to the strength of our constitutional system. A search for patterns in why or how they accomplished this reveals none, for these men represent the diversity of thought and political principle that has propelled our nation forward and made our form of government the envy of nations around the world.

The places from whence these men came must remain as they were, for to know them is to know ourselves. "After all," said John Kennedy, "history is people, and particularly, in great periods of history, presidents." Fortunately, we have come to realize the importance not only of preserving presidential homes but also of preserving presidential history by building presidential libraries — sometimes while a president is still in office — and stocking them with historical displays, gifts, souvenirs, mementos, and millions of important, as well as sometimes trivial, papers and documents. It was not always so.

Mount Vernon, the first of our historic presidential homes to be preserved, remained in the Washington family for many years after President Washington's death in 1799. By the mid-1800s, however, it had fallen into decline and become agriculturally unproductive and dangerously close to bankruptcy. The owner, John Augustine Washington, Jr., appealed to the federal government and the Commonwealth of Virginia, but neither was interested in assuming responsibility for the property.

An unlikely savior appeared in the person of Miss Ann Pamela Cunningham of South Carolina. As a girl, she had been injured in a fall from a horse, and the accident caused a painful and debilitating spinal injury. In constant pain and discomfort, she spent most of her time in South Carolina reading and resting. She did make frequent trips to Philadelphia for treatment from a specialist who provided relief, but not a cure.

One day in 1853, her mother left the semi-invalid Ann Pamela in Philadelphia and returned to Charleston by boat, a journey that took Mrs. Cunningham down the Potomac River past the forlorn and dilapidated Mount Vernon. In a now-historic letter, she wrote to her daughter:

> *I was painfully distressed at the ruin and desolation of the home of Washington, and the thought passed through my mind; why was it that the women of his country did not try to keep it in repair, if the men could not do it? It does seem such a blot on our country!*

Her mother's rhetorical question ignited a spark in the frail young woman lying in a rented room in Philadelphia. Surely, she reasoned, this was an urgent, important, and — yes — noble cause in which she could lead the women of America. This, she felt, was her destiny.

From the perspective of today's age of instant communication, it is difficult to grasp the enormity of the task facing Miss Cunningham, whose only tools were her pen and a fervent dedication to the cause of preserving the home, memory, and heritage of George Washington. After many years of emotional struggle, physical hardship, political manipulation (at a time when women didn't have suffrage), fundraising, ingenious organization, and gentle (and not-so-gentle) persuasion, her goal was attained. In 1860, on the very eve of the Civil War, the Mount Vernon Ladies' Association, which she had organized, took possession of Mount Vernon.

Many trials lay ahead. Efforts to raise funds to finance badly needed repairs continued. Mount Vernon was threatened physically because it lay in a no-man's-land between the opposing forces of the North and South. With communications disrupted by the war, the leading figures of the Ladies' Association were frustrated in their attempts to communicate with one another. It was not until 1866, thirteen years after the idea was originally suggested, that the first meeting of the Association took place at Mount Vernon. Miss Cunningham announced the group's final success:

> *Ladies of the Mount Vernon Association, it is with feelings whose particular depth and intensity I must fail to clothe in fitting words, that I greet you, sister guardians, on this proud, long-hoped-for day. Looking back from our present assured stand-point of an accomplished fact, my memory cannot fail to recall the early vicissitudes, the oft-discouraging progress of our labor of love, in redeeming from oblivion and sure decay the home and the grave of the immortal Washington! Then we lived on hope! We would not yield to despair! Now we rejoice, with intense satisfaction, to know that Mount Vernon is ours . . . the Nation's! And well may I feel almost overpowered to find myself, at this moment, in the midst of ladies representing the varied sections of our country, pledged to guard that sacred spot forever!*

She was the instigator, but Miss Cunningham had not worked alone. Ordinary citizens, women from every state, and sympathetic politicians had contributed time, money, effort, and influence. The most dramatic contribution may have been that of Miss Cunningham's secretary, Sarah Tracy, and Upton Herbert, Mount Vernon's first superintendent. Attended by a chaperone — this was 1861, after all — they resided at Mount Vernon throughout the four years of the Civil War. Always at the mercy of the surrounding military forces and often cut off from food supplies, they protected the ramshackle estate from man and nature.

The most active and successful fundraiser was a retired minister and college president, Reverend Edward Everett. Everett was well-known for his oratorical prolixity and, in particular, for a two-hour discourse on the life of Washington in which he dwelt on the need for national unity — certainly a pertinent issue during that troublesome time. Everett became interested in Miss Cunningham's crusade and delivered his speech all over the country, contributing all gate receipts to the Mount Vernon cause.

Without Everett's unique contribution and attendant publicity, the restoration effort might not have succeeded; thus, Edward Everett stands tall in the annals of the Mount Vernon Ladies' Association. Ironically, Everett is not remembered for his work on behalf of Mount Vernon, but for the long-winded two-hour speech he delivered at the dedication of the Gettysburg National Cemetery that preceded Abraham Lincoln's famous address.

The Mount Vernon Ladies' Association was the first national historic preservation society and still functions as the caring guardian-owner of America's most cherished historic home. The association's stewardship and activities in education, archaeology, and expansion have continued for more than a century and served as models for other preservation organizations that followed its inspiring example of enlightened volunteerism.

The charter of the Mount Vernon Ladies' Association includes old-fashioned yet simple and fervent words articulating its objectives — words paraphrased by charters of groups managing presidential homes everywhere:

> *To perpetuate the sacred memory of "The Father of His Country" and, with loving hands, to guard and protect the hallowed spot where rest his mortal remains. To forever hold, manage and preserve the estate, properties and relics at Mount Vernon, belonging to the Association, and, under proper regulations, to open the same to the inspection of all who love the cause of liberty and revere the name of George Washington.*

Many similar nonprofit historical organizations have been formed since 1858, initiated by hometown or home state friends and political constituents of the presidents. Like the Mount Vernon Ladies' Association, they have raised money, bought properties, collected artifacts, and refurbished or reconstructed buildings appropriate to the period of the presidential occupancy. Many continue to maintain and administer their facilities under state charters as educational foundations staffed by dedicated volunteers. All of the organizations, indeed all of us, owe a debt of gratitude to Ann Pamela Cunningham and the Mount Vernon Ladies' Association for their decades of responsible, practical, and inspirational leadership.

Prominent among historical organizations is the National Trust for Historic Preservation, a nonprofit organization chartered by congress in 1949 and now consisting of more than 250,000 members. The mission of the organization is to:

> *Encourage preservation of significant American buildings . .*
> *. . As a leader of the national preservation movement, it is committed to saving America's diverse historic environments and to preserving and revitalizing the livability of communities nationwide.*

The National Trust works with over two thousand local historic preservation organizations throughout the country and directly owns or operates twenty-six house museums, including four presidential sites described in this book — Montpelier (Madison), Decatur House (Van Buren), President Lincoln's Cottage, and the Woodrow Wilson House Museum.

Some preservation societies have chosen to present presidential homes to the federal government for maintenance, and others have been donated to the government in the form of family bequests. Once accepted by the government, the homes are placed under the aegis of the National Park Service, which currently serves as administrator of more than twenty presidential birthplaces or homes in the United States.

The National Park Service was conceived and authorized by congress in 1916, its mandate being to administer the parks, monuments, and other preserves under the jurisdiction of the Department of the Interior. In 1933, a number of facilities managed by the Forest Service and the War Department were transferred to the Park Service, a significant step forward in the development of the coordinated system that currently is responsible for the management of more than 350 natural, scenic, scientific, and historical places.

We may think of the National Park Service primarily as the overseer of the great national parks — such as Yellowstone, Grand Canyon, or Sequoia — but over half of the sites maintained by the park service are associated with events and activities important to the nation's history. These sites range from archaeological finds associated with prehistoric Indians to houses and museums memorializing individual Americans who have made significant contributions to our society.

Figure 3. The Franklin D. Roosevelt Library in Hyde Park, New York. Opened to the public in 1941, this was the first structure built specifically to house the personal papers and related materials of an American president. Figure courtesy of The Franklin D. Roosevelt Library; Daisy DePuthod, artist.

On December 10, 1938, President Franklin D. Roosevelt announced plans for an institution that would preserve his presidential papers and other historical materials related to his life and presidency. He proposed that a building, to be financed by private subscription, be erected on land donated from Roosevelt's Hyde Park estate. When completed, the project would be turned over to the National Archives to be maintained and administered at government expense. A joint resolution of congress formalized the plan and President and Mrs. Roosevelt deeded sixteen acres to the United States. The cornerstone of the Franklin D. Roosevelt Library was laid on November 19, 1939. On July 4, 1940, the government accepted the completed building (Figure 3). Since that time, the trend has been to follow Roosevelt's example by building presidential libraries and museums with private funds, then transferring the property to the American people, often with the still-living president in attendance at the dedication. The facilities usually consist of separate library and museum divisions, although both units may be under the same roof.

Presidential libraries are not public libraries in the traditional sense. Each is an archive of the valuable documents of an individual presidency.

Each administration creates and receives millions of pages of documents, including, in recent years, digital documents. Before the material placed in presidential libraries can be made available to the public, it must be reviewed and approved for access by an archivist working under the provisions of the Presidential Records Act of 1978. One part of this act distinguishes between presidential records, which are the property of the federal government, and presidential papers (personal records), which are the property of the president.

The National Archives and Records Administration, Office of Presidential Libraries, currently supervises the presidential libraries of presidents Hoover, Roosevelt, Truman, Eisenhower, Kennedy, Johnson, Nixon, Ford, Carter, Reagan, Bush, and Clinton. While use of the libraries is normally reserved for scholars, the museum sections, which are open to the public, chronicle the life, times, and contributions of the respective presidents through a variety of exhibits.

It is not surprising that our first five presidents were active in the War for Independence and founding of the nation. Even the sixth, John Quincy Adams, when he was just a boy, was reported to have witnessed the Battle of Bunker Hill from another hill near the back of his home. Six of the first ten presidents were manor-born Virginians, members of what was called the planter aristocracy. Their estates, still in existence, are reminders of the vast plantations and tobacco farms whose products were so important to the financial well-being and vitality of the Virginia Colony and the fledgling nation.

Several of the manor houses of these Virginia-born leaders are on the shores of the James and Potomac rivers, upon whose banks were shipping terminals essential to trade with England and the rest of the world. The farmers and planters who cultivated these vast acres were mostly descendants of English settlers who brought to the colonies not only their agricultural skills but an inherited sense of responsibility for public service — an implied duty to their fellow citizens.

Roaming the halls and rooms of the mansions, standing on the docks overlooking the mighty rivers or wandering the fields and woods, it is easy for us to conjure up thoughts of the hard work, dedication, and tenacity of our ancestors as they cleared forests and developed the land into rich farms and lush plantations. Perhaps, also, we can better understand their desire to enjoy the fruits of their new life without arbitrary direction and taxation being impressed upon them by an unresponsive government far across the sea.

A visit to Mount Vernon's slave graveyard or Monticello's slave quarters, however, reminds us of another side of life on the elegant estates. The success of many plantations was due, in great measure, to the efforts of slave labor. Washington, Jefferson, and many of their contemporaries were landowners whose products and profits depended on the enslavement of others. Slavery in the early days of our republic was legal until the sixteenth president, a man born in a log cabin, wrote and signed the Emancipation Proclamation in the midst of a bloody civil war. A century later, another president, himself born on a hardscrabble Texas farm, would sign into law the most comprehensive civil rights legislation since Lincoln's time.

There has been progress in our two hundred years of existence, from slavery to civil rights; from horseback to jet planes; from outhouses to indoor plumbing; from dispatch riders to television news; from periwigs to hair transplants. It's a long way from Andrew Jackson's duels in defense of his wife's honor to Harry Truman's letter to a music critic who dared write a negative review of daughter Margaret's Washington singing debut.

Progress also has meant expansion of our borders, and with expansion and time have come increased population and diversity. Six of the presidents who followed the Virginians were born in log cabins. They were poorly educated, but possessed native intelligence and ambition. All of them were imbued with the principle of hard work and held a strong belief in goodness and opportunity.

The log cabin in which Andrew Jackson, the first "western" president, was born, has been lost. His first farm home (Figure 4) stands as part of today's Hermitage estate near Nashville, Tennessee. His later residence, The Hermitage mansion, has been restored to its original beauty. Jackson's journey, from log cabin to the White House and back to The Hermitage as his final resting place, is but one shining example of the American dream coming full circle. When we visit the places identified in this book (Figure 5), then, we will be inspecting the presidents from the perspective of their origins, their homes, their most intimate environments; and perhaps we shall discover a different person from the one we came to know from the history books.

A. Cranston Jones, in his book, *Homes of the American Presidents*, has written:

> *These homes are a historic bequest providing us with an eloquent link to the past . . . . It was in homes very much like these across the nation that men and women met to discuss the issues of*

the day. This grass-roots fact the Presidents bore in mind as they mapped their political strategy. And it was to these front porches that their cheering fellow citizens came in torchlight procession with bands playing to hail the victor, or, more quietly, to console the loser. As such, these Presidents' homes have all known the limelight of history. For us today they can also be beacons, guiding us to the hearthstone of our great national heritage, quickening our awareness of the great personalities of the past, and vividly recreating our own history.

Figure 4. Andrew Jackson's first Hermitage home, the two-story log farmhouse, was converted into a one-story slave cabin in the early 1820s after the brick Hermitage mansion was built. It and adjacent slave-cabin/ kitchen buildings have been restored to the slave-cabin period and contain exhibits and interpretive panels. Photograph courtesy of The Ladies' Hermitage Association.

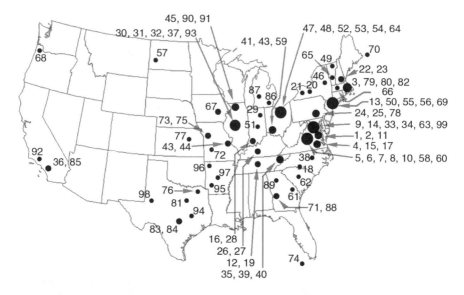

Figure 5. The distribution of homes, libraries, and museums commemorating presidents of the United States that are described in this book. The sites identified by numbers on the map are listed in Table 1.

Table 1: Homes, libraries, and museums of the presidents described in this book.

1. George Washington Birthplace National Monument
2. Mount Vernon
3. Adams National Historical Park
4. Tuckahoe Plantation
5. Monticello
6. Poplar Forest
7. Montpelier
8. James Madison Museum
9. The Octagon Museum
10. Ash Lawn-Highland
11. James Monroe Museum and Memorial Library
12. The Hermitage

13. Martin Van Buren National Historic Site
14. Decatur House
15. Berkeley Plantation
16. Grouseland
17. Sherwood Forest Plantation
18. President James K. Polk State Historic Site
19. James K. Polk Ancestral Home
20. Millard Fillmore Log Cabin
21. Fillmore House Museum
22. Franklin Pierce Homestead
23. The Pierce Manse
24. Buchanan Historic Site

(continued on next page)

Table 1 (continued)

25. Wheatland
26. Abraham Lincoln Birthplace National Historic Site
27. The Lincoln Museum (Hodgenville, Kentucky)
28. Lincoln Boyhood National Memorial
29. The Lincoln Museum (Fort Wayne, Indiana)
30. Lincoln's New Salem State Historic Site
31. Lincoln Home National Historic Site
32. Lincoln College Museum
33. President Lincoln's Cottage at the Soldiers' Home
34. Ford's Theatre National Historic Site
35. The Abraham Lincoln Library and Museum
36. Lincoln Memorial Shrine
37. Abraham Lincoln Presidential Library and Museum
38. Andrew Johnson Birthplace
39. Andrew Johnson National Historic Site
40. President Andrew Johnson Museum and Library
41. Grant Birthplace
42. U. S. Grant Boyhood Home
43. Ulysses S. Grant National Historic Site
44. Grants Farm
45. Ulysses S. Grant Home State Historic Site
46. Grant Cottage State Historic Site
47. Rutherford B. Hayes Presidential Center
48. James A. Garfield National Historic Site
49. President Chester A. Arthur Historic Site
50. Grover Cleveland Birthplace
51. President Benjamin Harrison Home
52. Saxton McKinley House
53. Wm. McKinley Presidential Library and Museum
54. McKinley Memorial Library, Museum, and Birthplace Home
55. Theodore Roosevelt Birthplace National Historic Site
56. Sagamore Hill National Historic Site
57. Maltese Cross Cabin
58. Pine Knot
59. William Howard Taft National Historic Site
60. Woodrow Wilson Presidential Library
61. Boyhood Home of President Woodrow Wilson (Augusta, Georgia)
62. Woodrow Wilson Family Home (Columbia, South Carolina)
63. Woodrow Wilson House Museum
64. President Harding's Home
65. President Calvin Coolidge State Historic Site
66. Calvin Coolidge Presidential Library and Museum
67. Herbert Hoover National Historic Site and Herbert Hoover Presidential Library and Museum
68. Hoover-Minthorn House

(continued on next page)

Table 1 (continued)

69. Home of Franklin D. Roosevelt National Historic Site and Franklin D. Roosevelt Presidential Library and Museum

70. Roosevelt Campobello International Park

71. FDR's Little White House

72. Harry S Truman Birthplace State Historic Site

73. Harry S. Truman National Historic Site

74. Harry S. Truman Little White House Museum

75. Truman Presidential Museum and Library

76. Eisenhower Birthplace State Historic Site

77. The Eisenhower Presidential Center

78. Eisenhower National Historic Site

79. John Fitzgerald Kennedy National Historic Site

80. The John F. Kennedy Hyannis Museum

81. The Sixth Floor Museum at Dealey Plaza

82. John F. Kennedy Presidential Library and Museum

83. Lyndon B. Johnson National Historical Park and Lyndon B. Johnson State Park and Historic Site

84. Lyndon B. Johnson Library and Museum

85. The Richard Nixon Presidential Library and Museum

86. Gerald R. Ford Library

87. Gerald R. Ford Presidential Museum

88. Jimmy Carter National Historic Site

89. Carter Presidential Center

90. Ronald Reagan Birthplace

91. Ronald Reagan Boyhood Home

92. Ronald Reagan Presidential Library and Museum

93. The Ronald Reagan Museum at Eureka College

94. George Bush Presidential Library and Museum

95. President Bill Clinton's 1st Home Museum

96. Clinton House Museum

97. The Clinton Presidential Center

98. George W. Bush Childhood Home

99. The White House

Section II

Homes, Libraries, and Museums of the Presidents

George Washington

First President — 1789–1797

Born February 22, 1732, Popes Creek Plantation, Virginia
Died December 14, 1799, Mount Vernon, Virginia

To the memory of the man, first in war, first in peace, and first in the hearts of his countrymen, he was second to none in the humble and endearing scenes of private life.

— "Lighthorse Harry" Lee

George Washington was born into a social class that had always taken an active role in the life of the Virginia Colony. This was the planter aristocracy, people whose ancestors had come to Virginia with attitudes derived from their English country gentry heritage. They believed strongly in participating in the civil and military affairs of the colony and in performing duties without complaint — even though such service might entail sacrifice of individual comfort and welfare.

That selfless philosophy may explain much about Washington's willingness to serve the cause of liberty; to participate in the building and function of government; to become the nation's first chief executive; and to live on as an inspiration and example for all who followed. As he noted in his first State of the Union message, "The welfare of the country is the great object to which our cares and efforts ought to be directed."

Washington's career was remarkable; at various times, and sometimes concurrently, he was surveyor, farmer, explorer, soldier, politician, and statesman. Twenty-five years of his life were devoted to military and political service unparalleled in our history. As the first son of his father's second marriage, Washington was ever conscious of his patrimony, a feeling that fed his ambition for personal wealth and social acceptance. He was a landowner at nineteen and an explorer and military officer in the west while still in his early twenties. His experiences there, both successes and failures, honed his sense of ambition and sharpened his military and leadership skills — discipline, patience, and courage under fire — attributes that made him, years later, the logical choice to lead America's revolutionary army to victory. Following that victory, his stature as the nation's most revered and heroic figure made him the overwhelming choice to lead the fledgling nation into its first critical years.

Washington never forgot his roots. Once, during the most trying times of the Revolutionary War, he wrote "No pursuit is more congenial with my nature and gratifications, than that of agriculture; nor none I so pant after as again to become a tiller of the Earth." Thus, when his service to the nation was completed in 1797, Washington returned to his beloved estate, Mount Vernon, where he spent his last years fulfilling his ambition of being a full-time farm manager.

> *I can truly say that I had rather be at Mount Vernon with a friend or two about me, than to be attended at the Seat of Government by the Officers of the State and the Representatives of every Power in Europe.*

> — George Washington

George Washington Birthplace National Monument

WESTMORELAND COUNTY, VIRGINIA

In the early part of the eighteenth century, George Washington's father, Augustine, bought property on Popes Creek where it fed into the Potomac River, forty miles east of Fredericksburg on Virginia's Northern Neck. The elder Washington planted the land in tobacco and built a fine house around 1725.

George Washington was born at Popes Creek in 1732 but spent just over three years there before the family moved upriver to Little Hunting Creek Plantation, which later became well-known as Mount Vernon. When George was seven, the family moved again, this time to Ferry Farm near Fredericksburg. Upon Augustine's death in 1743, Popes Creek became the property of George's half-brother, Augustine, Jr., and young George visited frequently. The main house at Popes Creek Plantation was named Wakefield by George's nephew, William, who had inherited the property in 1774. Wakefield was destroyed by fire in 1779, and William chose not to rebuild. The property lay fallow for many years and passed from the family in the early nineteenth century.

In the 1920s, a group of public-spirited ladies banded together to seek a more meaningful memorial of the house where George Washington was born and formed the Wakefield National Memorial Association, its purpose being to restore the site to its early eighteenth-century condition. With significant public support and additional funding from the Rockefeller family, 394 acres were purchased and dedicated as a National Historic Site in 1931, only a year before the two-hundredth anniversary of Washington's birth at Popes Creek.

Archaeological searches over the past seventy-five years have uncovered many artifacts, as well as the structural remains of the Main House, the smokehouse, the kitchen, and other buildings, some of which have been replicated. The Main House in which Washington was born has not been reconstructed. Rather, its original foundation has been marked with a strip of oyster shells.

The Memorial House, constructed near the location of the Main House and finished in 1931 in time for the dedication, represents a typical 1½-story upper-class home of the eighteenth century, with four rooms and a central hallway on each floor. The bricks used for the outer walls were handmade of clay from a nearby field, and the furnishings, although not original, are of the period when the Washington family resided at Popes Creek. The Memorial House (Figure 6), set in a grove of magnificent red cedars, dramatically illustrates the setting into which Washington was born and the lifestyle led by his family.

A "living history" farm, established in 1968, recreates scenes reminiscent of Washington's boyhood. The farm features a colonial herb and flower garden, livestock, poultry, and crops characteristic of the 1700s. Douglas Southall Freeman wrote:

As George came into consciousness and learned to walk, there was around him an amazing world of dogs and chickens and pigs and calves, as well as those towering creatures called cows.

The buildings, furnishings, animals, and crops at Popes Creek offer an experience of aesthetic and historic interest whereby visitors may view a bit of what life was like on the colonial river plantations of Tidewater Virginia.

Family plantations of that period were the focus of the colony's social and economic life; the planter was the patriarch of a self-contained community where even the architecture and design of the plantation reflected social differentiation — outbuildings, gardens, fields, and slave quarters surrounded the main house in informal symmetry. Large landowner-planters dominated the Virginia Colony, and perpetuated their fortunes and lifestyle through intermarriage and inheritance. Thus each planter, a member of what was basically a ruling class, not only bequeathed his sons the land, but ensured that they received a formal education and were taught a sense of honor, dignity, and dedication to public service. Love of glory and pursuit of fame and fortune also were considered noble virtues indicative of character. These

Figure 6. The Memorial House at George Washington Birthplace National Monument, Washingtons Birthplace, Virginia. Photograph by Richard Frear; use courtesy of National Park Service.

values, observed at all of the great Virginia plantations, were instilled in George Washington, a man of his time — planter by birth, public servant when chosen.

The visitor center features exhibits about Washington's early years and life on the Potomac River, and a fourteen-minute film, *A Childhood Place,* dramatizes life at the plantation in the late eighteenth century. The film is captioned.

DIRECTIONS: Washington Birthplace is 40 miles east of Fredericksburg, Virginia. From Fredericksburg, take SR 3E to SR 204, then proceed north-bound on SR 204 2 miles to Washington Birthplace (Figure 7).

PUBLIC USE: Season and hours: Daily, 9 AM-5 PM. Closed Thanksgiving Day, Christmas Day, New Year's Day. **Admission fee. Picnic area. Gift shop. For people with disabilities:** The park is accessible for people who use wheel-chairs.

FOR ADDITIONAL INFORMATION: Contact: George Washington Birth-place National Monument, 1732 Popes Creek Road, Colonial Beach, Virginia 22443-5115, (804) 224-1732. **Web site:** *www.nps.gov/gewa.* **Read:** (1) Charles E. Hatch. 1979. *Popes Creek Plantation.*

Mount Vernon

MOUNT VERNON, VIRGINIA

I have no objection to any sober or orderly person's gratifying their curiosity in viewing the buildings, Gardens &ct about Mount Vernon.

— George Washington, 1794

Little could President Washington have dreamed that two hundred years after he wrote those words, his beloved and treasured Mount Vernon would be visited each year by over one million people. Mount Vernon (Plate 1) is the most popular historic home in America.

Washington's elegant mansion overlooking the majestic Potomac River has been restored meticulously. The interior has been replicated to appear as it did during the last year of Washington's life. Bright green

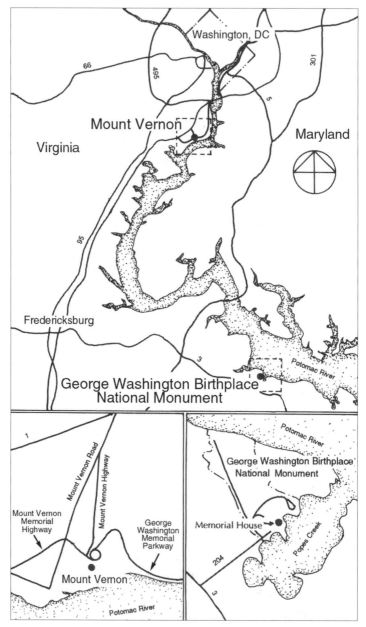

Figure 7. Location of George Washington Birthplace National Monument and Mount Vernon in northern Virginia.

and vivid blue walls, handsome wood grains, and dimity and satin window hangings all reflect the ambience and history of an exciting era. Fourteen rooms of the mansion are open for visitation. Each of these rooms is filled with original Washington pieces, and each is vibrant with rich window hangings, decorated ceilings, carved mantels, and polished woodwork. A featured hanging is a key to the Bastille presented by General Lafayette to Washington in 1790. In an accompanying letter, the Marquis wrote,

> Give me leave, my dear general, to present you with a picture of the Bastille, just as it looked a few days after I ordered its demolition, with the main key of the fortress of despotism. It is a tribute which I owe as a son to my adoptive father — as an aide-de-camp to my general — as a missionary of liberty to its patriarch.

An outdoor exhibition area contains more than thirty acres of colorful gardens and forests that are open for exploration by the public. Near the mansion are several outbuildings where much of the day-to-day maintenance of the plantation took place in Washington's time. Here bread was baked, wool and flax were woven into cloth, laundry was washed and ironed, and meat was cured.

A four-acre exhibition area introduces visitors to George Washington's pioneering work as a farmer. This working-farm exhibit highlights his experiments with crop rotation and other innovative agricultural methods. The main structure on the farm is a reproduction of Washington's unique sixteen-sided barn, built of trees cut on the estate and bricks made at Mount Vernon. All finishing work for the restoration was accomplished using eighteenth-century tools and methods. Just three miles from the main estate are on-original-site reproductions of George Washington's Gristmill and Distillery. Visitors are enabled to observe both operations in action and learn about a little-known aspect of Washington's entrepreneurial spirit.

The mansion at Mount Vernon was not built in its entirety at one time. Rather, it evolved from a simple 1½-story dwelling, probably built in the 1740s by George's half-brother Lawrence who named it Mount Vernon in honor of Admiral Edward Vernon, a British naval officer under whom he had served. When George Washington acquired the house by lease from Lawrence's widow in 1754, he enlarged and redecorated it and when he inherited the house outright in 1761, he added outbuildings, improved the gardens and fields, and continued to enlarge the house itself. The work was sporadic; one building project begun in 1757 was nearing completion when Washington brought his new bride to live at Mount Vernon in 1759. That entailed raising the structure to 2½ stories, adding exterior closets to the north and south gables, incorporating "rusticated" pine boards into the east and west facades to give the appearance of stone, and extensively redecorating the interior spaces. The work was interrupted several times for extended periods as Washington answered the many calls to his country's service, the labor supervised in his absence by a neighbor.

Mount Vernon, not completed until 1787, is an excellent example of colonial architecture, although there are indications of other influences in the Palladian windows and the originality of the front portico. The home is white, simple, uncluttered, and relaxed. It is one of America's greatest architectural and historic treasures, an evocation of eighteenth-century plantation life.

For nearly 150 years, Mount Vernon has been owned and operated by the Mount Vernon Ladies' Association, which continues to keep fresh and alive the lifestyle, heritage, and glory of George Washington. With that in mind, Mount Vernon dedicated two new buildings in 2006 — the Ford Orientation Center and the Donald W. Reynolds Museum and Education Center, both of which focus on Washington as a dynamic, fascinating hero rather than the popular elder statesman icon. When visitors enter the grounds, they pass through the orientation center to be greeted by life-sized bronze sculptures of the Washingtons and two of their grandchildren, then to enjoy a dramatic 18-minute movie mini-epic featuring pivotal moments of Washington's life. Another popular attraction is *Mount Vernon in Miniature,* an authentic, one-twelfth-scale exact replica of the mansion. It and descriptive stained glass panels prepare visitors for what they will experience in the real mansion nearby.

The Museum and Education Center features 23 gallery and theater experiences — many of them with interactive technology — that illuminate Washington's life story, including his military and political careers. These experiences cannot be covered in depth by a tour of the estate and mansion, which focuses on life at Mount Vernon. The Education Center also serves as Washington's presidential library with classroom space and computers providing access to more than 20,000 letters written by Washington during his lifetime.

In the Museum, over 500 objects are displayed in six galleries and a changing exhibit space. In the Education Center, visitors will be captivated by the use of computer imaging, LED map displays, dynamic graphics, surround-sound audio programs, "immersion" videos, illusionist lighting effects, dramatic staging, and touch-screen computer monitors. The state-of-the-art displays tell Washington's entire life story, from his childhood on the Northern Neck of Virginia through his adventures in the new American frontier, to his military leadership that brought victory to the Continental Army and his precedent-setting role as the first president of a new nation.

In planning the new Education Center, it was decided that physical appearance was a crucial element in learning about the real George Washington. As no extant portraits depicted Washington under the age of 40, a team was formed of a forensic anthropologist, computer scientists, historical researchers, and sculptors. Using special software, three-dimensional imaging equipment, historical documents, and the skill of expert artists, analysis was made of the Houdon bust, Washington's dentures (on display in the Education Center), clothing, and various portraits. The finished result was three lifelike wax heads with real human hair atop plaster bodies with realistic clothing depicting the young Virginia surveyor at 19, the 45-year-old noble general at Valley Forge, and the 57-year-old being sworn in as president on the balcony of Federal Hall in New York City.

A distance learning center, designed to connect communities to Mount Vernon with virtual teacher workshops, the library, lesson plans and other learning materials, and a hands-on history area for children further communicate the themes and ideas of the Museum and Education Center. Ann Pamela Cunningham, founder of the Mount Vernon Ladies' Association, could not have envisioned the modern methodology but would surely be thrilled to have her dream so completely fulfilled, "To perpetuate the sacred memory of 'The Father of His Country' . . . to open the same to the inspection of all who love the cause of liberty and revere the name of George Washington."

DIRECTIONS: By car, Mount Vernon is at the southern end of the George Washington Memorial Parkway, 8 miles south of Alexandria, Virginia (Figure 7). For Metro or bus schedules from Washington, DC, contact Metro Bus and Rail in Washington, (202) 637-7000 or Gray Line Tours, (202) 289-1995. By boat, the motor vessel *Potomac Spirit* sails from Washington, DC. Call (866) 211-3811 for schedules and prices. *Miss Christin* sails from Alexandria. Call (703) 684-0580 for schedules and prices. Prices for both ships include admission to Mount Vernon.

PUBLIC USE: Season and hours: Mount Vernon: April-August, 8 AM-5 PM; March, September, October: 9 AM-5 PM; November-February, 9 AM-4 PM.

Gristmill and Distillery: April-October, 10 AM-5 PM. **Admission fee. Food service:** Food and drink are not permitted on the grounds, but a full-service food court and a more formal restaurant are located in the Mount Vernon Inn complex just outside the main gate. **Gift shops:** *The Shops at Mount Vernon* are also in the complex. Recently expanded to 6600 square feet, the shops feature books, foodstuffs, regional crafts, collectibles, glassware, linens, and licensed reproductions. **For people with disabilities:** A limited number of wheelchairs are available on a first- come, first-served basis. The first floor of the mansion, restrooms, and many of the buildings are accessible.

FOR ADDITIONAL INFORMATION: Contact: Mount Vernon Ladies' Association, Box 110, Mount Vernon, Virginia 22121, (703) 780-2000. **Web site:** *www.mountvernon.org.* **Read:** (1) Charles Cecil Wall. 1988. "The Architect of Mount Vernon" in *George Washington: Citizen-Soldier*, pp. 92–103. (2) Charles Cecil Wall and others. 2001. *Mount Vernon: A Handbook.* (3) Wendell Garrett, ed. 1998. *George Washington's Mount Vernon.*

John Adams

Second President — 1797–1801

Born October 30, 1735, Braintree (now Quincy), Massachusetts
Died July 4, 1826, Braintree (now Quincy), Massachusetts

> *All of us in America are constantly bemused and astounded by this extraordinary golden age in our history which produced so many men of exceptional talent. . . . the record of the Adams family, this tremendous devotion to the public interest, this vitality which goes from generation to generation is, really, the most exceptional scarlet thread which runs through the entire tapestry of American political life.*

> — John F. Kennedy

Few families have so dominated the American political scene as has that of John Adams. Adams himself served as vice president under George Washington and was elected second President of the United States. He fathered our sixth president, John Quincy Adams; he was grandfather to an American minister to Great Britain, and other descendants included distinguished politicians, historians, and writers.

John Adams, a farmer's son, had ambitions that extended far beyond his home. He graduated from Harvard College with a bachelor's degree and then earned a degree in law. Adams had an unquenchable thirst for knowledge about the world, its history, its people, and especially its political institutions. His political writings brought him national attention as differences between England and her colonies widened. Adams was elected to be a delegate from

Massachusetts to the Continental Congress and later served as an invaluable American representative to the European states during the War for Independence.

Following the conflict, Adams returned to Massachusetts with the intention of becoming a farmer and attorney. While in Europe, he and his wife had purchased a farm and home south of Boston and named it Peacefield, both to emphasize the tranquility they hoped to enjoy there and to memorialize the Treaty of Paris that Adams had written and helped to negotiate. About Peacefield, he once said, "It is but the farm of a patriot," but he proved to be much more than a patriot farmer as the new nation called him to further service as vice president and president.

In 1801, John and Abigail Adams finally retired to Peacefield, nicknamed the "Old House" by their grandchildren. It was home to many family members, including son John Quincy Adams, by then on the way to his own singular and successful diplomatic and political career. John Adams died in his study at Peacefield on July 4, 1826, the fiftieth anniversary of the adoption of the Declaration of Independence. His last words included a reference to his old compatriot, Thomas Jefferson who, coincidentally, had passed away at Monticello only a few hours earlier.

The confluence of those tragic events had an almost mystical effect on the nation. Certainly the deaths of the two great patriots were to be mourned. But the coincidence of their deaths on such a significant anniversary day seemed to signal a divine blessing on the two men and the free nation they had helped bring forth and nurture.

Adams National Historical Park

QUINCY, MASSACHUSETTS

John Adams, our second president, was born in a house at 133 Franklin Street in Quincy, at that time called Braintree. The house at #133 is a New England "saltbox" building with multiple fireplaces around a central chimney. It originally consisted of two upper and two lower rooms, although additional rooms were added later. John Adams inherited the next door at #141 upon his father's death and utilized it as both a home and law office and, in 1769 it was the birthplace of his son, John Quincy Adams. The house at #141, built in 1663, is the oldest surviving presidential birthplace, while #133, dating to about 1681, is the next oldest. In 1779, #141 was the birthplace of the Massachusetts State Constitution, a document framed by Adams and others, that became the primary model used by members of the Constitutional Convention when they wrote the Constitution of the United States.

Both of the Adams houses are typical of New England homes built in the late seventeenth century. They are framed with huge beams secured with wooden pegs, floored with wide planks, and covered with clapboard siding over brick-filled walls designed to ward off the rigors of harsh winter weather. Ceilings were low and windows small; the houses were utilitarian and comfortable.

John Adams spent considerable time in Europe as a diplomatic representative of the young United States. In 1787 he and wife Abigail purchased a forty-acre farm and farmhouse, built around 1731, from Major Leonard Vassall, a wealthy West Indian sugar planter. The property, known as Peacefield or the "Old House" (Plate 1), was about one-and-one-half miles north of the houses on Franklin Street. It consisted of six rooms and a kitchen wing.

When the Adamses returned from Europe in 1788, they anticipated retirement from governmental affairs, but almost before they could unpack and settle into their new life at Peacefield, John was called to the capital in New York City to serve as George Washington's vice president. Upon Washington's retirement, John Adams was elected the second President of the United States. As a result, it was to be twelve long years before John and Abigail would retire to Massachusetts permanently.

During those twelve years, Mrs. Adams spent much time in Quincy running the farm and overseeing major improvements which included doubling the area of Peacefield when an east wing was added in 1800. Years later, grandson Henry Adams would recall the "Old House:"

> *The Old House at Quincy was 18th century. What style it had was its Queen Anne mahogany panels and its Louis XV chairs and sofa. The panels belonged to an old colonial Vassall who built the house; the furniture had been brought back from Paris in 1789 or 1801 or 1817, along with porcelain and books and much else of old diplomatic remnants; and neither of the two 18th century styles . . . was comfortable for a boy, or for anyone else. The dark mahogany had been painted white to suit daily life in winter gloom.*

After leaving the presidency, John joined Abigail at Peacefield, able at last to enjoy the garden, his books, children, and grandchildren. "I long for rural and domestic scenes," he noted, "for the warbling of birds and the prattle of my grandchildren." Abigail wrote to a friend, "the beauties which my garden unfolds to my view from the window at which I now write . . . all unite to awaken the most pleasing sensation."

Much has changed at Peacefield over two hundred years, but the garden's fragrance and beauty offer a link to the splendor and serenity of an earlier day. A white York rose brought from England by Abigail in 1788 thrives to this day, and a walk on the gravel paths through the orchards and colorful blooms engenders in today's visitors a renewed sense of the history, tradition, and quietude of Peacefield.

Son John Quincy Adams loved Peacefield as the home of his parents and used the house as a summer White House during his presidency. After the death of John Quincy Adams in 1848, his son Charles Francis Adams converted the property from a farm to a country gentleman's home and built a separate building, the Stone Library, to house the extensive John Quincy Adams library and other family papers. John Adams's papers are preserved at the Massachusetts Historical Society in Boston.

Brooks Adams, the fourth generation, remained in the "Old House" until his death 1927. Prior to his death, he formed the Adams Memorial Society which managed the house as a museum until 1946 when the Society deeded it to the federal government as a gift. The birth houses of John Adams and John Quincy Adams were the property of the City of Quincy until 1979 when they, too, were presented to the federal government. The two areas are managed as a single National Historical Park by the National Park Service.

DIRECTIONS: By car from Boston, take I 93 (Southeast Expressway) to Exit 7 (SR 3 southbound). The first exit will be Exit 18 (Quincy Adams T) that flows into Burgin Parkway. Proceed straight on Burgin Parkway through 6 sets of traffic lights. Turn right at the 7th light onto Dimmock Street and drive 1 block to Hancock Street, turning right on Hancock for 2 blocks to the visitor center on the left. Northbound from Cape Cod on SR 3, take Exit 19 (Quincy Adams T) which merges with southbound traffic from Boston, then follow the above directions with the flow into Burgin Parkway. By MBTA from Boston, take the Red Line to the Quincy Center Station. Exit on the Hancock Street side. The visitor center is across the street (Figure 8).

PUBLIC USE: Season and hours: Guided tours, starting at the visitor center, are conducted on a first-come, first-served basis from April 19-November 10,

9 AM-5 PM. The visitor center only is open November 10-April 19, Tuesday-Friday, 10 AM-4 PM. **Admission fee:** Admission includes entry to all three houses. **Book store. For people with disabilities:** The lower floors of Peacefield are accessible with a picture book available to help interpret the second floor. The Franklin Street houses are accessible. The National Park Service provides a trolley bus that offers transportation between the visitor center, Peacefield, and the Franklin Street homes.

FOR ADDITIONAL INFORMATION: Contact: Park Headquarters and Administrative Offices, Adams National Historical Park, 135 Adams Street, Quincy, Massachusetts 02169-1749, (617) 770-1177. Visitor center, 1250 Hancock Street, Quincy, Massachusetts 02169, (617) 770-1175. **Web site:** *www.nps.gov/adam*. **Read:** (1) Wilhelmina S. Harris. 1983. *A Family's Legacy to America.* (2) Paul Nagel. 1983. *Descent from Glory: Four Generations of the John Adams Family.* (3) David McCullough. 2001. *John Adams.*

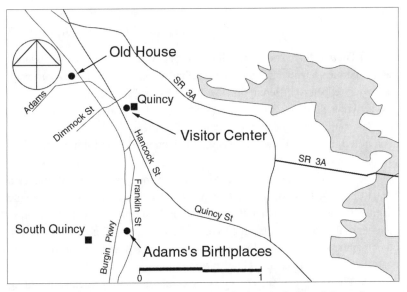

Figure 8. Location of Adams National Historical Park, Quincy, Massachusetts.

Thomas Jefferson

Third President — 1801–1809

Born April 13, 1743, Goochland County, Virginia
Died July 4, 1826, Monticello, Charlottesville, Virginia

> *I think this is the most extraordinary collection of talent, human knowledge, that has ever been gathered together at the White House, with the possible exception of when Thomas Jefferson dined alone.*

> — John F. Kennedy, hosting a dinner
> for Nobel Laureates, April, 1962

If Thomas Jefferson were still with us, he would be called a Renaissance man, or perhaps a Universal genius, for he had an eclectic mind, great curiosity, and high intellect. At different times, sometimes concurrently, he was a planter, lawyer, writer, politician, philosopher, scientist, architect, agronomist, diplomat, educator, statesman, and, not incidentally, President of the United States. It's been noted, too, that he was a reasonably accomplished violinist and had a fine singing voice!

Jefferson attended the College of William and Mary for two years, from 1760 to 1762. After that, he took the path to law and politics. He served in the Virginia Legislature and then the Continental Congress where he was made a member of the committee assigned to draft a Declaration of Independence. The other members deferred to Jefferson's rare writing skills, and the final document bears the singular marks of his lucid writing style.

Jefferson's presidency is noted for numerous achievements, including the Louisiana Purchase, but perhaps the most important day of his administration was the very first one. Many doubted that the new form of government, with its system of checks and balances, would really work. Would peaceful succession prove practical? Vice President Adams had followed George Washington into the presidency, but Jefferson would be the first opposition candidate to assume office. Would the system be a blessing or a curse? Would periodic changes of administration solidify citizens' rights to govern themselves, or would these changes result in chaos or, even worse, would they mean a return to the political and economic yoke of England?

The campaign between Jefferson and Adams in 1800 was bitter, with rancor on both sides. Even after the election the conflict continued, especially evident when Adams appointed his infamous "midnight judges" and left town before Jefferson was sworn into office on March 4, 1801. It would be many years before the rivals would reconcile. Nevertheless, the young nation passed its first great constitutional test as power efficiently flowed from the Federalists to the Democratic-Republican Party. The system had worked.

Thomas Jefferson left the White House in 1809 to live at his estate home, Monticello. For the next seventeen years he was a farmer-philosopher, honored by men and nations for his many contributions to the cause of freedom. Personally, he felt that his greatest accomplishment was the founding of the University of Virginia in Charlottesville. He had a hand in every facet of its birth — he served as head of its Board of Governors, he designed the buildings, he approved the curriculum, he hired the staff and he conducted the laying of the cornerstone on October 6, 1817. The university was chartered in 1819 and opened to students on March 17, 1825. A biblical passage frequently quoted in the university's publications is reflective of Jefferson's philosophy — a stirring and profound creed for free persons everywhere:

Ye shall know the truth and the truth shall make you free.

— John 8:32

Tuckahoe Plantation

RICHMOND, VIRGINIA

Tuckahoe Plantation (Figure 9) was founded in 1733 by William Randolph, who passed away in 1745. William's will stipulated that Peter Jefferson, who was married to William's cousin, Jane Randolph, should assume management of Tuckahoe during the minority of William's son, Thomas Mann Randolph. William further directed that a tutor be hired to direct the boy's education. Peter Jefferson's son, also named Thomas, joined young Thomas Randolph to take lessons from the same educator. The Jefferson family remained in residence at Tuckahoe for seven years.

The mansion at Tuckahoe, an H-shaped Georgian building, is considered by some architectural historians to be America's finest existing eighteenth-century plantation home. Professor Frederick Nichols of the University of Virginia wrote, "Not only is the house priceless because of its completeness, but it contains some of the most important architectural ideas of the early Georgian period." The Georgian style was English, and it is no surprise that many of the finer homes in colonial America copied it as a reminder of the mother country. The style was simple and balanced, with a planned relationship between the architecture and the landscape. It evolved in no small measure from the Palladian style.

The English adaptation of the Palladian style lay in the development of formal gardens and straightforward architecture that eliminated unnecessary decorations and made maximum use of the buildings. Primary examples at

Figure 9. The mansion of Tuckahoe Plantation, Richmond, Virginia. Photograph courtesy of Tuckahoe Plantation.

Tuckahoe are paired outside structures, one of which was an office and the other the schoolhouse where the two Thomases attended class. Both buildings still stand as parts of Tuckahoe's pleasant landscape of gardens and fields.

Tuckahoe is unique in another way, for little about the house has changed since it was built. There have been no additions or other modifications to its exterior, and the interior paneling and embellishments are original. The interior of the main house, in sparkling mint condition, contains outstanding carved staircases and paneling, built-in cupboards, and beautiful period furniture. All interior rooms face the outside, with a view of either the gardens, the fields, or the river. Jessie T. Krusen, in her book, *Tuckahoe Plantation*, wrote, "It is a rare old place endowed with many charms. It is restful, and the quiet of the fine old rooms makes one forget the worries of today — for at Tuckahoe all the world seems at peace."

Almost three centuries old, Tuckahoe remains a working farm and home, owned by a family partnership and managed by family members Mr. and Mrs. Addison Thompson who graciously open the mansion and grounds to visitors by appointment. Tuckahoe is also available as a picturesque venue for special events.

DIRECTIONS: From I 64, take the Gaskins Road Exit southbound to River Road. Turn right on River Road for 2.5 miles and enter a country lane through white pillars. From I 95, exit to Cary Street and follow it westbound. At the junction with Huguenot Road, Cary Street becomes River Road. Continue on River Road to Tuckahoe (Figure 10).

PUBLIC USE: Season and hours: 9:30 AM-5 PM, by appointment only. **Admission fee. Picnic area. Gift shop.**

FOR ADDITIONAL INFORMATION: Contact: Tuckahoe Plantation, 12601 River Road, Richmond, Virginia 23233, (804) 784-5736. **Web site:** *www.tuckahoeplantation.com.* **Read:** (1) Jessie T. Krusen. 1976. *Tuckahoe Plantation.* (2) Dumas Malone. 1948–1981. *Jefferson and His Time.* 6 volumes. Volume 1, *Jefferson the Virginian.*

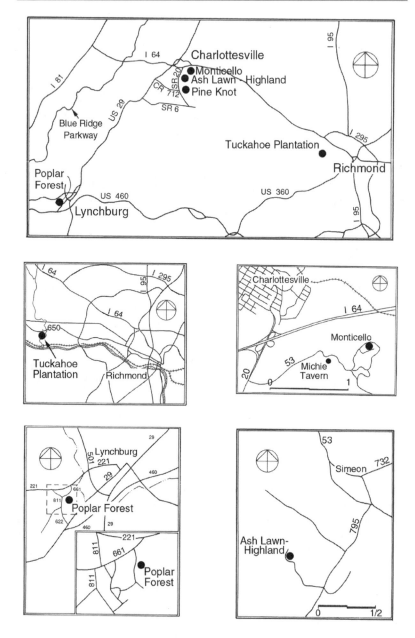

Figure 10. Location of Tuckahoe Plantation, Monticello, Poplar Forest, Ash Lawn-Highland, and Pine Knot in central Virginia.

Monticello

CHARLOTTESVILLE, VIRGINIA

Architecture is my delight, and putting up and pulling down, one of my favorite amusements.

— Thomas Jefferson

Monticello, or "Little Mountain" (Figure 11), stands proudly atop an 867-foot peak with a commanding view of the lush Virginia countryside. Rarely does a home more accurately reflect the personality of its owner than does Monticello, a testimony to Thomas Jefferson's ingenuity and breadth of interests. Jefferson began to clear the mountain top in 1768, and for the next forty years Monticello centered his thoughts. He designed and supervised its construction, and he never stopped changing the house or the grounds. Every facet of the home and the land around it mirrored the pleasure he found in architectural planning and design. Monticello's thirty-three rooms recall Jefferson's quest for perfection in artistic execution, with key elements existing in perfect balance. Everything in and around the mansion is a reminder of its

Figure 11. Monticello. Photograph courtesy of Thomas Jefferson Foundation/ Ray Van Doorn.

owner's keen mind and deep interest in the arts, sciences, agriculture, and architecture. The house has been restored to the splendor of its appearance in 1809 — 1809 generally accepted as the date when the house was "finished." Recently, the roof was restored to its appearance in 1825, the year that Jefferson, out of concern about fire hazards and leakage, put on a new roof of tin-plated iron shingles. Monticello is unquestionably one of America's great architectural treasures.

The house in its initial form was unlike anything ever seen in this country. Early sketches of the "first Monticello" reveal the neoclassic influence of Palladio, whose works were familiar to Jefferson. In 1782, the Marquis de Chastellux, a visitor to the house, described it as "consisting of a large, square pavilion." Even in that early stage of the house's evolution, Chastellux was compelled to remark, "Mr. Jefferson is the first American who has consulted the Fine Arts to know how he should shelter himself from the weather."

In 1784, Jefferson left on a diplomatic mission to Paris where he remained for five years, during which time he absorbed the classic art, literature, music, and architecture of the continent. Upon his return, he was inspired to redesign Monticello. The upper story was removed and walls were razed in order to add rooms and a new façade. He added a dome, its design inspired by an ancient Roman temple illustrated in Palladio's *The Four Books of Architecture.* The exterior look of Monticello is deceiving as it appears to be but one-story tall. Actually, Jefferson blended the mezzanine and lower windows into single units and hid the upper floor behind a balustrade. The interior halls and rooms are filled with Jefferson's gadgetry, such as a double-faced clock that may be read from both outdoors and indoors, alcove beds, and twin hall doors rigged so that both doors open as one.

Jefferson's interest in architecture was matched only by his interest in garden design and landscape architecture. His plans for Monticello included ornamental and vegetable gardens, orchards, vineyards, and even an ornamental forest. The gardens disappeared after his death, but researchers uncovered his sketches and meticulous records which have allowed for an unusually accurate restoration of the grounds, a project initiated by the Garden Club of Virginia. Today, as part of its interpretive programming, Monticello conducts lectures, nature walks, seminars, and special events ranging from apple tasting to gardening demonstrations.

The ornamental flower gardens of Monticello were designed to complement and beautify the property, to define the perimeters of the lawns, and to balance the aesthetics of the house, lawns, fields, and distant view. There are twenty oval-shaped flowerbeds around the house and a roundabout flower walk on the West Lawn. Jefferson used a large number of species, including some he had brought back from Europe. The beds now are filled with varieties that bloom at different times, thus ensuring constant flowering and color.

In addition to his accomplishments as a landscape architect, Jefferson was a horticultural scientist who tested hundreds of vegetables and herbs. In 1987, the Thomas Jefferson Center for Historic Plants was opened at Monticello as a living tribute to Jefferson's contributions to the study of plants. The center features gardens and a shop where historic varieties of seeds and plants are sold. This continuation of Jefferson's work would have suited his feelings:

> *No occupation is so delightful to me as culture of the earth, and no culture comparable to that of the garden . . . but though an old man, I am but a young gardener.*

Thomas Jefferson died at Monticello on July 4, 1826, more than $100,000 in debt. A dispersal sale held in 1827 included his slaves, crops, household items, and furniture. Monticello was leased to various tenants until 1923 when the Thomas Jefferson Memorial Foundation took over its management. Eventually the house and 2000 surrounding acres became a place for all people to visit, a memorial to Thomas Jefferson's extraordinary gifts and contributions to the United States.

Jefferson rests in the graveyard at Monticello where family tradition holds that he and his boyhood friend Dabney Carr studied under a favorite oak tree. The two friends had an agreement that, whichever of them died first, would be buried beneath the tree by the other. Jefferson buried Carr under the oak in 1773. Jefferson's grave is marked by an obelisk inscribed with an epitaph he wrote for himself:

> *Here was Buried Thomas Jefferson*
> *Author of the Declaration of American Independence*
> *Of the Statute of Virginia for Religious Freedom*
> *And Father of the University of Virginia*

A special premium signature tour of Monticello is available each Friday from April through September at 6:30 PM. Reservations are required and may be made via the Monticello web site *(www.monticello.org)*. Reserved tickets for scheduled, timed tours of the house are also available on the web site, but same-day tickets are always available at the ticket office.

In May 2006, Monticello initiated guided walking tours of Thomas Jefferson's Montalto, a nearby mountain peak (410 feet higher than Monticello) that offers unparalleled views of the surrounding countryside; three interpretive stations offer panoramic views of Monticello, Charlottesville, the University of Virginia, and a broad expanse that features the homes of some of Jefferson's notable neighbors. Montalto tours, which last approximately sixty minutes, depart from Monticello's ticket office twice every day, spring, summer, and fall. A maximum of twenty-four guests may be accommodated on each tour group which is transported to and from the summit of Montalto by shuttle bus. There is a separate charge for the Montalto tour.

A visitor center featuring a museum and an introductory film, *Thomas Jefferson: The Pursuit of Liberty,* is located at the intersection of SR 20 and I 64, just below Monticello. This center also sells combination tickets for Monticello, James Monroe's Ash Lawn-Highland, and Michie Tavern, an eighteenth-century pub located alongside the road that leads to both of the presidential sites.

A new visitor center currently under construction at the Monticello property will feature historical exhibitions, a museum shop, sit-down cafe, and a two-story history center. This new, modern facility is scheduled for completion late in 2008 with the dedication scheduled for Jefferson's birthday on April 13, 2009.

DIRECTIONS: Monticello is 3 miles south of Charlottesville, Virginia. From I 64, exit on SR 20 southbound to SR 53, go east on SR 53 and follow the historical markers to Monticello (Figure 10).

PUBLIC USE: Season and hours: March 1-October 31, 8 AM-5 PM; November 1-February 28/29, 9 AM-4:30 PM. Closed Christmas Day. Visitors are transported to the house by shuttle from the visitor center. All tours of the house are guided. **Admission fee. Food service:** Picnic tables are located near the parking area; a luncheonette is open April through October. **Museum shops:** One is at the visitor center, one is at Monticello. **For people with disabilities:** Fully accessible.

FOR ADDITIONAL INFORMATION: Contact: Monticello, Box 316, Charlottesville, Virginia 22902, (434) 984-9822. **Web site:** *www.monticello.org.* **Read:** (1) Edwin M. Betts and Hazelhurst Bolton Perkins.1986. *Thomas*

Jefferson's Flower Garden at Monticello. (2) Jack McLaughlin. 1988. *Jefferson and Monticello: The Biography of a Builder* (3) Marc Leepson. 2001. *Saving Monticello: The Levy Family's Epic Quest to Rescue the House that Jefferson Built*.

Poplar Forest

FOREST, VIRGINIA

In 1806, Thomas Jefferson began construction of a villa retreat in the foothills south of Lynchburg, his intent to enjoy the "solitude of a hermit" far from the intrusion of visitors to Monticello by which he was sometimes overwhelmed. He called his retreat Poplar Forest (Plate 2).

Mrs. Jefferson had inherited the 4819-acre working farm in 1773 but, with only a small house located on the property, the Jeffersons rarely spent time there. A notable exception occurred in 1781 when British forces appeared at Monticello in search of Virginia Governor Jefferson. Forewarned, the Jeffersons fled to the farm and took refuge in what is believed to have been the overseer's tiny cabin. It was not until 1806, well after his wife's death and near the end of his presidency, that Jefferson laid the foundation for an unusual and creatively designed octagonal house. The living space that occupied one floor was a series of elongated octagons surrounding a 20-foot x 20-foot x 20-foot cube-shaped room illuminated by a skylight. "When finished," Jefferson wrote, "it will be the best dwelling house in the State, except that of Monticello, perhaps preferable to that, as more proportioned to the faculties of a private citizen."

In 1984, the historic property was purchased by the nonprofit Corporation for Jefferson's Poplar Forest and was opened to the public in 1986. Restoration of the house continues, as does archaeological exploration for Jefferson's original landscape design and the search for other clues to the ideas, plans, and activities of its genius owner. Exterior restoration was completed in the summer of 1998, and interior structural restoration of the walls and floor system followed. Restoration of the east wing's service rooms is ongoing.

Throughout the year, Poplar Forest offers a series of public programs in the form of lectures, family days, concerts, and living history demonstrations. An Independence Celebration is held every July 4th, and field schools in architectural restoration and archaeology are offered in the summer months. Exhibits on general history, archaeology, architecture, restoration, and the plantation community are available to all visitors. A hands-on history center featuring activities representative of Jefferson's era is open for school groups periodically throughout the summer season.

DIRECTIONS: From Washington, DC, and Charlottesville, take SR 29 south-bound. After crossing the James River, exit onto SR 460 westbound toward Lynchburg/Roanoke and remain on SR 460 for approximately 14 miles to its intersection with SR 811. Turn right on SR 811 (Thomas Jefferson Road) and continue approximately 4.2 miles to the intersection with SR 661 (Bateman Bridge Road). Go 1 mile on Bateman Bridge Road to the entrance to Poplar Forest on the right. From Roanoke and I 81, take US 460 eastbound for 40 miles. At SR 811, turn left and proceed for 4.4 miles. At SR 661, turn right and proceed for 1 mile to Poplar Forest (Figure 10).

PUBLIC USE: Season and hours: April-November, guided tours daily except Tuesday, 10 AM-4 PM. Closed Thanksgiving Day. Group tours of 20 or more are available year-round by appointment. **Admission fee. Museum shop. For people with disabilities:** Limited accessibility.

FOR ADDITIONAL INFORMATION: Contact: The Corporation for Jefferson's Poplar Forest, Box 419, Forest, Virginia 24551-0419, (434) 525-1806. **Web site:** *www.poplarforest.org.* **Read:** (1) Allen S. Chambers, Jr. 1993. *Poplar Forest and Thomas Jefferson.* (2) Joan Horn. 2002. *Thomas Jefferson's Poplar Forest: A Private Place.* Lynchburg: Thomas Jefferson's Poplar Forest. (3) Janet Shaffer. 2004. *Thomas Jefferson: From Shadwell to Poplar Forest.*

James Madison

Fourth President — 1809–1817

Born March 16, 1751, Port Conway, King George County, Virginia
Died June 28, 1836, Montpelier, Orange County, Virginia

*I believe there are more instances of the abridgment of freedom
of the people by gradual and silent encroachment of those in power
than by violent and sudden usurpation.*

— James Madison

Madison, like predecessors Washington and Jefferson, was a member of the planter aristocracy; his family had prospered in the Virginia Colony since 1653. Provided with the best possible education that included private tutoring and matriculation at the College of New Jersey, now Princeton University, Madison struggled with the question of whether to pursue a religious vocation after graduation, but ultimately he chose a career in law. He distinguished himself as a member of the Virginia House of Delegates, and when the War for Independence was over he was elected a delegate to the Constitutional Convention where his intelligence and clarity of thought were instrumental in developing and writing the Constitution of the United States.

A year later, in 1787, Madison, Alexander Hamilton, and John Jay began to write a series of essays known collectively as the *Federalist Papers.* These documents were distributed to citizens of the new nation in an effort to explain the new constitution and they are still studied as examples of brilliantly cogent constitutional thought.

In 1794, Aaron Burr introduced the forty-three-year-old bachelor Madison to Dolley Payne Todd, a twenty-six-year-old widow with a small child. Soon after, they married and began a life of fine living, entertaining, political service, and deep devotion to the nation and to one another. Madison served as a United States congressman and later as Secretary of State in the cabinet of Thomas Jefferson before being elected President of the United States in 1809.

Dolley served as White House hostess during the presidency of the widower Thomas Jefferson, then for eight years during her husband's term, forever defining the formal and ceremonial role of the president's wife. She was the first wife of a president to be referred to as the "First Lady."

> *I can say conscientiously that I do not know in the world a man of purer integrity, more dispassionate, disinterested and devoted to genuine republicanism; nor could I in the whole scope of America and Europe point out an abler head.*

> — Jefferson on Madison, 1790

Montpelier

MONTPELIER STATION, VIRGINIA

> *I wish you had just a country home as this. It is the happiest and most independent life.*

> — Dolley Madison

The tract of land that was to become the Montpelier estate was settled by the Madison family in 1723. The core of the present mansion house was built around 1760 by James Madison's father who bequeathed the estate to his son James in 1801. Madison himself enlarged the house twice — in 1797 and in the 1810s. Montpelier became a retreat which Madison referred to as "a squirrel's jump from heaven." He and Dolley returned to the estate again and again through a long, productive, and distinguished life in public service.

Upon James's retirement from the presidency, he and Dolley moved to Montpelier permanently. They remained involved in national and world affairs as James's voluminous correspondence and Dolley's lavish entertaining kept them in the public eye.

The original main house at Montpelier seems to have combined some principles of Georgian architecture with a vernacular style. Its simple lines include a colonnade designed by Dr. William Thornton and a broad porch that offers a sweeping view of the lawn and the distant Blue Ridge Mountains.

The derivation of the name Montpelier is unclear. Montpellier, a medieval French term for "Mount of the Pilgrim," was the name of a popular resort and university town in France. Since the Madisons had no ties to the town, however, it is more likely that the name is associated with the beauty, clean air, and healthy climate of the Montpellier area of France.

James Madison died at Montpelier in 1836. Dolley sold the estate in 1844 and returned to Washington, DC, where she died in 1849. Montpelier changed hands and appearances many times before it was acquired in 1901 by William and Annie duPont who made extensive alterations that included the enlargement of the main house, the addition of outbuildings, and the establishment of a formal garden. The estate remained in the duPont family until 1983 when Marion duPont Scott bequeathed it to the National Trust for Historic Preservation. Montpelier opened to the public in 1987 and is now administered by the Montpelier Foundation.

Late in 2003, the Foundation announced plans to restore Montpelier to the home that James and Dolley knew in the 1820s. The ambitious project will remove alterations made to the mansion after President Madison's death, including elimination of the wings added by the duPont family. Plaster facing, including that on the pillars, already has been removed to bring the core of the mansion down to its original brick. The restoration will reduce the mansion from fifty-five to twenty-two rooms. A restoration celebration is scheduled for Constitution Day (September 17), 2008 (Plate 3).

National Trust President Richard Moe said, "The restored mansion will bring the era of James and Dolley Madison alive in a way that has not been possible . . . when this ambitious project is completed, Montpelier will be one of the nation's most distinctive historic sites, offering visitors a unique first-hand encounter with America's heritage."

The home remains open for tours throughout the restoration period, as will exhibits at the education center located just beyond the back lawn of the mansion. The Madison exhibits feature *The Treasures of Montpelier*, a gallery exhibit of Madison family furniture grouped in vignettes to show how the Madisons relied on, related to, and used these items. Other popular exhibits are a recreation of the Madison dining room, representing a dinner held in honor of the Marquis de Lafayette in 1824; and Dolley's bedchamber, resplendent in crimson and featuring her large four-poster tester bed.

Features of Montpelier that remain in place include (1) the Madison family cemetery, the final resting place for James and Dolley; (2) the slave cemetery; (3) the James Madison Landmark Forest; (4) a formal garden; (5) a landscape arboretum; (6) Madison's temple, which covers an underground ice house that he built, and which serves as the symbol of Montpelier; and (7) the Gilmore Cabin and Freedman's Farm which tells the story of the journey from slavery to freedom.

Madison was interested in both botany and horticulture. The James Madison Landmark Forest is a 200-acre old-growth forest that has been designated as a National Natural Landmark and is the best surviving remnant of the original hardwood forests that once blanketed the American Piedmont. The mature tulip poplars in the forest, known colloquially as the "Big Woods," are 250 years old and date to President Madison's lifetime. A series of interlocking trails about two miles in length open the natural treasure to visitors. The formal garden that James and Dolley enjoyed was a four-acre feature designed by a French gardener, Bizet. Then, in the early 1900s, Annie duPont designed a two-acre garden on the same site. Traces of the original garden survive in the scheme of the paths and parterres. In creating his arboretum, Madison corresponded with horticulturists throughout America and Europe and imported a number of exotic plants. Two large Cedars-of-Lebanon and a row of walnut trees date to the Madison residency.

At a rededication ceremony in 1998, honored guest First Lady Hillary Rodham Clinton said, "We need to be educated and inspired time and again by the American story written here by James and Dolley Madison — because it is only by understanding where we came from — looking squarely at our past, appreciating the sacrifices and difficulties others endured for us to be enjoying what we enjoy today — that we can hold dear those ideals and values that should be cherished, and pass them on to our own children and grandchildren."

DIRECTIONS: Montpelier Station is 4 miles southwest of Orange, Virginia, on SR 20 (Figure 12).

PUBLIC USE: Season and hours: April-October, 9:30 AM-5:30 PM; November-March, 9:30 AM-4:30 PM. Closed Thanksgiving Day, Christmas Day. **Admission fee. Picnic area. For people with disabilities**: The main floor of the mansion and many trail segments are wheelchair accessible. Due to the restoration process, it would be prudent to call ahead for current information.

FOR ADDITIONAL INFORMATION: Contact: James Madison's Montpelier, Box 911, Orange, Virginia 22960, (540) 672-2728. **Web site:** *www.montpelier.org.* **Read:** (1) Ann L. Miller. 1990. *Historic Structure Report-Montpelier, Orange County, Virginia: Phase II: Documentary Evidence Regarding the Montpelier House 1723–1983.* (2) Ralph J. Ketcham. 1990. *James Madison: A Biography.*

James Madison Museum

ORANGE, VIRGINIA

The James Madison Museum (Figure 13) contains permanent exhibits that delineate the life and times of Madison and his enormous contributions to our political system, and thereby provides an interesting complement to the nearby Montpelier estate. The museum contains a number of Madison

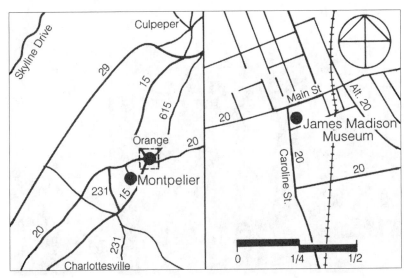

Figure 12. Location of Montpelier near (left), and the James Madison Museum in (right), Orange, Virginia.

artifacts, including furnishings from Montpelier, some of the Madisons's correspondence and books, plus accessories and textiles associated with Dolley.

The Orange County Room provides information about the history of Orange County. A Hall of Transportation and Agriculture on a lower floor is dedicated to James Madison, whom Thomas Jefferson called "the best farmer in the world." A collection of antique farm tools, machines, and an original 16-foot x 16-foot land grant "cube house" built in 1733 are on display.

DIRECTIONS: The James Madison Museum is located on US 20 (Caroline Street) in Orange, Virginia, immediately south of the intersection with Main Street (Figure 12).

PUBLIC USE: Season and hours: March-December, Monday-Friday, 9 AM-5 PM; Saturday, 10 AM-5 PM; Sunday, 1 PM-5 PM. Closed Thanksgiving Day, Christmas Day, New Year's Day, Easter Sunday. **Admission fee. For people with disabilities:** Partially accessible.

FOR ADDITIONAL INFORMATION: Contact: James Madison Museum, 129 Caroline Street, Orange, Virginia 22960, (540) 672-1776. **Web site:** *www.jamesmadisonmuseum.org.* David K. Gleason. 1989. *Virginia Plantation Homes.*

Figure 13. The James Madison Museum, Orange, Virginia. Photograph courtesy of The James Madison Museum.

The Octagon Museum

WASHINGTON, DC

During the War of 1812, the President's House was partially destroyed by British invaders. When President Madison returned to the capital following the British departure, Colonel John Tayloe, III, the owner of Octagon House, graciously offered him use of the Octagon as his temporary headquarters until the President's House could be repaired.

Octagon House is a misnomer; the structure is only six-sided. The building was designed by Dr. William Thornton, the first architect of the US Capitol building, for Colonel Tayloe, a wealthy Virginia plantation owner who wanted to build a fine townhouse in the new capital city. The house hosted many distinguished guests and its historical significance was cemented in 1815 when President Madison, in residence, signed the Treaty of Ghent that established peace between the United States and Great Britain. The Treaty Room on the second floor contains a pivoted, circular rent table upon which it is believed President Madison signed the treaty. As one climbs the oval staircase and tours the splendor that is the Octagon, one may think of Dolley Madison as she reigned as hostess of this magnificent building (Figure 14).

The Octagon House gradually deteriorated until rescued by the American Institute of Architects (AIA), which purchased the Octagon in 1902 and used the building as its national headquarters until ownership was transferred in 1968 to the nonprofit AIA Foundation (now the American Architectural Foundation, or AAF). The AAF was mandated to maintain and operate the house as a historic landmark. Today, visitors delight in the grand stair hall and brilliant colors of this home.

The Octagon is the oldest museum in the United States devoted to architecture and design, enabling the AAF to increase awareness of the power of architecture and its influence on the quality of our lives.

DIRECTIONS: The Octagon Museum is located at the intersection of New York Avenue and 18th Street in Washington, DC (Figure 15).

PUBLIC USE: Season and hours: The Octagon is available for pre-arranged, appointment-only group tours of no less than 10 and up to 25 guests. Walk-in visitors will not be accommodated. **Admission fee. For people with disabilities:** The first floor is accessible.

Figure 14. The Octagon Museum, Washington, DC. Photograph courtesy of The Octagon Museum of the American Architectural Foundation, Washington, DC.

FOR ADDITIONAL INFORMATION: Contact: The Octagon Museum, 1799 New York Avenue, NW, Washington, DC 20006, (202) 638-3221. **Web site:** *www.archfoundation.org/octagon.* **Read:** (1) Kenneth R. Bowling. 1988. *Creating the Federal City, 1774–1800: Potomac Fever.* (2) Orlando V. Rideout. 1989. *Building the Octagon.* (3) Barbara G. Carson. 1990. *Ambitious Appetites.*

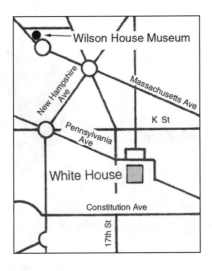

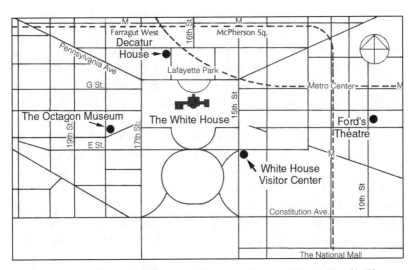

Figure 15. Location of the Octagon Museum, Decatur House, Ford's Theatre National Historic Site, Woodrow Wilson House Museum, The White House, and the White House Visitors Center, Washington, DC.

James Monroe

Fifth President — 1817–1825

Born April 28, 1758, Westmoreland County, Virginia
Died July 4, 1831, New York City, New York

> *The American continents are henceforth not to be considered
> as subjects for future colonization by any European powers.*

— The Monroe Doctrine

James Monroe was one of four Virginians who served as President of the United States during thirty-two of the country's first thirty-six years. Monroe came from a middle-class background, but he received an excellent education at the College of William and Mary in Williamsburg, Virginia. At eighteen, he interrupted his education to join the Continental Army during the Revolutionary War in which he served with distinction, including being wounded at Trenton and suffering with Washington at Valley Forge.

Following the conflict, Monroe returned to Virginia to finish his education, after which he applied himself to law and politics. Monroe's political resume has rarely been equaled as it includes service as delegate to the Virginia Assembly; member of the Virginia Convention to ratify the Constitution of the United States; United States Senator; Governor of Virginia; Minister to France, Spain, and England; Secretary of State; Secretary of War during the War of 1812, and, of course, fifth President of the United States.

Monroe's term as president became known as the "Era of Good Feelings." He was so popular that he ran for a second term unopposed, an honor shared only with George Washington. One member of the Electoral

College disregarded public opinion, however, and cast his vote for John Quincy Adams, which gave Monroe a plurality of 231 to 1 and thus assured George Washington the singular honor of being the only president elected unanimously.

Ash Lawn-Highland

CHARLOTTESVILLE, VIRGINIA

Highland was the name of James and Elizabeth Monroe's home from 1799 to 1823. They had moved to Charlottesville, in Albemarle County, at the urging of Thomas Jefferson, who admired Monroe and wished to create a social and intellectual community close to Monticello. Jefferson even selected the site for the Monroe home, which was located only two miles from Monticello. Less imposing than Jefferson's mansion, Highland reflected Monroe's less prosperous background and his belief in the simple life of a farmer, although from our modern perspective, Highland was hardly simple. The house was a modest frame structure that, with additions made through the years, grew to encompass almost 4400 square feet.

Like other farms of the era, Highland was a community unto itself that employed the services of resident craftsmen and housed from forty to fifty slaves. There were numerous outbuildings (threshing barns, a saw mill, slave quarters, plantation office, smoke house, and other farm buildings) and the property included forests, orchards, vineyards, and fields that eventually contained an imposing 3500 acres.

Monroe sold Highland in 1826. A subsequent owner changed the name to Ash Lawn, and both names are used today. In 1931, philanthropists Jay and Helen Johns purchased Ash Lawn-Highland and opened it to visitors. In 1974, they bequeathed the property to Monroe's alma mater, the College of William and Mary, with the stipulation that it be operated "as a historic shrine for the education of the general public."

Today, Ash Lawn-Highland (Plate 3) is a house museum, working farm, and center for the performing arts. The Summer festival includes musical performances and family activities staged in the boxwood gardens and Highland Pavilion.

The entrance to the Monroe house features Monroe family and White House china, while the adjoining Exhibit Room showcases Monroe's Revolutionary War service and the Monroe Doctrine. The latter warned European powers not to intervene in the affairs of nations in the Western Hemisphere and was gratefully received by our southern neighbors. One relevant item on display is a magnificent drop-leaf table carved from a single section of Honduras mahogany, a gift of appreciation to President Monroe from the people of Santo Domingo, now the Dominican Republic.

James Monroe and his family spent several years living abroad while on diplomatic assignments for Presidents Washington and Jefferson, and they returned home with newly acquired furnishings, fashions, and manners. Monroe referred to his house at Highland as his "cabin-castle" alluding, perhaps, to its being modest in size yet richly furnished. Many of Highland's original French furnishings survive, and over the past few years a number of pieces on loan from the James Monroe Museum in Fredericksburg, Virginia, have been beautifully restored and placed on view in the newly refurbished interiors at Ash Lawn-Highland. French wallpapers and period paintings provide a fitting background for the Monroe treasures.

Outside, visitors may explore the still-active farm and watch craft demonstrations. A particularly popular activity is to stroll through the historic boxwood gardens — now enlivened by colorful, strutting peacocks. Young people, always intrigued by the chickens, sheep, and cattle, also enjoy rolling hoops on the lawn.

A nonprofit subsidiary of the College of William and Mary, Ash Lawn-Highland seeks to fulfill its educational agenda with income from a variety of sources — admission fees, donations, and grants. These funds support the maintenance and restoration activities of the facility as well as the expansion of educational programs that serve the general public and thousands of students each year. Monroe would be touched by such a living memorial, for in 1818 he wrote:

> *The principal support of free government is to be derived from the sound morals and intelligence of the people; and the more extensive means of education, the more confidently we may rely upon the preservation of our public liberties.*

DIRECTIONS: From I 64 in Charlottesville, take Exit 121 and proceed southbound on SR 20 toward Scottsville. Move into the left lane immediately and turn left on SR 53. Go approximately 4 miles and turn right on SR 795 (James

Monroe Parkway) which will take you to the entrance of Ash Lawn-Highland (Figure 10). See previous directions to Monticello for information about the visitor center that serves both homes.

PUBLIC USE: Season and hours: April-October, 9 AM-6 PM; November-March, 11 AM-5 PM. Closed Thanksgiving Day, Christmas Day, New Year's Day. **Admission fee:** Visitors may purchase tickets at Ash Lawn-Highland. The Presidents Pass for discounted admission to Ash Lawn-Highland, Monticello, and Michie Tavern can be purchased at any of the three sites or at the visitor center located on SR 20 at I 64. **Picnic area.** Picnic tables and lawn spaces are available year-round. Catered lunches for groups are available by advance reservation. **Museum shop. For people with disabilities:** Fully accessible, including Braille material and facilities for the hearing impaired.

FOR ADDITIONAL INFORMATION: Contact: Ash Lawn-Highland, 1000 James Monroe Parkway, Charlottesville, Virginia 22902-8722, (434) 293-9539. **Web site:** *www.ashlawnhighland.org.* **Read:** (1) James E. Wootton. 1987. *Elizabeth Kortright Monroe.* (2) Harry Ammon. 1991. *James Monroe: The Quest for National Identity.* (3) Ash Lawn-Highland. 1999. *Ash Lawn-Highland: A Guide.* (4) Daniel Preston. 2000. *The Presidency of James Monroe. (5)* Daniel Preston. 2001. *The Life of James Monroe.*

James Monroe Museum and Memorial Library

FREDERICKSBURG, VIRGINIA

James Monroe practiced law in Fredericksburg for several years before he moved on to a brilliant career in politics and diplomatic service. The James Monroe Museum and Memorial Library (Figure 16) is on land that he might have owned and is possibly on the site of his former law office.

Monroe served as the United States Minister to France from 1794 to 1797 and again from 1803 to 1807. While in Paris, the Monroes purchased several suites of exquisite Louis XVI furniture which they used while in the White House when Monroe was president. Several pieces of this handsome furniture are displayed in the James Monroe Museum, a favorite piece being the desk upon which President Monroe signed his annual message to

Figure 16. James Monroe Museum and Memorial Library, Fredericksburg, Virginia. Photograph courtesy of James Monroe Museum and Memorial Library.

congress in 1823, a portion of which became known as the Monroe Doctrine. Mrs. Monroe's impressive gem collection, costumes worn by the couple at the Court of Napoleon, other personal and historically significant items, changing exhibits, and special events all serve to make a visit to the museum a rewarding experience.

The James Monroe Museum and Memorial Library is located in Fredericksburg's expansive Historic District. The museum is owned by the Commonwealth of Virginia and administered by the University of Mary Washington, also located in Fredericksburg.

DIRECTIONS: From I 95, exit eastbound on SR 3 and go into Historic Fredericksburg, then go south on Charles Street 0.5 block to the museum on the right (Figure 17).

PUBLIC USE: Season and hours: March-November, Monday-Saturday, 10 AM-5 PM; Sunday, 1 PM-5 PM. December-February; Monday-Saturday, 10 AM-4 PM. Sunday, 1 PM-4 PM. Closed Thanksgiving Day, December 24, 25, 31 and New Year's Day. **Admission fee. Museum shop. For people with disabilities:** Partially accessible.

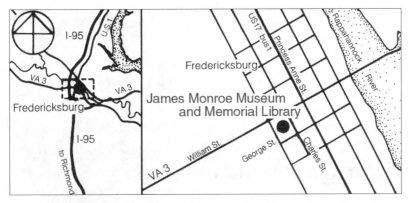

Figure 17. Location of James Monroe Museum and Memorial Library.

FOR ADDITIONAL INFORMATION: Contact: James Monroe Museum and Memorial Library, 908 Charles Street, Fredericksburg, Virginia 22401-5810, (540) 654-1043. **Web site:** *www.umw.edu/jamesmonroemuseum.* **Read:** (1) James Monroe. 1959. *The Autobiography of James Monroe.* (2) Lee Langston-Harrison. 1992. *Images of a President: Portraits of James Monroe.*

John Quincy Adams

Sixth President — 1825–1829

Born July 11, 1767, Braintree (now Quincy), Massachusetts
Died February 23, 1848, Washington, DC

> I want a garden and a park
> My dwelling to surround
> A thousand acres (bless the mark!)
> With walls encompassed round,
> Where flocks may range and herds may low,
> And kids and lambkins play
> And flowers and fruits comming led grow
> All Eden to display.
>
> — John Quincy Adams

John Quincy Adams was the first son of a president to attain the same high office once held by his father. The younger Adams was ascetic, impatient, and often aloof in his relationships with others, although his love of country and deep devotion to public service were unquestionably sincere.

As a youngster, John Quincy had accompanied his father on diplomatic assignments to Europe, so it was not surprising that his own political career began with similar diplomatic postings. He spent considerable time overseas before returning to the United States to serve as Secretary of State in the cabinet of James Monroe, wherein he was influential in framing the Monroe Doctrine.

In 1824, Adams ran for president, but none of the presidential candidates received a majority of the popular or electoral votes. As a result, the election was thrown into the House of Representatives. In the first tabulation, Adams was second to Andrew Jackson, but the influential senator Henry Clay swung his considerable support to Adams, who won on the second ballot by a single vote. When Adams subsequently named Clay Secretary of State, the appointment was looked upon unkindly by the suspicious electorate who, four years later, swept Jackson into the presidency.

Adams's constituents in Massachusetts were loath to lose his brilliance and political influence, however, and elected him to congress, making him the first ex-president to so serve. He remained in congress for almost eight terms until he suffered a stroke on the floor of the chamber. To his last breath he was a passionate political fighter for his personal beliefs, the good of Massachusetts, and the glory of the nation.

Where could death have found him, but at the post of duty?

— Senator Thomas Hart Benton

The Adams National Historical Park (see pages 34–37) is a memorial to a remarkable legacy in our political heritage, a tribute to one of the Founding Fathers, John Adams, and to his son, John Quincy Adams, who continued the valuable family tradition of public service.

Andrew Jackson

Seventh President — 1829–1837

Born March 15, 1767, The Waxhaws, South Carolina
Died June 8, 1845, The Hermitage, Nashville, Tennessee

[Jackson is] incompetent both by his ignorance and by the fury of his passions. He will be surrounded and governed by incompetent men, whose ascendancy over him will be secured by their servility and who will bring to the Government of the nation nothing but their talent for intrigue.

— John Quincy Adams, during
the 1824 presidential campaign

Faults he had, such faults as often belong to an ardent, generous, sincere nature — the weeds that grow in rich soil. Notwithstanding this, he was precisely the man for the period in which he fell and nobly discharged the duties demanded of him by the times.

— William Cullen Bryant, 1836

Today, Andrew Jackson might be considered a "troubled youth." His father died before he was born, his family was poor, and he was a hellion — an undisciplined and constant mischief-maker. Jackson often told the story of having participated in the Revolutionary War as a messenger when he was only thirteen. He and one of his brothers were captured by the British and held prisoner. When feisty Andrew was ordered to polish the boots of an officer, he refused. His penalty was a blow on the head by the officer's sword. Jackson carried the scar proudly through life.

Jackson had an innate sense of his own ability and a compelling determination to overcome his impoverished background. He moved west to Salisbury, North Carolina, where he read for the law and qualified for the bar in 1787. He then settled in the western district of North Carolina, the part that would become Tennessee, where he served as attorney general for the district and established his own successful private practice. He served in the Tennessee Constitutional Convention and in the United States Congress before moving to Nashville to sit on the Tennessee Supreme Court.

In 1802, Jackson was elected major general of the Tennessee militia. During the War of 1812, he received a commission as a major general in the United States Army after he had defeated the Creek Indians at Horseshoe Bend, Alabama. As commander of United States forces, Jackson won a dramatic victory over the British military at New Orleans which earned him national attention and initiated a political boom that would lead to the presidency. Although he lost his first bid for that office in the disputed presidential election of 1824, he was elected handily in 1828 and reelected in 1832. He proved to be an active chief executive who greatly expanded the power and prestige of the office.

The Hermitage

NASHVILLE, TENNESSEE

The 425-acre Hermitage Plantation that Andrew and Rachel Jackson bought in 1804 was a far cry from The Hermitage that visitors enjoy today (Plate 3). When the Jacksons acquired the property, it was merely a clump of log buildings — storerooms, slave quarters, and a two-story house (Figure 4) where the Jacksons lived until 1821, when they moved into a more fashionable home built in the Federal style popular in America at that time. The house was plain, its symmetrical facade embellished only with a fan-lighted entry. In 1831, Jackson began the addition of two wings and a colonnade.

Three years later, The Hermitage was partially destroyed by fire; the upper floor was lost and the ground floor was severely damaged. Jackson, who was serving as president at the time, had the house rebuilt within the original walls and foundation, but the rooflines were changed and columns were added to the portico in the Greek Revival style then becoming popular. The interior was totally renovated; rooms were enlarged and new wallpaper, carpeting, and furniture were added. To unify the elements of the house and complete the Greek Revival look, the front brick walls were painted white, although the other sides remained brick red.

As Jackson prospered, the plantation grew to include more than 1000 acres worked by 140 slaves. Jackson entertained simply but constantly, and The Hermitage, with its large rooms and handsome furniture, reflected a gracious lifestyle. After Jackson's death in 1845, however, the property fell into decline. By 1856, Andrew Jackson, Jr., Jackson's adopted son, had come into financial difficulty and was forced to sell the mansion and five hundred acres of property to the State of Tennessee. The state had intended to propose that The Hermitage become a branch of the United States Military Academy, but that scheme died and the Jackson family was invited back to manage the state-owned property.

During the Civil War, The Hermitage was protected from physical damage but the loss of agricultural productivity was ruinous. With its viability in doubt, the state considered converting the estate into a home for indigent Confederate soldiers. But at the same time, Amy Jackson, wife of Andrew Jackson, III, inspired by the success of the Mount Vernon Ladies' Association, formed a similar women's organization in Nashville to reclaim The Hermitage. On February 19, 1889, The Ladies' Hermitage Association was officially recognized under charter of the State of Tennessee. Over a century later, the Association remains the custodian of The Hermitage.

Today, visitors to The Hermitage enter a sprawling visitor center that houses a museum shop, restaurant, and a small but impressive museum that contains original Jackson artifacts, memorabilia, and graphic displays that trace Jackson's career and the history of The Hermitage. Self-guided tours of the property begin with the screening of a sixteen-minute orientation film, then move into the mansion where trained interpreters are stationed to answer questions. The most frequently asked question pertains to the panoramic wallpaper covering the entire front hall. Scenic wallpaper was popular in fine homes of the period; in this case, the paper depicts the epic legend of Telemachus searching for his father Odysseus on the Island of Calypso.

Another popular item is Rachel Jackson's portrait that hangs over the mantel in the president's bedroom. Mrs. Jackson died only weeks after the 1828 election, and Jackson had his friend Ralph E. W. Earl paint a copy of his portrait of Rachel to be placed opposite his bed at the White House "so it might be the first object to meet my eyes when my lids open in the morning and the last for my gaze to leave when they close in sleep at night."

The grounds at The Hermitage are colorful, lush, and manicured. The walk from the visitor center to the mansion winds past a guitar-shaped driveway bordered by cedar trees, some planted in 1838. Tragically, a devastating tornado in 1998 destroyed many of the old cedars and hundreds of other trees, but the cedars along the drive have been replanted. To the east is "Rachel's Garden," an excellent example of a southern plantation garden. Over an acre in size, it is maintained with the same kinds of flowers that were available when Rachel Jackson gathered bouquets for departing guests or made floral arrangements for the house. There are over fifty varieties of flowers, shrubs, herbs, and trees; the central beds are arranged in a formal geometric design, with brick borders. At the southeast corner of the garden is the Jackson tomb, a stone monument built along classic Greek lines with a copper dome supported by fluted columns.

To the rear of the mansion are a number of outbuildings which include the smokehouse, three original log buildings, and a springhouse. Just down Rachel's Lane stands Tulip Grove, the residence of Andrew Jackson Donelson, Rachel's nephew and the president's private secretary. Nearby is the Old Hermitage Church, built on land donated by Jackson in 1823. Jackson attended services at this church regularly and became a member in 1838. Both Tulip Grove Mansion and Old Hermitage Church are accessible as parts of a visit to The Hermitage.

The Hermitage conducts an extensive research and educational program including summer garden tours and a "hands-on" history series for children. In the summer months, visitors may watch archaeological excavations that are revealing much about life on The Hermitage plantation.

At The Hermitage, Jackson was the opposite of his public persona — the tough old general or stern, squabbling politician. Childless, the Jacksons adopted one of Rachel's nephews and eventually the mansion filled with friends, children, and grandchildren, all of whom delighted Jackson, "The Old Spoiler." The Hermitage was a friendly house, filled with joy and security. It is easy to understand why Jackson, frequently absent in service to the nation, always returned home to The Hermitage.

DIRECTIONS: The Hermitage may be reached by taking the Old Hickory Boulevard Exit from I 40 eastbound, I 65 northbound, or I 24 northbound from Nashville, Tennessee (Figure 18). The entrance onto Old Hickory Boulevard off I 40 is prominently marked.

PUBLIC USE: Season and hours: 9 AM-5 PM. Closed Thanksgiving Day, Christmas Day and Tuesday-Friday of the third week in January. **Admission fee. Food service:** There is a public restaurant on site, plus two outdoor picnic areas. **Museum shop. For people with disabilities:** Accessible, with the exception of the second floor of the mansion and Tulip Grove mansion.

FOR ADDITIONAL INFORMATION: Contact: The Hermitage, 4580 Rachel's Lane, Nashville, Tennessee 37076-1344, (615) 889-2941. **Web site:** *www.thehermitage.com.* **Read:** (1) Stanley Horn. 1976. *The Hermitage.* (2) Patricia L. Hudson. 1990. "Old Hickory's House."

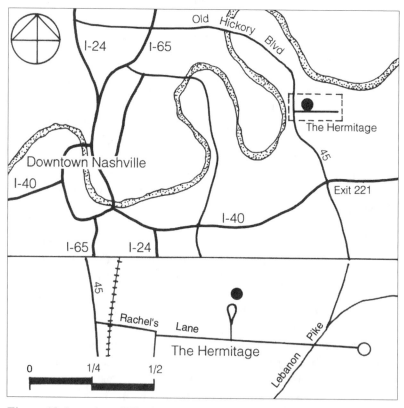

Figure 18. Location of The Hermitage, Nashville, Tennessee.

Martin Van Buren

Eighth President — 1837–1841

Born December 5, 1782, Kinderhook, New York
Died July 24, 1862, Kinderhook, New York

> *I, Martin Van Buren . . . heretofore Governor of the State and more recently President of the United States, but for the last and happiest years of my life, a Farmer in my native town.*

> — Martin Van Buren, the start of his will

Martin Van Buren was the first president to have been born as a citizen of the United States and was the first Governor of New York to seek the presidency. Born in 1782 in the tiny hamlet of Kinderhook, New York, as the son of a tavern keeper, he attended local schools, studied law, gravitated to politics, and served as a United States senator, New York's governor, and secretary of state and vice president under Andrew Jackson.

Van Buren was elected to the presidency in 1836, but his term was clouded by the financial panic of 1837, which began almost immediately upon his inauguration and contributed to his failed bid for reelection. The 1840 campaign highlighted his dismal economic record — actually inherited from the Jackson presidency — and was notable as a masterpiece of political prowess carried out by his opponents.

Van Buren's opposition nominated William Henry Harrison, a Virginia aristocrat with a distinguished frontier military record. Harrison was craftily portrayed by the Whigs as "a man of the people" and "the candidate of hard cider and a log cabin." On the other hand, Van Buren, who was a man of humble beginnings and had been born in his parents' tavern, was depicted as a champagne-swilling dilettante who used silver spoons and dainty tea cups in the White House. The tactic was successful, and Harrison and the Whigs carried the day.

Van Buren's single term has been described by scholars as undistinguished, but a linguistic legacy of his final run for office, the everyday expression "OK," remains with us to this day. There are conflicting theories as to the derivation of this bit of American slang, but one of the more interesting is that it stands for "Old Kinderhook," one of Van Buren's nicknames. The first recorded use of the expression to signify approval took place in 1839 when a newspaper referred to a Democratic Party meeting of "roarers, the butt-enders, ringtails, and O.K.s," the last allusion apparently being to those who marked ballots "O.K." for Martin Van Buren.

Van Buren's political nickname was "The Little Magician," as he was a master of cool, competent persuasion — one of the first great political manipulators in our history. Defeated by Harrison, but unbowed, he sought the Democratic nomination for president once again in 1844, only to be defeated by James K. Polk. In 1848, never-say-die Van Buren switched political affiliation to run as the presidential candidate of the Free-Soil party, a group opposing the extension of slavery. His subsequent defeat finally ended his remarkable political career.

Martin Van Buren National Historic Site

KINDERHOOK, NEW YORK

Martin Van Buren returned to Kinderhook in 1841. Two years earlier he had paid $14,000 for a two-story red brick house situated on a fine piece of prime farm land once owned by his ancestors. He named the place "Lindenwald," German for "Grove of Linden Trees," after the lovely trees that surrounded the property (Plate 4).

Belying his humble background, Van Buren, by now a wealthy and fastidious man with expensive tastes, lavished money and attention on extensive renovations to Lindenwald, both inside and out. For the exterior he decided upon a "Venetian Villa" appearance that involved a third story and the addition of a library wing, a porch, a 4½-story tower and additional rooms.

The red brick exterior was painted yellow and the interior was refurbished with fresh hangings, new furniture, and spectacular wallpaper. The front hall was handsomely decorated with fifty-one panels of rich French wallpaper depicting a European hunting scene.

Van Buren's daughter-in-law once described her young son's "little shrieks of delight [that] can be heard all over the house when he is shown the dogs and cows of the hall paper." Modern visitors share that delight when visiting Lindenwald. The paper, fine paintings, expensive furnishings, and what may be his White House china recall a time when gentleman farmer Martin Van Buren "drank the pure pleasure of a rural life" at his retirement home.

After a number of ownerships and lack of interest in the property's historical significance, Lindenwald was purchased by the National Park Service in 1976 and restored to the charm it possessed when owned by "The Red Fox of Kinderhook," Martin Van Buren.

DIRECTIONS: From the Taconic Parkway, go westbound on SR 23 for 6 miles to US 9H, then go northbound for 10.5 miles to Lindenwald. From I 90E, take Exit 12 onto US 9, go 5 miles to US 9H, then go southbound 5 miles to Lindenwald (Figure 19).

PUBLIC USE: Season and hours: Mid-May to October 31, 9 AM-4:30 PM. **Admission fee. For people with disabilities:** There is a wheelchair lift to the first floor. The basement and second floor are not accessible although there is a visual tour available for those who are disabled.

FOR ADDITIONAL INFORMATION: Contact: Martin Van Buren National Historic Site, 1013 Old Post Road, Kinderhook, New York 12106, (518) 758-9689. **Web site:** *www.nps.gov/mava.* **Read:** (1) John Niven. 1983. *Martin Van Buren, the Romantic Age of American Politics.* (2) Donald Cole. 2004. *Martin Van Buren and the American Political System.* (3) Ted Widmer. 2005. *Martin Van Buren.*

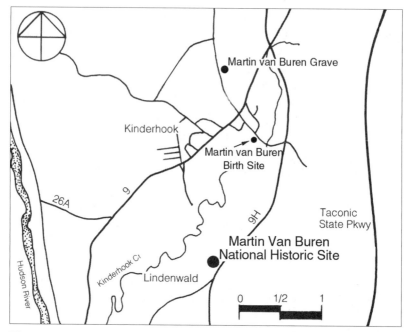

Figure 19. Location of Martin Van Buren National Historic Site, Kinderhook, New York.

Decatur House

WASHINGTON, DC

While serving as secretary of state in the cabinet of Andrew Jackson, Martin Van Buren resided in Decatur House (Figure 20), an elegant Federal-style red brick townhouse designed by Benjamin H. Latrobe. Decatur House is on the northwest corner of Lafayette Square, one block north of The White House just across Pennsylvania Avenue.

Decatur House was built in 1818 for Commodore Stephen Decatur, hero of the War of 1812 and of conflicts with the Barbary Pirates. It also has served as home to cabinet officers, congressmen, secretaries of state, foreign ministers, and other important political and diplomatic figures. As a gathering place for politicians and statesmen, Decatur House has played an important part in our nation's progress.

Figure 20. Decatur House, Washington, DC. Photograph courtesy of Decatur House, a museum property of National Trust for Historic Preservation.

On the darker side, however, was the construction in the late 1830s of a two-story attachment to the rear of the house, a dependency utilized as slave quarters. At least thirteen enslaved people lived there until President Lincoln signed the District of Columbia Emancipation Act on April 16, 1862, months prior to the more famous Emancipation Proclamation. Slaves in Washington were freed in the only compensated emancipation in the nation, as owners were paid for their "losses" by the federal government. This important and little-known part of Black History in America is recounted as part of a tour of Decatur House and its slave quarters.

Following the Civil War, during which it served as a clothing depot, Decatur House was purchased by General Edward Beale, a close personal friend and confidante of Ulysses S. Grant. The Beale family was socially prominent and the house was host to hundreds of distinguished visitors including Grant, who stayed with the Beales during a much-publicized return visit to Washington shortly after the end of his presidency. In 1956, its last owner, Mrs. Marie Oge Beale, bequeathed Decatur House to the National Trust for Historic Preservation under whose attention the mansion is now maintained as a museum representing 175 years of residential living in Washington. The ground floor rooms reflect the Federal style of the Decatur era; the formal parlors on the second floor remain decorated in the Victorian style used by the Beale family.

DIRECTIONS: Decatur House is located on Jackson Place NW opposite the west side of Lafayette Park at the center of Washington's most famous historic district (Figure 15).

PUBLIC USE: Season and hours: Tuesday-Saturday, 10 AM-5 PM; Sunday, 12 M-4 PM. Guided tours leave every hour on the quarter hour. Closed Thanksgiving Day, Christmas Day, New Year's Day. **Museum shop. For people with disabilities:** Fully accessible.

FOR ADDITIONAL INFORMATION: Contact: Decatur House, 1610 H Street, NW, Washington, DC 20006, (202) 842-0920. **Web site:** *www.decaturhouse.org.* **Read:** (1) Marie Beale. 1954. *Decatur House and its Inhabitants.* (2) Helen Duprey Bullock. 1967. "Decatur House."

William Henry Harrison

Ninth President — March, 1841–April, 1841

Born February 9, 1773, Charles City, Virginia
Died April 4, 1841, Washington, DC

> What has caused this great commotion
> All the country through?
> It is the ball a-rolling on
> For Tippecanoe and Tyler too.

> — Campaign song, 1840

Campaign songs and rhetoric to the contrary, William Henry Harrison was anything but a common man. His father, Benjamin, was a signer of the Declaration of Independence and a three-time Governor of Virginia, and William Henry was born at Berkeley, a great James River plantation that had been in the family for a century.

William Henry was an eighteen-year-old medical student when his father died. Attracted by the West and the idea of fighting the British who still occupied parts of the western territories, the ambitious young man visited his father's old friend George Washington and obtained a commission as ensign in the fledgling American army. He was assigned to the western frontier where he remained for many years.

In 1800, when only twenty-two years old, Harrison was appointed Governor of Indiana Territory and made his military and residential headquarters in Vincennes. He wrote, "I am much pleased with this country. Nothing can exceed its beauty and fertility."

Although engaged in periodic conflicts with Indians (in the most famous of these encounters he defeated the Shawnee at the Tippecanoe River, which earned him his famous nickname, "Old Tippecanoe"), it was during this period that Harrison began construction of a home, designed in a style reminiscent of his boyhood home, Berkeley Plantation in Virginia. He called it Grouseland because of the many birds on the property. He and his family resided at Grouseland until 1812 when they moved to Ohio. In 1814, Harrison retired from the military to begin a career in local and regional politics. In 1836, to his surprise and that of many others, he was nominated for the presidency by the newly formed Whig party. He was defeated, but ran a strong enough race to be nominated again in 1840. With the nation's economy in disarray, he easily defeated incumbent Martin Van Buren.

Harrison's time in office was shockingly brief. He died of pneumonia only one month into his term, the first president to die while in office.

Berkeley Plantation

CHARLES CITY, VIRGINIA

Berkeley Plantation (Plate 4) is famous as the ancestral home of the Harrison family; it is the birthplace of William Henry Harrison, our ninth president, and Benjamin Harrison V, a signer of the Declaration of Independence. Its legacy dates to 1619 when thirty-eight Englishmen calling themselves the Berkeley Company put ashore to establish a colony under a grant from the London Company. On December 4, the tiny group fell to their knees in thankful prayer, an act recognized by some as the first Thanksgiving in America. The Berkeley settlement was tragically short-lived, however, as it fell victim to a bloody Indian uprising in 1622.

The Harrisons, a family of English descent who had been in the Virginia Colony for two generations, acquired the Berkeley property in 1691. They expanded the estate to include a shipyard and tobacco warehouse, but it was not until 1726 that Benjamin Harrison IV built the Georgian mansion that subsequently became the base for the family's commercial and agricultural empire.

The manor house, the oldest three-story brick house in Virginia that can prove its date, is situated on a landscaped hilltop within a nearly 1000-acre estate. The grounds include a formal boxwood garden and textured lawns that slope from the front door of the mansion to the banks of the James River. Handsome Adam woodwork and double arches in the "Great Rooms" were installed in 1790 at the direction of Thomas Jefferson.

By the middle of the nineteenth century, financial setbacks caused the Harrison family to lose Berkeley. During the Civil War, the house was appropriated as headquarters for General George McClellan leading the Army of the Potomac. During that bivouac, McClellan's aide, General Daniel Butterfield, composed the plaintive *Taps,* played for the first time at Berkeley by company bugler O. W. Norton. A commemorative plaque on the grounds marks the historic event. President Abraham Lincoln visited Berkeley twice during the war to confer with General McClellan.

Following the war, the estate declined until 1907 when it was purchased by Scottish-born John Jamieson, formerly a drummer boy in McClellan's army. Jamieson's son and daughter-in-law, Malcolm and Grace, inherited Berkeley in 1927 and are responsible for the restoration of the property to the state that appears much the same as it did in the glory days when owned by the Harrisons. Visitors are particularly interested in the 1726 manor house, as all of the interior rooms are furnished with authentic furniture and fine antiques. William Henry Harrison returned to Berkeley after his election to the presidency to write his inaugural address in the room where he was born.

As Parke Rouse, Jr. and Susan Burtch remark in their book, *Berkeley Plantation and Hundred*:

> *Berkeley Hundred Plantation stands today as a reminder of those men of vision, Americans of long ago who worked and fought to make this country free and prosperous. It is at once a birthplace and an inheritance: not only a plantation home, but in a very real sense, an ancestral home common to Americans nationwide.*

DIRECTIONS: Berkeley Plantation is on Virginia SR 5 between Richmond and Williamsburg (Figure 21).

PUBLIC USE: Season and hours: Guided tours conducted daily, 9 AM-5 PM; last tour leaves at 4:30 PM. Tours of the grounds are self-conducted. Closed Christmas Day, Thanksgiving Day. **Admission fee. Gift shop. Museum.**

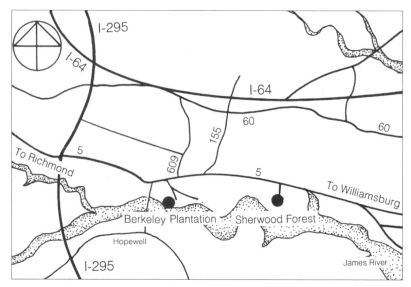

Figure 21. Location of Berkeley Plantation and Sherwood Forest, Charles City, Virginia.

For people with disabilities: Accessibility is limited. Some assistance is available with advance notice.

FOR ADDITIONAL INFORMATION: Contact: Berkeley Plantation, 12602 Harrison Landing Road, Charles City, Virginia 23030, (804) 829-6018 *or* 1-888-466-6018. **Web site:** *www.berkeleyplantation.com.* **Read:** (1) Clifford Dowdey. 1957. *The Great Plantation.* (2) Parke Rouse, Jr. and Susan Burtch. 1980. *Berkeley Plantation and Hundred.* (3) John Coski. 1989. *The Army of the Potomac at Berkeley Plantation: The Harrison's Landing Occupation of 1862.* (4) Bruce Roberts. 1990. *Plantation Homes of the James River.*

Grouseland

VINCENNES, INDIANA

I wish that my husband's friends had left him where he is, happy and contented in retirement.

— Anne Harrison, leaving for Washington
to become First Lady and learning of her husband's death.

In 1800, William Henry Harrison was appointed first Governor of Indiana Territory, then part of the western frontier of the United States. Accustomed to living well in Virginia, he began construction, between 1803 and 1804, of a house that was similar in appearance to his boyhood home at Berkeley Plantation and that would be a visible symbol of civility and style on the frontier. He named the house Grouseland in acknowledgment of the numerous game birds found on the property.

There were, however, many significant structural differences between Grouseland and Berkeley. The threat of Indian raids in Indiana was real, and consequently the brick outer walls of Grouseland were eighteen inches thick. In addition, the walls and ceilings were reinforced against the stress caused by the weight of the Harrisons's many guests. Grouseland (Figure 22) contains seventeen rooms and ten fireplaces. The rooms were always filled as the Harrisons had eight children, entertained frequently, and offered a haven for their neighbors in the event of an Indian attack.

After the Harrisons moved to Ohio in 1812, Grouseland underwent many changes of occupancy. A period of ignominy included its use as a grain storage facility and later as a less-than-four-star hotel while the railroad was being built. Shortly after the Civil War, Grouseland was reclaimed as a private residence, but by 1909 it was decaying and was scheduled for demolition to make room for a water company's settling tank.

Grouseland was saved from the wrecker's ball by the intervention of the newly formed Francis Vigo Chapter, Daughters of the American Revolution, who were granted custody of the historic home. The ladies filled the house with genuine Harrison possessions and other period pieces, and opened the house for visitation in 1911. In 1998, the Frances Vigo Chapter created the Grouseland Foundation to maintain the mansion and attend to the requirements of its placement on the National Register of Historic Places.

Figure 22. Grouseland, Vincennes, Indiana. Photograph courtesy of Francis Vigo Chapter, Daughters of the American Revolution.

The basement of the mansion serves as a museum, and the dependency is used for historical displays — war materiel, uniforms, maps, and other artifacts delineating the life and career of the hero of the Battle of Tippecanoe and the War of 1812 — a man who served our young nation with distinction, then achieved another distinction when he led that country as its ninth president for only thirty-one days.

DIRECTIONS: From US 50 (Business) in Vincennes, take the 6th Street Exit. Go northbound on 6th to Harrison, then west on Harrison Street to North 1st Street, then go south on North 1st to Scott Street, then west on Scott 1.5 blocks to Grouseland, located on the southern boundary of the Vincennes University campus (Figure 23).

PUBLIC USE: Season and hours: January-February, 11 AM-4 PM; March-December, Monday-Saturday, 9 AM-5 PM; Sunday, 11 AM-5 PM. Closed Thanksgiving Day, Christmas Day, New Year's Day. **Admission fee. Museum shop. For people with disabilities:** No special facilities.

FOR ADDITIONAL INFORMATION: Contact: Grouseland Foundation, Inc., 3 West Scott Street, Vincennes, Indiana 47591, (812) 882-2096. **Web site:** *www.grouselandfoundation.org.* **Read:** (1) Loretha Hamke. 1985. *All about William Henry Harrison.* (2) Freeman Cleaves. 1990. *Old Tippecanoe: William Henry Harrison and His Time.*

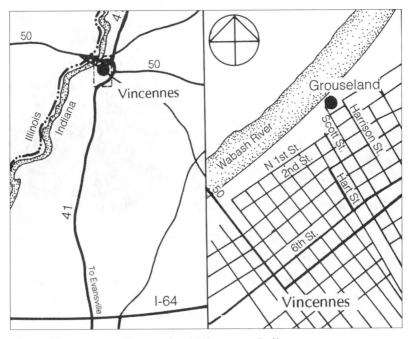

Figure 23. Location of Grouseland, Vincennes, Indiana.

John Tyler

Tenth President — 1841–1845

Born March 29, 1790, Charles City, Virginia
Died January 18, 1862, Richmond, Virginia

> *My daughters, you are now occupying a position of great importance.*
>
> *I desire you to bear in mind three things: show no favoritism, accept no gifts, receive no seekers after office.*

> — John Tyler's admonition to his family
> at his inauguration.

John Tyler was the first vice president to succeed a president who died in office. Fletcher Webster, son of Daniel Webster, was dispatched from Washington to Williamsburg, Virginia, to inform Vice President John Tyler that President Harrison had died — only thirty-one days into his term. Tyler was asleep when Webster arrived on horseback at one o'clock in the morning.

Tyler's ascent to the presidency shocked the nation, particularly some political leaders who found the country under the direction of a new president not under their control and influence. Some even suggested that Tyler resign and not assume the presidency, but Tyler stood firm on strong constitutional grounds and refused to be swayed by such sentiments. He wrote:

> *I can never consent to being dictated to. I, as President, shall be answerable for my administration. My resignation would amount to a declaration to the world that our system of government has failed.*

Thus Tyler set a legal and moral precedent for vice presidents who have followed. Another constitutional crisis passed; the trial and error process of the new democracy — and the strength and courage of John Tyler — had resulted in victory for the people. "His Accidency," as he was called by some of his enemies, proved to be a man of vigor and honesty, with solid beliefs in the Constitution and the evolving democracy it guided.

In 1842, early in his term, Tyler's wife, Letitia, died, the first First Lady to pass away in the White House. In 1844, the president remarried, taking twenty-four-year-old Julia Gardiner as his bride in a ceremony held in her home state, New York. With this marriage, Tyler became the first president to marry while in office. The couple enjoyed the remaining eight months of his presidency, during which time they campaigned together for the annexation of Texas into the Union. Tyler signed the annexation into law only two days before his term ended, and he presented Julia with the golden pen used to sign the bill into law. She wore it on a necklace to the inauguration of James K. Polk, and later to her grave. Upon their departure from the White House, the Tylers moved to Sherwood Forest, their retirement estate along the James River in Virginia.

Sherwood Forest Plantation

CHARLES CITY, VIRGINIA

While serving as president, John Tyler, anticipating retirement, purchased a plantation along the James River not far from where he had grown up. He christened the house Sherwood Forest since he considered himself a political Robin Hood. Sherwood Forest (Plate 4) was a Georgian clapboard structure that Tyler renovated in the Greek Revival style and increased in size by connecting the law offices to the main house with a sixty-eight-foot-long ballroom. Three stories tall and only one room deep, the completed house ended up with a three-hundred-foot façade, the longest frame house in America.

The large house was necessary to accommodate Tyler's second family of seven children. His prolificacy remains a presidential record; he had fathered eight children by his first wife. Sherwood Forest's spacious rooms include a family sitting room occupied by a two-hundred-year-old ghost, the

Gray Lady. Legend has it that she descends a hidden staircase each night and rocks until dawn in a non-existent rocking chair. Presumably, she is the only ghost to haunt a presidential home.

The Gray Lady notwithstanding, Sherwood Forest has been owned and occupied continuously by direct descendants of President Tyler. The property is still a 1600-acre working plantation, and remains the repository of treasures of the Tyler family.

A number of original outbuildings are located on the grounds. The colorful gardens and lush woods also appeal to visitors. Among the more than eighty varieties of century-old trees found on the grounds is a large ginkgo tree from Japan. Captain Matthew C. Perry, who opened trade between the United States and Japan in 1853, presented the tree to the Tylers to commemorate the president's success in opening trade with China in 1844.

DIRECTIONS: Sherwood Forest Plantation is located on Virginia SR 5 (Figure 21).

PUBLIC USE: Season and hours: The 26 acres of grounds immediately adjacent to the mansion of Sherwood Forest Plantation are open 9 AM-5 PM daily. The mansion, however, is an active residence and may be visited only with advance reservations.

FOR ADDITIONAL INFORMATION: Contact: Sherwood Forest Plantation, 14501 John Tyler Memorial Highway, Charles City, Virginia 23030, (804) 829-5377. **Web site:** *www.sherwoodforest.org.* **Read:** (1) Robert Seager, II. 1963. *And Tyler, too.* (2) Oliver Perry Chitwood. 1990. *John Tyler: Champion of the Old South.* (3) Bruce Roberts. 1990. *Plantation Homes of the James River.* (4) Jane C. Walker. 2001. *John Tyler: A President of Many Firsts.*

James Knox Polk

Eleventh President — 1845–1849

Born November 2, 1795, Pineville, North Carolina
Died June 15, 1849, Nashville, Tennessee

> *I would relieve the burdens of the whole community as far as possible, by reducing the taxes. I would keep as much money in the treasury as the safety of the Government required, and no more. I would keep no surplus revenue there to scramble for, either for internal improvements, or for anything else. I would bring the Government back to what it was intended to be . . . . a plain economical Government.*
>
> — James K. Polk

James K. Polk is recognized today as a strong and forceful president. A compromise candidate for his party's nomination, he won the general election and went on to accomplish every goal of his administration — the acquisition of California, settlement of the Oregon boundary dispute, reduction of a tariff which he felt favored the industrializing north and hurt southern development, and the establishment of an independent treasury. These remarkable achievements are a credit to Polk's singular dedication, sincerity, and business-like conduct of government affairs.

Polk was born on a North Carolina farm, the first child of a strict, God-fearing Presbyterian family. When he was eleven, his family moved west to Tennessee where their determination and hard work led to financial success.

James graduated from college with honors, practiced law, and entered politics as a protégé of Andrew Jackson. He represented Tennessee in congress for seven terms, then returned to Nashville to run for governor of Tennessee. He served a single term before resuming his law practice. When the Democratic Convention of 1844 deadlocked, his name was brought forward as "Jackson's Choice" and "Young Hickory," as he was dubbed, was nominated as the darkest of dark horses.

As he had promised, Polk served but a single term. Physically exhausted by the pressures of the presidency, he passed away a few months after returning home to Tennessee. At the news of his death, James Buchanan said of him:

> *He was the most laborious man I have ever known, and in a brief period of four years had assumed the appearance of an old man.*

President James K. Polk State Historic Site

PINEVILLE, NORTH CAROLINA

James K. Polk, like other early presidents, was a son of the soil. His life began on a one hundred-fifty-acre farm worked by his parents on the Carolina Piedmont in what is today southern North Carolina. The President James K. Polk State Historic Site (Figure 24) lies on twenty-one acres of the original farm. Visitors to the memorial can imagine young James performing his daily chores — feeding the animals, planting, hoeing and reaping. The work was hard, the only rewards the development of industry, family responsibility, frugality, and devotion — ingrained qualities that served Polk and the nation well throughout his tenure of public service. Reconstructed buildings representative of the Polk homestead — log house, kitchen house, and the barn — have been furnished with period items to approximate their appearance at the time of the Polk residency.

The Polk Memorial is owned by the State of North Carolina and administered by the Division of State Historic Sites. A visitor center features a thirteen-minute film plus colorful exhibits illustrating significant events in Polk's personal and presidential life.

Figure 24. President James K. Polk State Historic Site, Pineville, North Carolina. Photograph by Larry Misenheimer; use courtesy of North Carolina Department of Archives and History.

DIRECTIONS: From I 485 at Pineville, take US 521 southbound through Pineville for 3 miles to the President James K. Polk State Historic Site on the east (Figure 25).

PUBLIC USE: Season and hours: Tuesday-Saturday, 10 AM-4 PM. Closed major holidays. **Gift shop. For people with disabilities:** The visitor center is accessible.

FOR ADDITIONAL INFORMATION: Contact: President James K. Polk State Historic Site, Box 475, Pineville, North Carolina 28134, (704) 889-7145. **Web site:** *www.polk.nchistoricsites.org.* **Read**: Charles C. Sellers. 1957. *James K. Polk: Jacksonian,* 1795–1843.

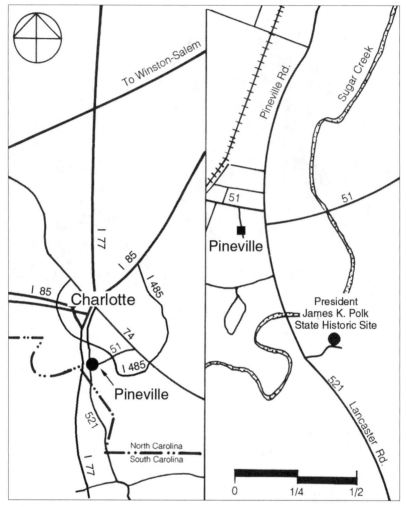

Figure 25. Location of President James K. Polk State Historic Site, Pineville, North Carolina.

James K. Polk Ancestral Home

COLUMBIA, TENNESSEE

Searching for a more secure future, the Samuel Polk family moved west from North Carolina when son James was eleven. They settled in Columbia, Tennessee, where Samuel subsequently prospered as a farmer and land surveyor. Financial success enabled him to build a comfortable home (Plate 5), a two-story Federal-style structure of handmade bricks. James lived with the family in this home until he married in 1824.

The interior of the Polk home was typical of a well-to-do Tennessee farmer of the time. It had a double parlor off the entrance hall and three bedrooms on the second floor. Outside, there were gardens and a separate kitchen building. The house next door was home to Polk's sisters, a building similar in design to the main house, which now serves as the visitor center to the Polk Ancestral Home. Later residents nicknamed the house "Sisters."

Tours of the Polk property begin at the visitor center with the screening of an orientation film, and then move to a museum area with exhibits that feature Polk's life and career. Visitors are always intrigued by the "National Fan," an inauguration gift from the new president to Mrs. Polk, a gift which she carried to the inaugural ball. On one side of the fan are miniature portraits of Polk and the ten previous presidents, with "President-elect" written above Polk's picture. On the reverse side is a rendering of the signing of the Declaration of Independence. Other popular items on exhibit include Sarah Polk's satin ball gown and the Bible upon which James Polk swore his oath of office as president. Also on display is the first daguerreotype photograph of a president and his cabinet, taken in the White House. Guests are then taken next door to the Polk home, which contains original furniture, silver, crystal, and Polk's set of White House china, decorated with Tennessee wildflowers and bordered by the shield of the United States.

In anticipation of retirement from the presidency, the Polks purchased a colonnaded mansion in Nashville that, together with formal gardens, occupied a full city block. It was called "Polk Place" and was where former president Polk passed away in 1849. Mrs. Polk lived in the home until her death in 1891. Contrary to Polk's explicit instructions, "Polk Place" was razed, a tragedy for all Americans who love, appreciate, and gain inspiration from the places where great men once lived.

DIRECTIONS: From I 40 westbound, proceed southbound on I 440 (Exit 213) to I 65, then southbound to Saturn Parkway. Turn right (westbound) to US Route 31 and proceed southbound to Columbia. In Columbia, turn right on West 7th Street to the Polk house. From I 40 eastbound, take I 440 southbound (Exit 206) to I 65 southbound and follow the preceding directions (Figure 26).

PUBLIC USE: Season and hours: April-October, Monday-Saturday, 9 AM-5 PM; Sunday, 1 PM-5 PM. November-March, Monday-Saturday, 9 AM-4 PM; Sunday, 1 PM-5 PM. Closed Thanksgiving Day, Christmas Eve Day, Christmas Day, New Year's Day. **Admission fee. Gift shop. For people with disabilities:** Partially accessible.

FOR ADDITIONAL INFORMATION: Contact: James K. Polk Ancestral Home, Box 741, Columbia, Tennessee 38402, (931) 388-2354. **Web site:** *www.jameskpolk.com.* **Read:** Betty D. Elder. 1980. *A Special House.*

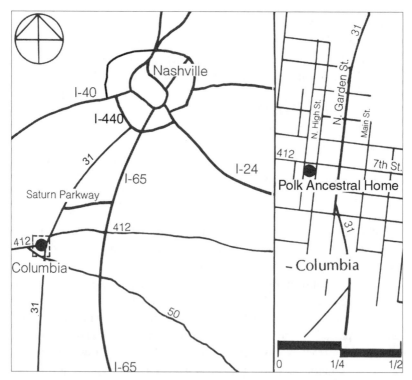

Figure 26. Location of James K. Polk Ancestral Home, Columbia, Tennessee.

Zachary Taylor

Twelfth President — 1849–1850

Born November 24, 1784, Montebello, Virginia
Died July 9, 1850, Washington, DC

> *It would be much more congenial to my feelings to be sitting with you under your own vine and fig-tree discussing the best mode of raising cotton.*

> — Zachary Taylor to son-in-law Jefferson Davis

Zachary Taylor, nicknamed "Old Rough and Ready," was the first career army officer to attain the presidency. Taylor was born into a military family of modest means, although their home was filled with warmth and affection. Throughout his own frequent moves to rugged and sometimes primitive frontier posts, Taylor recalled his boyhood with fondness.

Taylor rode into history during the War with Mexico by virtue of a brilliant military victory against overwhelming odds at Buena Vista. Although he had no formal affiliation with any political party — he had never even voted — his sudden, new-found fame propelled him to the presidency soon after the war with Mexico ended. Only sixteen months into his term, he died of pneumonia, a problem brought on by fatigue, fever, and the effects of his arduous military campaigning.

The only Taylor home in existence is a boyhood home in Louisville, Kentucky, where he had lived when his father was stationed near that frontier settlement on the Ohio River. Named Springfield, it is privately owned and closed to the public.

Millard Fillmore

Thirteenth President — 1850–1853

Born January 7, 1800, Locke, New York
Died March 8, 1874, Buffalo, New York

> *God knows I detest slavery . . . . but we must endure it and give it such protection as is guaranteed by the Constitution, till we can get rid of it without destroying the last hope of free government in the world.*

— Millard Fillmore

Millard Fillmore, as much as any other man, epitomized the Horatio Alger-type story of personal movement from "rags to riches, log cabin to the White House and poverty to worldly success." Fillmore was born in a two-room log cabin on a frontier farm in upstate New York, in a home where everyone had to work, and with precious little food or attention to go around. Under the circumstances, his parents apprenticed Millard to a cloth maker when he was only fourteen years of age. Historical lore tells us that the ambitious lad used whatever spare time he could find to study, and that by eighteen he had purchased his freedom and was studying the law while paying his way as an itinerant preacher.

Just out of his teens, he fell in love with a pretty schoolteacher who recognized latent talent in the raw, unlettered youth. With her encouragement, he continued to work even harder, and at twenty-three, he passed the New York bar, obtained employment with an East Aurora law firm, and felt secure enough to marry his schoolteacher-mentor, Miss Abigail Powers.

After a few years in East Aurora, the Fillmores moved to Buffalo where the young attorney caught the eye of political impresario Thurlow Weed, who fostered Millard's career. Fillmore spent the next fifteen years in a succession of elected and appointed political capacities. In 1848, he was nominated as Vice President of the United States in an effort to "balance the ticket" with westerner Zachary Taylor. Fillmore assumed the nation's highest office upon Taylor's death in 1850.

As president, Fillmore proved to be more than a political hack; his short administration was one of stable competence. His party, nevertheless, refused to nominate him for a full term in 1852, although he was persuaded to run four years later as the candidate of the "Know-Nothings," a fringe party that sought to unite the country against foreigners and aliens in hopes of diverting attention from the divisive issue of slavery.

Fillmore was badly defeated in 1856 and retired to Buffalo to live in baronial splendor, a far cry from the log cabin and impoverished boyhood he had experienced on the farm in rural New York. The home occupied by Fillmore in Buffalo has not survived.

Millard Fillmore Log Cabin

MORAVIA, NEW YORK

> *Deep dark woods, log cabin below,*
> *everywhere the drifting snow.*
> *Raw wind whistling through the trees,*
> *Never a place to take one's ease.*
> *Ever on watch for wolf or bear,*
> *Wildcat catching one unaware*
> *Who in that wilderness could foresee*
> *A youth destined for history.*

— Ruby Morse

In 1921, the citizens of Moravia, New York dedicated a local park to the memory of Millard Fillmore, who had been born in Locke, a few miles away. Four years later, the State of New York opened the park to the general public

Figure 27. The Millard Fillmore Log Cabin, Fillmore Glen State Park, Moravia, New York. Photograph by Robert Scarry.

as Fillmore Glen State Park that now encompasses 938 acres of woodlands, playgrounds, camping, and fishing facilities, and other family attractions. Fillmore Glen lies in the middle of one of New York's most beautiful vacation areas, at the southern end of Owasco Lake, one of the famous Finger Lakes.

The log cabin in which Millard Fillmore was born has been lost to time and the elements, but in the 1960s efforts were begun to replicate the cabin within Fillmore Glen State Park. Construction of the cabin (Figure 27) was completed in 1965. With the exception of a hidden cement foundation, the materials used in building this reconstruction are from Fillmore's period; the logs, nails, glass, and bricks were reclaimed from cabins that had survived in the area. Building techniques were authenticated and supervised by architectural scholars and historians. One newspaper reported:

> *With the pluck of pioneers . . . and no state aid . . . the citizens of Moravia have held a cabin raising to honor a log cabin President and the area's most distinguished native, Millard Fillmore.*

Robert Scarry, a biographer of Fillmore, noted:

> *It is hoped that this cabin will serve as an inspiration to the young people of America in years to come in that it exemplifies the*

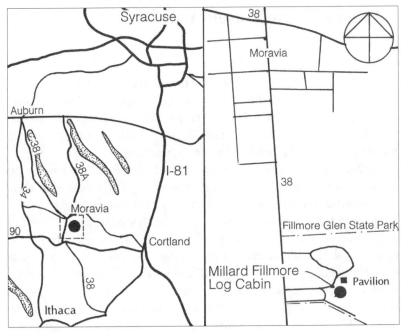

Figure 28. Location of the Millard Fillmore Log Cabin, Fillmore Glen State Park, Moravia, New York.

American dream, that a person from humble surroundings can rise to hold the highest office in the land.

DIRECTIONS: From I 81, take Exit 12 (Homer) northbound on SR 281, go 0.5 mile to SR 90, then go westbound to Locke. At Locke, turn northbound on SR 38 and proceed to the park (Figure 28).

PUBLIC USE: Season and hours: Mid-May-mid-October, dawn to dusk. **Admission fee:** There is a park entrance fee for vehicles between the hours of 9 AM and 6 PM. **Picnic area. For people with disabilities:** Accessible.

FOR ADDITIONAL INFORMATION: Contact: Fillmore Glen State Park, 1686 State Route 38, Moravia, New York 13118, (315) 497-0130. **Web site:** *www.nysparks.state.ny.us.* **Read:** Robert Scarry. 1993. *Millard Fillmore: Thirteenth President of the United States.*

Fillmore House Museum

EAST AURORA, NEW YORK

Millard and Abigail Fillmore's time in East Aurora, from the time of their marriage in 1826 until 1830, was an important period in Millard's odyssey from log cabin to the White House. During this time he practiced law and became interested in politics, and their first child was born in a modest frame house that Fillmore had built by hand on Main Street.

Eventually the house was abandoned and stood in disrepair until 1930 when it was purchased by a local artist who moved it to its present location and converted it to a studio. In 1975, the Aurora Historical Society bought the house with the intention of restoring it to the style of 1826 and the time of the Fillmore occupancy. Extensive research uncovered the original floor plans, paint colors, and other details of the interior. These were combined with period furniture that included the Fillmores's bed, scrub table, and other nineteenth-century artifacts, along with President Fillmore's tall law desk, to recreate the sense of a typical small dwelling of the Federal period (Plate 5). Special pieces are the bookcase Abigail purchased to start the first permanent library in the White House and daughter Mary's Gothic Revival-style harp.

On the exterior, the East Aurora Garden Club has researched and executed the grounds and gardens. All of the trees, shrubs, and flowers are historically authentic. The four-season garden, for example, displays a variety of roses grown before 1840 supplemented with flowering and evergreen shrubs, perennials, and annuals. Mrs. Fillmore's dooryard herb garden depicts a simple, functional garden of her time with aromatic, culinary and dyeing herbs.

DIRECTIONS: From SR 400 (Aurora Expressway) in East Aurora, exit southbound at Maple Street and proceed to Main Street, then go west on Main 1 block to Shearer Avenue, then go north on Shearer to the Fillmore House on the east (Figure 29).

PUBLIC USE: Season and hours: June-October, Wednesday, Saturday, Sunday, 1 PM-4 PM. Group and private tours are available. Call (716) 652-4985. **Admission fee. For people with disabilities:** Not accessible

FOR ADDITIONAL INFORMATION: Contact: Aurora Historical Society, Box 472, East Aurora, New York 14052, (716) 652-8875. **Web site:** *www.millardfillmorehouse.org.* **Read:** Robert J. Rayback. 1959. *Millard Fillmore.*

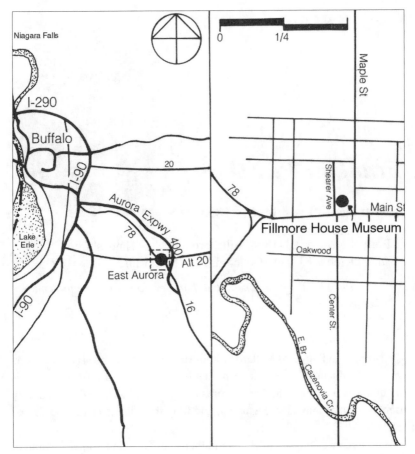

Figure 29. Location of the Fillmore House Museum, East Aurora, New York.

Franklin Pierce

Fourteenth President — 1853–1857

Born November 23, 1804, Hillsborough, New Hampshire
Died October 8, 1869, Concord, New Hampshire

> *Some men are so constituted that they do not incline to bend before a storm.*

— Franklin Pierce

Franklin Pierce, as Millard Fillmore before him, has been called a "Forgotten President." His single term has been considered unsuccessful, although it is doubtful whether any president could have halted the runaway train of disharmony, distrust, anger, and folly that characterized the United States in 1853.

Pierce was the son of Benjamin Pierce, a bluff, determined veteran of the Revolutionary War. Able and ambitious, he had overcome a background of poverty to attain prosperity, a good reputation, business success, and two terms as Governor of New Hampshire. Franklin inherited his father's political instincts as well as his principles of hard work and a strong belief in public responsibility. He served New Hampshire as legislator, speaker of the house, United States Congressman, and United States Senator.

In 1852, Pierce was chosen on the forty-ninth ballot by the Democratic Party as a compromise candidate for president, and went on to win the election by a deeply divided electorate. Exacerbating an already volatile and hopeless situation, Pierce entered the White House bearing the scars of a personal tragedy so horrifying that presidential scholars are convinced it affected his ability to govern. Only two months before Inauguration Day,

Franklin and Jane Pierce, along with their only surviving son — two others had died in infancy — were involved in a railway accident. Pierce and his wife were uninjured, but young Benjamin was killed before their eyes. Mrs. Pierce never recovered from her deep trauma, and Franklin's gloom and sense of guilt haunted him for the rest of his life.

As president, Pierce proved to be a strict constitutional constructionist. Every attempt he made toward appeasement and understanding between the political forces of the North and South failed. He pleased no one. When elected, he was the most popular political figure in New Hampshire, but when he returned home four years later, the capital city of Concord refused him an official welcome.

Nevertheless, the Pierces apparently had several good years following his presidency. Mrs. Pierce's health, often frail, improved when they traveled to the Bahamas and Europe. She had never liked politics, was happy to be away from it, and putting distance and time between them and young Benjamin's death helped her spirits. Mrs. Pierce died in 1863, after which Franklin lived alone, suspected of harboring a drinking problem, until his own death in 1869.

Franklin Pierce Homestead

HILLSBOROUGH, NEW HAMPSHIRE

In 1804, Benjamin Pierce built a fine Colonial House (Figure 30) of fourteen rooms in Hillsborough and finished it in time to welcome his son Franklin into the world. The pioneer era was passing in New England by the early part of the nineteenth century as settlers moved west, and the Pierce home reflected a new age of comfort and luxury. Its spacious rooms, dazzling with bright colors (following English fashion), hand stenciling on the walls, imported wallpaper, and fine paintings were indications of prosperity, good taste, and gracious living. The Pierce house even featured a second-floor ballroom that became the center of important political gatherings and grand social affairs. It echoed with inspirational, sometimes conspiratorial, discussions of public affairs during this period of development and maturation in America's democratic history. It was here that Franklin Pierce was exposed to

Figure 30. Franklin Pierce Homestead, Hillsborough, New Hampshire. Photograph courtesy of The Hillsborough Historical Society.

the excitement of politics and the thrill of debate. Governor Pierce was determined that his son reap benefits denied him and set a firm patriarchal example of ambition, discipline, strong religious beliefs, and absolute determination of purpose, qualities that Franklin desperately needed when faced with the rigors of the presidency many years later.

The Pierce Homestead, restored to its 1820s glory both outside and in, is an outstanding example of fine living in the early part of the nineteenth century.

DIRECTIONS: The Pierce Homestead is in Hillsborough on SR 31, 100 yards north of SR 9 (Figure 31).

PUBLIC USE: Season and hours: July-August, Monday-Saturday, 10 AM-4 PM; Sunday, 1 PM-4 PM. June and September, weekends only; Memorial Day, July 4th, Labor Day, Columbus Day, 10 AM-4 PM. Special tours are available May-October by appointment. **Admission fee. For people with disabilities:** The second floor is not accessible but a video of the rooms is provided.

FOR ADDITIONAL INFORMATION: Contact: The Hillsborough Historical Society, Box 896, Hillsborough, New Hampshire 03244, (603) 478-3165. **Web site:** *www.franklinpierce.ws/homestead/contents.html*. **Read:** (1) Larry Gara. 1991. *The Presidency of Franklin Pierce*. (2) Peter A. Wallner. 2004. *Franklin Pierce, New Hampshire's Favorite Son*.

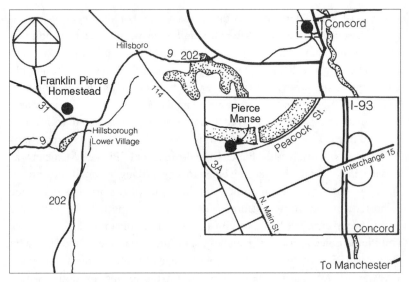

Figure 31. Location of Franklin Pierce Homestead, Hillsborough, New Hampshire, and The Pierce Manse, Concord, New Hampshire.

The Pierce Manse

CONCORD, NEW HAMPSHIRE

Franklin Pierce was serving his second term in congress when his wife, unhappy in Hillsborough and devastated by the death of their infant son, persuaded her husband to move their permanent home to Concord, New Hampshire (Plate 5). Mrs. Pierce considered Washington a place of exile and dread, so Pierce resigned from politics in 1842 and purchased a home in Concord close to his law office. The couple and their two young children resided in the house from 1842 to 1848. The new surroundings were to bring little happiness, however, as a second son, at only four years of age, died of typhus in 1843, soon after they moved into the house.

In 1847, not long after the outset of the Mexican War, Pierce enlisted as a private in the US Army, but due to his political experience and influence he was immediately promoted to brigadier general, a post in which he served with great distinction. Shortly after he entered the military, the Pierces's house in Concord was sold, most likely due, at least in part, to the lingering memories of the death of their son. After the war, Pierce was plucked from political obscurity and named the Democratic candidate for president in 1852.

The Concord house, a two-story white Greek Revival with multiple chimneys, is similar to dozens of others scattered throughout New England. The kitchen, parlor, and dining room are on the first floor, and the bedrooms are above. The house was saved from demolition associated with urban renewal in 1971 by a group of citizens interested in preserving Pierce's heritage. Calling themselves the Pierce Brigade in honor of Pierce's Mexican War service, they kept the house from being lost by moving it from its downtown site to an outlying piece of property in the Concord Historic District. Once relocated, the house was refurbished to represent the time of the Pierce family occupancy. The house is furnished with a combination of period pieces and Pierce objects, some of which were brought from the White House by Pierce in 1853. The word "Manse" was selected from a contest run by the Brigade in 1968, during their search for a name for the house that would differentiate it from other homes associated with President Pierce. In 1993, a barn that fit the dimensions and age of the original Pierce carriage house was brought in pieces from Belmont, New Hampshire, and rebuilt board by board. The barn is currently being renovated to contain new exhibition spaces and staff offices.

In 2004, the Pierce Brigade became affiliated with the New Hampshire Political Library in order to further promote the preservation of history and political traditions in New Hampshire. The Library and Brigade jointly maintain the Manse as a unique historical and educational site for the public.

DIRECTIONS: From I 93, take Exit 15W to downtown Concord; after the set of blinking yellow lights take a hard right at the traffic light onto North Main Street. The Manse is located at the end of North Main Street (Figure 31).

PUBLIC USE: Season and hours: Mid-June-Columbus Day weekend, Tuesday through Saturday, 11 AM-3 PM. Closed holidays. Groups are admitted only by appointment. **Admission fee. Gift shop. For people with disabilities:** A wheelchair ramp provides entry to the house through the barn. A photo album of the second floor exhibits is available for those unable to use the stairs.

FOR ADDITIONAL INFORMATION: Contact: The Pierce Manse, 14 Horseshoe Pond Lane, Box 425, Concord, New Hampshire 03301, (603) 225-4555. **Web site:** *www.piercemanse.org*. **Read:** Roy Nichols. 1958. *Franklin Pierce: Young Hickory of the Granite Hills.*

James Buchanan

Fifteenth President — 1857–1861

Born April 23, 1791, Cove Gap, Pennsylvania
Died June 1, 1868, Lancaster, Pennsylvania

> *If you are as happy, dear sir, on entering this house as I am on leaving it and returning home, you are the happiest man in the country.*

— James Buchanan at the inauguration of Abraham Lincoln

James Buchanan was born in Pennsylvania in his father's log cabin trading post at a place called Cove Gap, an area on the edge of civilization as the surrounding Allegheny Mountains formed a formidable barrier to the west. The trading post was profitable and enabled the Buchanans to move into Mercersburg to open a small dry goods store. James performed well in school and graduated from nearby Dickinson College. He then settled in Lancaster where, as a young attorney, he gravitated to politics and began a distinguished career that included service in the Pennsylvania State Legislature and the United States Congress, ambassadorial appointments to Russia and Great Britain, and an appointment as Secretary of State.

Buchanan's fate, of course, was to be elected president at a time when the national crisis over states' rights was all but impossible to solve. His attempts to appease the South only alienated important factions in the North and did nothing to reduce Southern militancy. He left office strongly supporting the Union and Lincoln's policies, but was happy to return to Lancaster, far from the daily pressures and cares of the White House.

Buchanan Historic Site

MERCERSBURG, PENNSYLVANIA

Mercersburg is a picturesque small town nestled in the beautiful Cumberland Valley of southern Pennsylvania. Unspoiled by the hustle and bustle of modern life, Mercersburg is a community proud of its roots, its present, and its future. In 1975, as part of its 225th anniversary celebration, Mercersburg created a historic district to preserve many of the town's fine structures, some of which dated to the early eighteenth century and, more significantly, to perpetuate and celebrate a lifestyle that was in danger of being lost forever. Included in the redevelopment project was the restoration and refurbishing of several buildings associated with President James Buchanan who had grown up in Mercersburg. Those places included:

Stoney Batter: An early trading post operated by the Buchanan family in Cove Gap. Buchanan's father named the post Stoney Batter after his ancestral home in Northern Ireland. This birth site of James Buchanan is but a few miles from downtown Mercersburg and is marked by a stone monument within the grounds of the eighteen-acre Buchanan Birthplace State Park.

Log Cabin: Buchanan's actual birth cabin (Figure 32) has been relocated to a woody copse on the campus of Mercersburg Academy. Its single room is unfurnished and may be viewed through a picture window.

Lane House: Harriet Lane, Buchanan's niece and ward, served the bachelor president as White House hostess and became the belle of Washington. Her childhood home, a Georgian-style house that dates to 1828, is part of a self-conducted walking tour of Mercersburg's historic district. The house is privately owned and the interior is not open to the public.

James Buchanan Hotel: When James was five, the family moved from Cove Gap to Mercersburg to open a small store. The family's living quarters were on the second floor. Years later, the store was converted to a hotel whose owner honored Buchanan by naming the hostelry for him. It is still open as a pub and residential hotel.

Mansion House: In 1856, Buchanan gave a speech from the balcony of the Mansion House, a speech that launched his campaign for the presidency. Once a dormitory for Marshall College, it is now utilized for stores and offices. The balcony is not open for visitation.

On June 17, 2000, the 250th anniversary of Mercersburg, a life-size statue of James Buchanan was dedicated in the town's public square.

DIRECTIONS: Mercersburg is on SR 16, 10 miles west of I 81. From the North, use Exit 6 (Greencastle) and follow US 30 westbound to SR 416, proceeding 8 miles southbound to Mercersburg. From the South, take Exit 2 or 3 (Greencastle) and proceed 10 miles westbound on SR 16 that becomes Main Street. From the Pennsylvania Turnpike, take Exit 13 (Fort Littleton) to US 522 southbound to McConnellsburg, then SR 16 eastbound to Mercersburg (Figure 33).

PUBLIC USE: Season and hours: Mercersburg is a thriving community, active the year-round.

FOR ADDITIONAL INFORMATION: Contact: Mercersburg Area Chamber of Commerce, 21C North Main Street, Mercersburg, Pennsylvania 17236, (717) 328-5827. **Web site:** *www.presidentialavenue.com/jb.cfm.* **Read:** Philip Shriver Klein. 1967. "Bachelor Father — James Buchanan as a Family Man." *Western Pennsylvania Historical Magazine* 50 (July): 199–214.

Figure 32. Log Cabin, Buchanan Historic Site, on the campus of Mercersburg Academy, Mercersburg, Pennsylvania. Photograph by William G. Clotworthy.

Figure 33. Location of Buchanan Historic Site, Mercersburg, Pennsylvania.

Wheatland

LANCASTER, PENNSYLVANIA

I am now residing at this place, which is an agreeable country
residence about a mile and a half from Lancaster . . . . I hope you
may not fail to come this way . . . . I should be delighted with a visit.

— James Buchanan, in a letter to a friend.

Wheatland (Plate 6), built in 1828 by a wealthy Lancaster banker, was
named for the rich wheat fields that surrounded the house. In 1848, the house
was purchased by Secretary of State James Buchanan as a country estate.
Buchanan loved his time at Wheatland and praised "the comforts and tranquility of home as contrasted with the troubles, perplexities, and difficulties
of public life." Wheatland was destined, however, to become a much more
public arena than Buchanan initially envisioned, especially since its library
became the center of political activity during Buchanan's presidential campaigns in 1852 and 1856. It was not until his retirement from the White House
that tranquility returned to Wheatland and it became, once again for Buchanan,
"the beau ideal of a statesman's abode."

The house, with its four acres of woodlands, was purchased in 1936 and restored by the James Buchanan Foundation for the Preservation of Wheatland, an educational, nonprofit organization. The foundation has succeeded brilliantly not only in preserving the residence, but in recreating the lifestyle of a wealthy country gentleman — a lifestyle that included liveried servants, leisurely dinners for twenty-five guests, and entertainment that comprised piano music and lively conversation.

Tours of Wheatland begin in the converted carriage house with the screening of an orientation film, then move into the residence, led by guides in period costumes. The rooms are spacious, a necessity considering Buchanan's extensive social and political activities. Original furnishings include a Chickering grand piano, which was played by Harriet Lane, Buchanan's niece and hostess.

In his description of Wheatland, author A. Cranston Jones said:

> *The great charm in visiting Wheatland is that so much of the tang and aroma of this pastoral existence can still be sensed. So magnificently are the rooms maintained, with their Lancaster hostesses in period crinolines, that one almost expects to catch sight of Miss Hetty tidying up the parlor, Harriet Lane once again adjusting her skirts before her fingers ripple the first chords on the Chickering grand, or find elegant and reserved President Buchanan himself standing at the head of the table, ceremoniously greeting each guest in turn.*

DIRECTIONS: Wheatland is 1.5 miles west of Lancaster on SR 23 (Marietta Avenue). From US 30 eastbound, take SR 23 eastbound and follow the historical markers. From US 30 westbound, take SR 23 westbound through downtown Lancaster (Figure 34).

PUBLIC USE: Season and hours: April 1-October 31, daily, 10 AM-4 PM. Sunday, 12 M-4 PM. November; Friday, Saturday, Monday, 10 AM-4 PM. Sunday, 12 M-4 PM. December, Saturday, Sunday and Monday, 12 M-4 PM. For winter hours, inquire via the information number or e-mail address listed below. **Admission fee. Food service:** Beverages and snacks are sold in the Carriage House and there is a picnic area. **Gift shop. For people with disabilities:** There are two steps to the porch. The main floor is accessible. A photographic tour of the second floor is available.

FOR ADDITIONAL INFORMATION: Contact: James Buchanan Foundation, 1120 Marietta Avenue, Lancaster, Pennsylvania 17603, (717) 392-8721.

Web site: *www.wheatland.org.* **Read:** (1) Sally Smith Cahalan. 1988. *James Buchanan's Wheatland.* (2) Sally Smith Cahalan. 1989. *At Home with James Buchanan.* (3) Philip Shriver Klein. 2003. *The Story of Wheatland.*

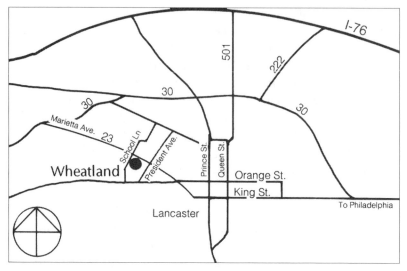

Figure 34. Location of Wheatland, Lancaster, Pennsylvania.

Abraham Lincoln

Sixteenth President — 1861–1865

Born February 12, 1809, Hardin County (now Larue County), Kentucky
Died April 15, 1865, Washington, DC

We can see the past, though we may not claim to have directed it; and by seeing it . . . . we feel more hopeful and confident for the future.

— Abraham Lincoln

Heritage, environment, and human associations all combine to shape our thoughts into beliefs, prejudices, and attitudes. Abraham Lincoln's work ethic and ambition were molded by hard farm life. His compassion was learned from his beloved mother and caring stepmother. His attitude toward slavery may have been defined by his first teacher, a determined emancipationist, or perhaps by the sight of slaves being driven down the road past the Lincoln cabin in Kentucky.

When Abraham was seven, the Lincoln family was evicted from the Kentucky farm on Knob Creek due to land title problems. They moved farther west to Indiana where, during the next fourteen years, young Abe helped carve a farm from the wilderness. During this time he also experienced the emotional wrench of his mother's death and his father's remarriage. His education was sporadic; he was, to a great extent, self-taught. All these experiences were critical elements of his development as he matured from child to adult.

Lincoln eventually struck out on his own and moved to New Salem, Illinois, where he worked in a general store and established his reputation as

"Honest Abe." A voracious reader with a thirst for knowledge and an insatiable curiosity about society and his fellow man, he continued to pursue his scattered education until he was admitted to the Illinois bar at the age of twenty-eight.

Lincoln's experiences in New Salem were a crucible for the skills and dogged determination that propelled him to future professional and political successes — a journey that would begin just twenty miles down the road, in the state capital of Springfield and would end in the national capital of Washington, DC.

Abraham Lincoln Birthplace National Historic Site

HODGENVILLE, KENTUCKY

My earliest recollection is of the Knob Creek place.

— Abraham Lincoln

In December, 1808, Thomas and Nancy Lincoln settled onto land in central Kentucky that came to be called the Sinking Spring Farm. Two months later, their son Abraham was born. When Abraham was two, the family moved about ten miles north and established a farm alongside Knob Creek. Here the family lived for five years before moving to Indiana in 1816. Both Sinking Spring Farm and Knob Creek Farm are administered by the National Park Service as units of the Abraham Lincoln Birthplace National Historic Site. The child of two remembered little of the Sinking Spring Farm, but the five years during which the Lincolns farmed Knob Creek were important ones for the maturation of Abraham. Years later, he recalled incidents from those years — listening to his mother read from the Bible, observing dealers driving slaves past the cabin, attending school for the first time, and experiencing the sheer joy of boyhood on the farm.

The Lincoln Memorial Building (Figure 35), the centerpiece of the Sinking Spring Farm unit, was dedicated in 1911 by President William Howard Taft as a memorial to the birthplace and legacy of the sixteenth president of the United States. The structure, situated on a low hilltop, is approached by

Figure 35. Abraham Lincoln Birthplace National Historic Site, Hodgenville, Kentucky. Photograph courtesy of National Park Service.

a flight of fifty-six steps, each representing one year of Lincoln's life. At the entrance, framed by six granite columns, are inscribed what are some of Lincoln's most famous words, "with malice toward none, with charity for all." This imposing neoclassical structure of marble and granite may seem a bit grandiose as a memorial to such a simple man as Thomas Lincoln's son Abraham, but those stone walls shelter a tiny, crude log cabin that symbolizes well the primitive, rugged environment that surrounded Abraham Lincoln during his earliest years.

The cabin is not Lincoln's actual birth cabin, but is representative of the same construction methods, size, and historical period as the building in which he was born. The cabin is, however, located on the same farmland, and is surrounded by the same forests and fields upon which and into which Abraham came and first melded with the Kentucky frontier. At the birthplace one is moved — hearing the same sounds, smelling the same natural aromas, walking the same ground — while vicariously sharing much of the same environment experienced by Lincoln almost two hundred years ago.

The National Park Service has developed a self-guided walking tour through the historic Sinking Spring Farm site that demonstrates the resourcefulness of the early American settlers in this region. Interpretive materials help visitors understand the forest and its importance as a source of food, building materials, kitchen utensils — even the thread and buttons used in making clothing. An environmental study area is available for the use of school groups.

The Abraham Lincoln Boyhood Home at nearby Knob Creek (Plate 6) was acquired by the National Park Service in 2001 as part of the National Historic Site. The cabin itself has been lost to time but was replicated in 1931 with the use of logs from a neighboring cabin. Construction was directed by Robert Thompson, whose father, a childhood playmate of Abraham Lincoln, had helped tear down the original Lincoln cabin in 1870.

DIRECTIONS: The Sinking Spring Farm lies astride US 31E immediately south of Hodgenville. Knob Creek Farm is 7 miles east of Hodgenville on US 31E (Figure 36).

PUBLIC USE: Season and hours: *Sinking Spring Farm:* Memorial Day-Labor Day, 8 AM-6:45 PM (EDT). Remainder of year, 8 AM-4:45 PM (EDT). *Knob Creek Farm:* Daylight hours year-round. Interpretive staff on premises April 1-October 31. **Book shop.** At Sinking Spring Farm. **For people with disabilities:** The main features of the Sinking Spring Farm site are accessible.

FOR ADDITIONAL INFORMATION: Contact: Abraham Lincoln Birthplace National Historic Site, 2995 Lincoln Farm Road, Hodgenville, Kentucky 42748, (270) 358-3137. **Web site:** *www.nps.gov/abli*. **Read:** Louis A. Warren. 1929. *Lincoln's Parentage and Childhood.*

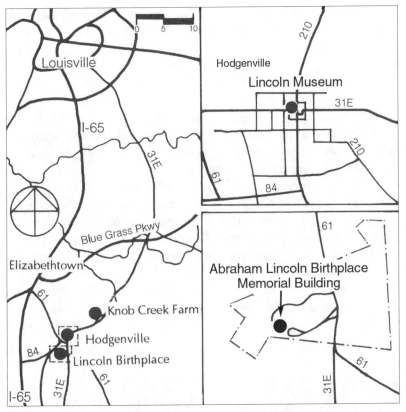

Figure 36. Location of Abraham Lincoln Birthplace National Historic Site and The Lincoln Museum, Hodgenville, Kentucky.

The Lincoln Museum

HODGENVILLE, KENTUCKY

Hodgenville Square, in the center of town, is dominated by A. A. Weinmann's bronze statue "The Great Emancipator," commissioned by Congress and erected in 1909. This memorial to Abraham Lincoln was enhanced by another effort to commemorate Hodgenville's most famous son when The Lincoln Museum, Kentucky's official museum in honor of the sixteenth president, opened on the town square in 1989 (Figure 37).

Hodgenville had not acted on earlier attempts to honor Abraham Lincoln until a retired museum curator came to town in 1986 looking to sell some used wax figures of the former president. The wax figures became the impetus for The Lincoln Museum, now one of the town's most valuable tourist attractions. The figures represent twelve significant episodes in Lincoln's life. "The Railsplitter," "Gettysburg Address," and "Ford's Theatre" are three of the scenes depicted in vivid, life-like detail in the museum. The second level of the museum is devoted to both permanent and traveling exhibits, an original Lincoln art collection and an audio-visual area where visitors are treated to a film, *Lincoln's Kentucky*.

Hodgenville Square is the centerpiece of many special events that include a Lincoln's Birthday Commemoration in February and "Lincoln Days," a festival held in October. The festival features rail-splitting tournaments, pioneer games, Abraham and Mary Lincoln look-alike contests, and an art contest where the winning work is purchased and added to the collection at The Lincoln Museum.

As the National Bicentennial Celebration of Lincoln's birthday approaches, the museum will open its Lincoln Library, along with several new exhibits, pertaining to early Hodgen's Mill history as well as the Centennial Celebration.

Figure 37. The Lincoln Museum, Hodgenville, Illinois. Photograph courtesy of the Lincoln Museum.

DIRECTIONS: Hodgenville is on US 31E (Figure 36). Take US 31E to the center of town and the town square.

PUBLIC USE: Season and hours: Monday-Saturday, 8:30 AM-4:30 PM; Sunday, 12:30 PM-4:30 PM. Closed Thanksgiving Day, Christmas Day, New Year's Day, Easter Sunday. **Admission fee. Gift shop. For people with disabilities:** Fully accessible.

FOR ADDITIONAL INFORMATION: Contact: The Lincoln Museum, 66 Lincoln Square, Hodgenville, Kentucky 42748, (270) 358-3163. **Web site:** *www.lincolnmuseum-ky.org.* **Read**: Harold Holzer and Mark E. Neely, Jr. 1960. *The Lincoln Family Album.*

Lincoln Boyhood National Memorial

LINCOLN CITY, INDIANA

The things I want to know are in books. My best friend is the man who'll get me a book I ain't read.

— Abraham Lincoln

In 1816, the slavery issue, in addition to the lawsuits over their Kentucky farm, induced the Thomas Lincoln family to move west to Indiana. There they carved out a farm from the wilderness and remained for fourteen years. On that farm, young Abraham Lincoln shared family life, learned to work, and earned his first money. He experienced joy and tragedy as he grew from boy to man.

Lincoln Boyhood National Memorial (Figure 38) is an ideal place to learn about young Lincoln, his times, and the circumstances that molded him. An integral part of the memorial is a living historical farm. The buildings are not original but were built as a part of the interpretive program to depict a typical farm of the period during which the Lincolns lived in Indiana. One theme of the farm is self-sufficiency and use of the natural environment. Farm workers dress in period clothing and demonstrate daily activities of Lincoln's time, including domestic arts and crafts, animal husbandry, farming, and gardening.

A visitor center contains two halls with a connecting cloister, a small auditorium, and five sculpted panels marking important periods in Lincoln's

Figure 38. Lincoln Boyhood National Memorial, Lincoln City, Illinois. Photograph by Richard Frear; use courtesy of National Park Service.

life. The Nancy Hanks Lincoln Hall is a retreat; its design and furnishings are representative of early Indiana and create a sense of the simplicity and warmth of pioneer homes.

Abraham Lincoln Hall is utilized for meetings, church services, weddings, and other special events. The stone and wood construction is meant to reflect the grandeur, yet simplicity, of Lincoln himself. A church-like ambience engenders a feeling of reverence and respect, and visitors are urged to pause and "think about the meaning — to America and you — of this great American's life."

The grave of Lincoln's beloved mother, Nancy Hanks Lincoln, is located on a knoll overlooking the farm.

DIRECTIONS: From I 64, take Exit 57 southbound on US 231 to Gentryville, then go eastbound on SR 162 to the Memorial (Figure 39).

PUBLIC USE: Season and hours: *Memorial site:* December-February, 8 AM-4:30 PM; March-November, 8 AM-5 PM. Closed Thanksgiving Day, Christmas Day, New Year's Day. *Farm:* Mid-April-September, 8 AM-5 PM. During the rest of the year, the farm is an exhibit in place, but the farm buildings and demonstrations are closed. **Admission fee. For people with disabilities:** Most facilities are accessible.

FOR ADDITIONAL INFORMATION: Contact: Lincoln National Boyhood Memorial, Box 1816, Lincoln City, Indiana 47552, (812) 937-4541. **Web site:** *www.nps.gov/libo*. **Read:** (1) Don Davenport. 1991. *In Lincoln's Footsteps: A Historical Guide to the Lincoln Sites in Illinois, Indiana and Kentucky*. (2) Walter Miller and Bill Gaetner. 1992. *Lincoln Lived Here.*

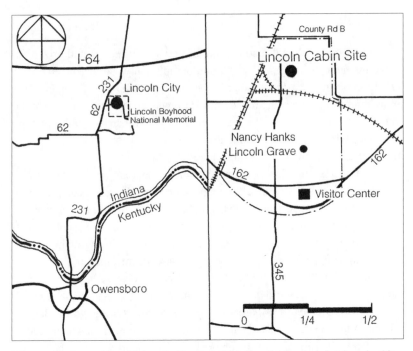

Figure 39. Location of Lincoln Boyhood National Memorial, Lincoln City, Illinois.

The Lincoln Museum

FORT WAYNE, INDIANA

An honest man is the noblest work of God.

— Abraham Lincoln

In 1905, Abraham Lincoln's son, Robert Todd Lincoln, authorized the use of his father's image and sent a photograph that was reproduced on the letterhead of a new business, Lincoln National Life Insurance Company. One of the founders of the company, Arthur Hall, was a long-time admirer of the sixteenth president and by the 1920s he felt the company should repay the debt owed Abraham Lincoln for the success the company achieved by using his name and picture that so represented integrity.

Arthur Hall met Louis Warren, a Lincoln scholar, and invited him to Fort Wayne to establish a Lincoln memorial project. Warren began work on February 12, 1928, with a mandate from Mr. Hall, "No motive of commercialism or profit entered into our plans to assemble this wealth of Lincolniana — we seek merely to provide the means and the channel through which there may continue to flow an ever increasing volume of information concerning Lincoln, especially to the youth of our land, that they may be influenced to think and to live as Lincoln did — 'with malice towards none and charity for all.'"

Thus the museum (Figure 40) is the repository for the world's largest private collection devoted to the life of Abraham Lincoln. Items of particular interest are the original photograph provided by Robert Lincoln, the Pickett bronze bas-relief plaque used at the dedication of the first company-owned building in 1923, and a white rose bud from Lincoln's casket given to Arthur Hall by his mother in 1912.

An overview of the museum's current collection includes over 18,000 volumes, numerous Lincoln artifacts, 300 Lincoln manuscripts, more than 10,000 nineteenth-century photographs, prints, broadsides, political cartoons, and the Lincoln family's personal photographs. The museum owns thousands of artifacts, including the inkwell Lincoln used in signing the Emancipation Proclamation, Lincoln's pocketknife, legal wallet, and shawl. In 1998 the museum acquired an extremely rare edition of the Emancipation Proclamation signed by Lincoln. On March 25, 2005, the museum unveiled one of thirteen copies of the 13th Amendment to the Constitution of the United

Figure 40. Lobby of the Lincoln Museum, Fort Wayne, Indiana. Photograph courtesy of the Lincoln Museum.

States signed by Abraham Lincoln. Of those copies, only three were also signed by members of the Senate. This is one of those three.

DIRECTIONS: From I 69 southbound, take Exit 111 to US 27 southbound that becomes US 33 (Clinton Street). The museum is on the southeast corner of Clinton and Berry streets. From I 69 northbound, take Exit 105 and proceed eastbound on Illinois Road that becomes Jefferson Street. Continue on Jefferson Street and turn north on Lafayette Street for 3 blocks and turn left on Berry Street for 2 blocks to the museum (Figure 41).

PUBLIC USE: Season and hours: Tuesday-Saturday, 10 AM-5 PM; Sunday, 1 PM-5 PM. Closed major holidays. **Admission fee.** The museum is open free of charge the first Sunday of each month. **Museum shop. For people with disabilities:** Fully accessible.

FOR ADDITIONAL INFORMATION: Contact: The Lincoln Museum, 200 E. Berry Street, Fort Wayne, Indiana 46802, (260) 455-3864. **Web site:** *www.thelincolnmuseum.org.* **Read:** (1) Harold Holzer and Mark E. Neely, Jr. 1960. *The Lincoln Family Album.* (2) Carolyn Texley, ed. 2000. *The Lincoln Museum.*

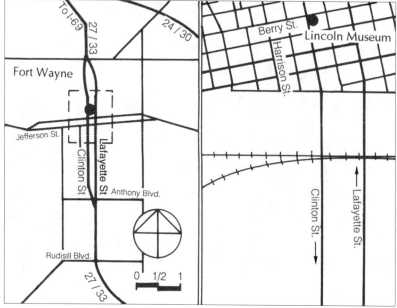

Figure 41. Location of the Lincoln Museum, Fort Wayne, Indiana.

Lincoln's New Salem State Historic Site

PETERSBURG, ILLINOIS

All my successes were because of that opinion of me which the people express when they call me "Honest Abe."

— Abraham Lincoln

Young Abraham Lincoln stopped in the village of New Salem in 1831 while piloting a flatboat on the Sangamon River and decided to settle there. He spent six years of his early adulthood in New Salem where he grew from a gangling youngster with no objectives, a self-admitted "aimless piece of driftwood," into a man of purpose. He clerked in a store, chopped wood, served as postmaster and surveyor, enlisted in the army during the Black Hawk War and was elected to his first public office. Most important to his

Figure 42. A log cabin and outbuildings in winter at Lincoln's New Salem State Historic Site, Petersburg, Illinois. Photograph courtesy of Lincoln's New Salem State Historic Site.

future, and to that of the nation, was that while living in New Salem, Lincoln began his study of law.

In 1839, two years after Lincoln left New Salem, the Menard County Seat was established in nearby Petersburg and the fortunes of New Salem declined. In the early part of the twentieth century, interest in New Salem's history was resurrected and the village was reconstructed over a period of time by the State of Illinois, the Chautauqua Association, the Old Salem Lincoln League, and the Civilian Conservation Corps. Today, New Salem consists of a reconstituted village representing life in the Sangamon Valley during the 1830s (Figure 42), part of Lincoln's New Salem State Historic Site, which includes the Theater in the Park and 700 acres of recreational facilities such as hiking trails, picnic areas, and campgrounds.

Visits to New Salem begin at a modern visitor center which shows an orientation film and contains exhibits that describe the town and his life when Abraham Lincoln was a resident. One then steps into the reconstructed village and strolls through a nineteenth-century living landscape that includes twenty-three structures; stores, mills, tavern, a schoolhouse/church, and others representing or interpreting the period. Many authentic artifacts from the period have been used to furnish the houses and to equip the farms and industrial shops. Interpreters in period dress go about the daily work of the town — farming, carding wool, blacksmithing, shop keeping, cooking, and other activities.

A walk through the winding paths of New Salem brings history to life, affording witness to a time and place that profoundly influenced the personality, principles, and career of Abraham Lincoln.

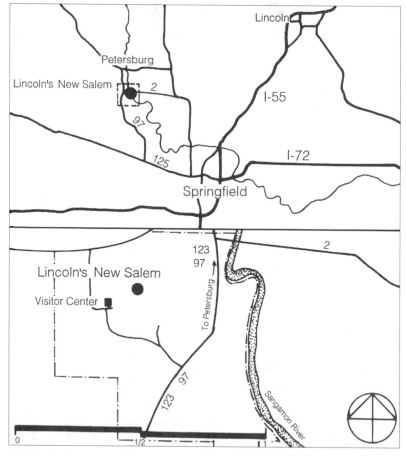

Figure 43. Location of Lincoln's New Salem State Historic Site, Petersburg, Illinois.

DIRECTIONS: Lincoln's New Salem is 2 miles south of Petersburg on SR 97 (Figure 43).

PUBLIC USE: Season and hours: March 1-April 15, Wednesday-Sunday, 9 AM-5 PM. April 16-Labor Day, daily, 9 AM-5 PM. Day after Labor Day-October 31, Wednesday-Sunday, 9 AM-5 PM. November 1-end of February, Wednesday-Sunday, 8 AM-4 PM. Closed Thanksgiving Day, Christmas Day, New Year's Day, Martin Luther King's Birthday, Washington's Birthday, Veterans' Day. **Food service:** The New Salem Deli and Pizzeria is open April through October. **Gift shop. For people with disabilities:** The visitor center is accessible; the village is partially accessible.

FOR ADDITIONAL INFORMATION: Contact: Lincoln's New Salem State Historic Site, 15588 History Lane, Petersburg, Illinois 62675, (217) 632-4000. **Web site:** *www.lincolnsnewsalem.com.* **Read:** Walter Miller and Bill Gaetner. 1994. *Lincoln Lived Here.*

Lincoln Home National Historic Site

Springfield, Illinois

> *No one, not in my situation, can appreciate my feeling of sadness at this parting. To this place, and the kindness of these people, I owe everything.*

— Lincoln's farewell, Springfield, 1861

The Lincoln Home (Figure 44) at Eighth and Jackson streets is the centerpiece of a four-square-block restoration project of the National Park Service intended to create a historic district that will preserve the nineteenth-century neighborhood where Abraham and Mary Todd Lincoln lived for seventeen years. It was in the Lincoln home, within this Springfield neighborhood, that Abraham Lincoln fully matured. His farewell remarks make clear his sense of connection to the town: "Here I have lived a quarter of a century, and have passed from a young man to an old man. Here my children have been born, and one is buried . . . ." Here he practiced law, served in the state legislature, gained national recognition as an orator and political thinker, learned of becoming a candidate for president, and heard, finally, of his election as the sixteenth President of the United States.

Figure 44. Lincoln Home National Historic Site, Springfield, Illinois. Photograph by Richard Frear; use courtesy of National Park Service.

In 1844, shortly after the birth of his first son, Lincoln purchased a house on Eighth Street. The Greek Revival structure was 1½ stories high, built of wood, with a cistern, well, privy, barn, and an attached carriage house. An exterior retaining wall was built in 1850, and major changes were effected in 1856 to make room for the Lincoln's growing boys; the house was expanded to two full stories with the addition of bedrooms and a storage room. Approximately fifty Lincoln-associated artifacts are on exhibit in the home.

In addition to the Lincoln Home, the National Historic Site includes two other restored houses that are open to the public. The Harriet Dean House interprets the history of the Lincoln Home and the Lincoln family in the exhibit "What a Pleasant Home Abe Lincoln Has." The Charles Arnold House explains the process of preserving and restoring historic houses, using the Arnold House as an example, in the exhibit "If These Walls Could Talk: Saving an Old House." Both houses are located across the street from the Lincoln Home.

Springfield is justly proud of Abraham Lincoln, and the city features many other attractions associated with him. The Lincoln-Herndon Law

Offices State Historic Site, the family pew at the First Presbyterian Church and the Old State Capitol State Historic Site where he served in the state legislature — all have been preserved and are open to the public. The Illinois State Historical Library's Lincoln Collection — one of the largest and most valuable single collections of papers, documents, letters, and memorabilia devoted to the life and times of Abraham Lincoln — has recently moved to the new Abraham Lincoln Presidential Library and Museum in Springfield.

All attractions are within walking distance of the Lincoln Home, including the Great Western Railroad Depot where the president-elect made his farewell address to Springfield's citizens before boarding the train for the inauguration journey to Washington — and into history. Five years later, another train would stop at Springfield, this one bearing the body of the martyred president. The president is buried in Oak Ridge Cemetery on the outskirts of Springfield where Lincoln, his wife Mary, and three of their children rest in an impressive monument building.

Following her husband's assassination, Mary Lincoln did not return to Springfield until 1880 when she came back to reside with her sister. The Lincoln house was rented until 1887 when Robert Todd Lincoln deeded it to the State of Illinois. In 1972, it was designated a National Historic Site to be administered by the National Park Service.

DIRECTIONS: From I 55 southbound, take Exit 98B (Clear Lake Avenue, becomes Madison going one-way west) westbound to 7th Street, then go south on 7th Street 5 blocks to the visitor center at 426 South Seventh Street (Figure 45).

PUBLIC USE: Season and hours: Ranger-conducted tours are conducted 8:30 AM-5 PM. Closed Thanksgiving Day, Christmas Day, New Year's Day. **Admission fee:** There is a parking fee. **Museum shop. For people with disabilities:** The visitor center, Dean house, Arnold house and the first floor of the Lincoln home are accessible to wheelchairs. If assistance is required, advise the staff at the visitor center. Wheelchairs are available for use within the site.

FOR ADDITIONAL INFORMATION: Contact: Superintendent, Lincoln Home National Historic Site, 413 South Eighth Street, Springfield, Illinois 62701-1905, (217) 492-4150. **Web site:** *www.nps.gov/liho.* **Read:** Wayne C. Temple. 1984. *By Squares and Compasses: The Building of Lincoln's Home and its Saga.*

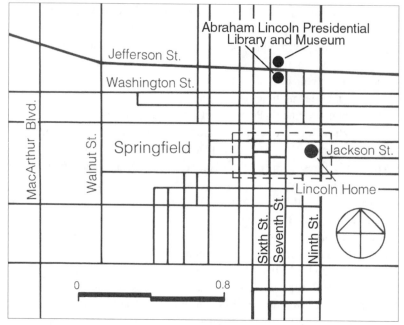

Figure 45. Location of Lincoln Home National Historic Site and Abraham Lincoln Presidential Library and Museum, Springfield, Illinois.

Lincoln College Museum

LINCOLN, ILLINOIS

In 1853, the first lots were sold in a new real estate development north of Springfield, Illinois. Attorney Abraham Lincoln had prepared the papers of incorporation. It was decided that the new town should bear his name, and he was asked to christen it. The story goes that he leaned back in his chair and remarked, "Nothing named Lincoln ever amounted to much." That notwithstanding, he traveled to Lincoln, took a watermelon, split it open, and duly baptized the little town with watermelon juice!

One cannot develop a complete picture of Abraham Lincoln without visiting Lincoln and surrounding Logan County, for it was in this area that he rode the circuit as a young attorney, invested in property, and spoke as a political candidate. The town of Lincoln was immensely proud when Abraham

Lincoln became president. On February 12, 1865, his last birthday, the town dedicated Lincoln University. Now Lincoln College, it was the first institution of higher learning to have been named in his honor during his presidency.

On the campus, McKinstry Memorial Library (Figure 46) houses two small museums, one of which is dedicated solely to Abraham Lincoln. It displays over two thousand volumes, pamphlets, pictures, and other significant items, including the original plat delineating the town of Lincoln as approved by attorney Lincoln in 1853. The second museum, a Hall of Presidents, is located at the main entrance to the facility. This hall is a shrine to those men who have served as chief executive, and contains documents signed by every president and many first ladies. The Lincoln Museum and the Hall of Presidents dramatize American history, inspire further study, and remind us, as Lincoln once said, that "freedom is the most valuable property of an individual." The museum also publishes *The Lincoln Newsletter,* a quarterly publication that features articles about Lincoln's life and artifacts or information in the museum's collections.

The exterior of the library is honored by Merrell Gage's bronze statue, "Lincoln, the Student."

Figure 46. The Lincoln College Museum, Lincoln, Illinois. Photograph courtesy of Lincoln College Museum.

DIRECTIONS: From I 55, take the Woodlawn Exit and go eastbound until it becomes Keokuk Street. McKinstry Memorial Library is a few blocks farther, on the left (Figure 47).

PUBLIC USE: Season and hours: Monday-Friday, 9 AM-4 PM; Saturday-Sunday, 1 PM-4 PM. Closed major holidays except for Lincoln's Birthday. Other times by appointment. **Museum shop. For people with disabilities:** Accessible.

FOR ADDITIONAL INFORMATION: Contact: Lincoln College Museum, 300 Keokuk Street, Lincoln, Illinois 62656, (217) 735-5050 (ext. 295). **Web site:** *www.lincolncollege.edu/museum.* **Read:** Don Davenport. 1991. *In Lincoln's Footsteps: A Historical Guide to the Lincoln Sites in Illinois, Indiana and Kentucky*

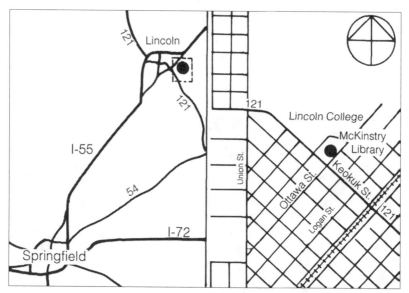

Figure 47. Location of the Lincoln College Museum, Lincoln, Illinois.

President Lincoln's Cottage at the Soldiers' Home

W<small>ASHINGTON</small>, DC

Following the Mexican War, General Winfield Scott, Robert Anderson, and Jefferson Davis founded a haven for retired and disabled US soldiers on a tract of land located three miles north of, and 300 feet higher than, downtown Washington, DC. This property was acquired by the federal government in 1851 as a "military asylum" and became known as the Soldiers' Home. The architectural centerpiece of the property, a 2½-story Gothic Revival "cottage" (Figure 48) that had been built in 1842 by a prosperous local banker, was considered at the time to be one of the finest homes in Washington, DC.

Presidents Buchanan, Lincoln, Hayes, and Arthur all used the Soldiers' Home campus to escape the heat and humidity of the summertime city, but

Figure 48. President Lincoln's Cottage, Washington, DC. Robert C. Lautman Photography 2005.

President Lincoln spent almost a quarter of his presidency in residence there during a crucial period of national tumult. Lincoln sought the Soldiers' Home as a haven of rest and renewal in the countryside. Each June of 1862–1864, the Lincolns moved some of their household effects to the rural, hilltop cottage, and resided there until November. It was while living at the cottage during that first summer that Lincoln worked on drafting the Emancipation Proclamation.

In 2000, President William J. Clinton declared Lincoln's seasonal retreat the President Lincoln and Soldiers' Home National Monument, noting "It's where Lincoln lived and worked, where his son played and his wife found solace, where ideas took shape and his last, best hope for America took flight."

Work to preserve the cottage and create public programs there for visitation began in the fall of 2001 under the aegis of the National Trust for Historic Preservation, which still manages the structure and operates the public programming. The property remains in federal hands; the Soldiers' Home campus now is known as the Armed Forces Retirement Home, and is

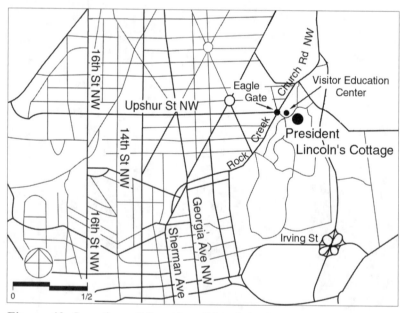

Figure 49. Location of President Lincoln's Cottage in northcentral Washington, DC.

home to about 1,200 retired or disabled veterans. President Lincoln's Cottage and the Robert H. Smith Visitor Education Center, accessible at this time only via Eagle Gate, opened to the public in February, 2008.

DIRECTIONS: President Lincoln's Cottage is in northcentral Washington at the intersection of Rock Creek Church Road and Upshur Street, NW. Entrance for the public is via Eagle Gate off of Rock Creek Church Road (Figure 49).

PUBLIC USE: Season and hours: Access to President Lincoln's Cottage is limited and advance reservation is strongly recommended. Please see web site — *www.lincolncottage.org* — for hours, directions, and tickets.

FOR ADDITIONAL INFORMATION: Contact: President Lincoln's Cottage, (202) 829-0436. **Web site:** *www.lincolncottage.org*. **Read:** (1) Matthew Pinsker. 2003. *Lincoln's Sanctuary: Abraham Lincoln and the Soldiers' Home.* (2) Elizabeth Brownstein. 2005. *Lincoln's Other White House.* (3) Kim A. O'Connell. 2008. "New directions for the old retreat."

Ford's Theatre National Historic Site

WASHINGTON, DC

On the evening of April 14, 1865, President and Mrs. Lincoln arrived at Ford's Theatre in downtown Washington, DC, looking forward to a performance of the comedy *Our American Cousin.* During the third act, scene III, the president was shot by John Wilkes Booth, a southern political activist who supported the Confederacy. Dr. Charles Leale, a young doctor from New York, rushed to Lincoln's theatre box and examined the stricken president. "His wound is mortal. He cannot recover," the doctor declared. The president, shot in the brain, was removed to a back room of the Petersen Boarding House, directly across the street, where doctors attempted to make him as comfortable as possible while awaiting the inevitable. Lincoln's great heart stopped at 7:22 AM the next day.

The nation was plunged into deep mourning as Lincoln, who had struggled to preserve the Union through the long and bloody Civil War, himself became yet another victim of senseless violence.

A few months after the assassination, Ford's Theatre was gutted and converted into a three-story government office building. In 1893, the building collapsed, killing twenty-two workers and injuring sixty-eight others. The building reopened the next year as a warehouse.

Restoration began in 1964. The building was again gutted and a basement was added. The interior was made to appear similar to, although not exactly like, its 1865 appearance. The façade, however, is the same as it was on that fateful day of Lincoln's last visit (Figure 50). Actress Helen Hayes reopened the stage in January, 1968.

A Museum of Lincolniana is located in the basement of Ford's Theatre. Exhibits include objects associated with his life and death, among which are the clothes he wore that fateful night and the pistol used by Booth.

The Petersen House, also known as The House Where Lincoln Died, has been restored. The Petersen House and the Theatre complex make up Ford's Theatre National Historic Site — a site that reminds us of the troubling events of 1865, yet serves to perpetuate the spirit, hopes, and ideals that Abraham Lincoln upheld for all Americans.

In June, 2007, Ford's Theatre closed for an $8.5 million upgrade that will include improved access for the disabled. The National Park Service plans to reopen the theatre in February, 2009. The Petersen House remains open to visitors during the renovation period.

Figure 50. Ford's Theatre National Historic Site, Washington, DC. Photograph courtesy of Ford's Theatre National Historic Site.

DIRECTIONS: Ford's Theatre is located at 516 10th Street, NW (Figure 15).

PUBLIC USE: Season and hours: 9 AM-5 PM. Closed Christmas Day. Talks by rangers are scheduled in the morning and afternoon. The theatre is closed when rehearsals or matinees (Thursday 12 M-3:30 PM, Sunday 2 PM-5 PM) are in progress, thus calling ahead is recommended. The museum and the Petersen Boarding House are open during the above hours. **Museum shop.** **For people with disabilities:** Limited access at the theatre, none at the Petersen House.

FOR ADDITIONAL INFORMATION: Contact: Ford's Theatre National Historic Site, 900 Ohio Drive, SW, Washington, DC 20024, (202) 426-6924. **Web site:** *www.nps.gov/foth.* **Read:** (1) Dorothy Meserve Kunhardt and Philip Kunhardt, Jr. 1985. *Twenty Days.* (2) National Park Service. 1991. *Ford's Theatre and the House Where Lincoln Died.*

The Abraham Lincoln Library and Museum

HARROGATE, TENNESSEE

On the subject of education, I can only say that I view it as the most important subject in which we as people can be engaged.

— Abraham Lincoln

In September, 1863, Union General O. O. Howard's corps was to be transferred from the eastern theater to the western. When he met with President Lincoln regarding the transfer, Lincoln pulled down a map and pointed to Cumberland Gap, an area where many eastern Tennessee residents had remained pro-Union, despite the fact that Tennessee was a Confederate state. The president suggested that, after the war, maybe they could "do something for these people." It was thirty years before Howard returned to Cumberland Gap, but he remembered Lincoln's words and founded Lincoln Memorial University in 1897 to help establish a better way of life for the people of southern Appalachia.

The Abraham Lincoln Library and Museum, located on the university's beautiful campus, (Figure 51) was conceived by the university's administration as a vehicle to provide the institution with a philosophical direction and:

Figure 51. Abraham Lincoln Library and Museum, Harrogate, Tennessee. Photograph courtesy of Abraham Lincoln Library and Museum.

To provide the public with a moving and creative portrayal of Abraham Lincoln's dramatic commitment to the American way of life and confront each of us with the need to reaffirm that commitment.

The museum houses an outstanding collection of books, manuscripts, relics, and pictures related to Lincoln and the Civil War period. As a research center, it provides an opportunity for students and scholars to research original materials. Among the many exhibits are a heroic sculpture of the martyred president by Gutzon Borglum and the cane the president carried on the night of his assassination.

DIRECTIONS: Lincoln Memorial University is in Harrogate, Tennessee, on US 25E (Figure 52).

PUBLIC USE: Season and hours: Monday-Friday, 9 AM-4 PM; Saturday, 11 AM-4 PM; Sunday, 1 PM-4 PM. Closed major holidays and at university closings. **Admission fee. Museum shop. For people with disabilities:** The first floor is accessible, but there is no access to the mezzanine gallery. There is a virtual tour available for those unable to access the mezzanine.

FOR ADDITIONAL INFORMATION: Contact: The Abraham Lincoln Library and Museum, Cumberland Gap Parkway, Harrogate, Tennessee 37752, (423) 869-6235. **Web site:** *www.lmu2.lmunet.edu/museum.* **Read:** (1) Weldon Petz. 1973. *In the Presence of Lincoln.* (2) Joseph Suppiger. 1997. *Phoenix of the Mountains.*

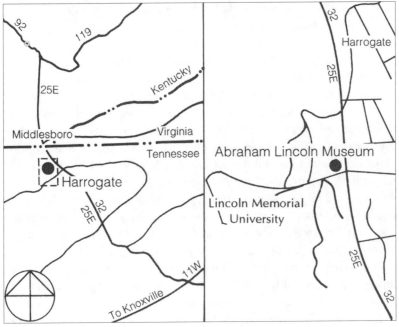

Figure 52. Location of Abraham Lincoln Library and Museum, Harrogate, Tennessee.

Lincoln Memorial Shrine

REDLANDS, CALIFORNIA

> *Those who deny freedom to others deserve it not for themselves.*

— Abraham Lincoln

Robert Watchorn emigrated from England to the United States in 1880. Impoverished and without an education, he was, nonetheless, ambitious to a fault and worked hard to become a highly successful and respected labor leader, government official, corporate president, and philanthropist. Watchorn, fascinated with Abraham Lincoln and the Civil War period, believed that people throughout the world could benefit from a more complete knowledge of Lincoln's principles, character, and life of public service. He began to formulate plans for a museum-memorial that would contain his extensive personal collection of Lincolniana. His dream came true when Lincoln Memorial Shrine (Figure 53), dedicated in 1932, was presented by Mr. Watchorn to the City of Redlands as a tribute to Lincoln and as a memorial to the Watchorns's late son who had died of injuries suffered in World War I.

The shrine is an imposing structure of reinforced concrete with Indiana limestone plates upon which are inscribed excerpts from Lincoln's speeches and writings. Bookcases, polished black walnut furniture, and display cases line the interior that is centered by Sculptor George Grey Barnard's magnificent bust of "The Great Emancipator," a major piece of art that inspired the building's design. Also displayed is Norman Rockwell's "The Long Shadow of Lincoln," painted as a *Saturday Evening Post* cover in February, 1945, and presented to the Shrine at Mr. Rockwell's request as its proper historic repository. The center of the painting is of a disabled American soldier gazing up at the bust of Lincoln, evoking the president's powerful image as a symbol of freedom and union. Around the edges sit allegorical representations of the blessings of liberty for which we, as Americans, were fighting, a message as powerful and meaningful today as it was in that earlier period of national peril.

The City of Redlands expanded the shrine in 1998 by adding two 1350-square-foot wings that allowed the museum to add thirty new displays and make room for larger group meetings. The Lincoln Memorial Shrine is the only tribute in the form of a museum to Abraham Lincoln west of the Mississippi River. At the dedication ceremony in 1932, Mr. Watchorn said:

Figure 53. Lincoln Memorial Shrine, Redlands, California. Photograph courtesy of Collection of the Lincoln Shrine.

I have no speeches, my speech is over there. . . . [the Shrine] will stand for generations to be inspired by the example of the great American who turned the current of freedom into the souls of millions of fellow men.

DIRECTIONS: From I 10, take the Orange Downtown Exit in Redlands and turn right on Eureka Street. The A. K. Smiley Library is just past the third traffic light on Vine Street. The shrine is behind the Library (Figure 54).

PUBLIC USE: Season and hours: Tuesday-Sunday, 1 PM-5 PM. Closed holidays except for Lincoln's Birthday. **Museum shop. For people with disabilities:** Fully accessible.

FOR ADDITIONAL INFORMATION: Contact: Lincoln Memorial Shrine, 125 West Vine Street, Redlands, California 92373, (909) 798-7632. **Web site:** *www.lincolnshrine.org*. **Read:** (1) Larry Burgess. 1981. *The Lincoln Memorial Shrine Genesis: Prelude to the Golden Jubilee*. (2) Larry Burgess. 1982. *The Lincoln Memorial Shrine Golden Jubilee: History Looking to the Future*. (3) Joseph Hosler. 1992. "A Shrine in the Golden State."

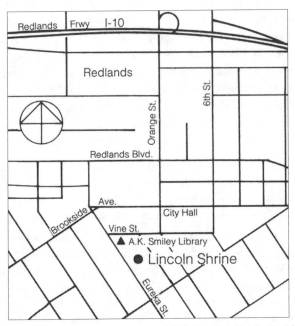

Figure 54. Location of the Lincoln Memorial Shrine, Redlands, California.

Abraham Lincoln Presidential Library and Museum

SPRINGFIELD, ILLINOIS

The Abraham Lincoln Presidential Library and Museum comprises two separate buildings located across the street from one another. The Library, which opened in October, 2004, is archival, containing twelve million documents, books, and other artifacts relating to areas of Illinois history. The 46,000-item Lincolniana collection of the Illinois State Historical Society, which is headquartered in the new library building (Figure 55), is also included. The Museum, which opened in April, 2005, combines scholarship and showmanship by communicating the times and life of Abraham Lincoln in unforgettable ways. The master architectural plan is a "hub and spoke," with galleries and other facilities arranged around a central plaza. Included are "Mrs. Lincoln's Attic," where children may try on clothing, build a log cabin, and enjoy other activities designed to engage their imaginations and involve them personally in the Lincoln story; "The Journey, Part I," in which visitors enter the early nineteenth century through a log cabin and visualize Lincoln's early life on the frontier; "The Journey, Part II," the story of the Lincolns's White House years; and "Ask Mr. Lincoln," an interactive theater that allows visitors to ask questions and obtain answers from Abraham Lincoln in his own words. There is also the Illinois Gallery with changing exhibits, the Treasures Gallery that displays actual Lincoln items, and The Union Theater, a multi-venue special effects theater featuring "Lincoln's Eyes," a fully automated special effects film giving a broad overview of Lincoln's life.

DIRECTIONS: From the visitor center at the Lincoln Home National Historic Site (see directions on page 128), walk north on Seventh Street 4 blocks to Jefferson Street, then left on Jefferson. The library is on the south side of the street, the museum on the north, between Sixth and Seventh streets (Figure 45).

PUBLIC USE: Season and hours: *Library research hours:* Monday, Tuesday, Thursday, Friday, 9 AM-4:30 PM; Wednesday, 9 AM-8:30 PM; Saturday, 8:30 AM-3:30 PM. Closed Sunday. *Museum:* Wednesday, 9 AM-8:30 PM. All other days, including Sunday, 9 AM-5 PM. The Library is closed all official state holidays. The Museum is closed Thanksgiving Day, Christmas Day, New Year's Day. **Admission fee**: Museum only. **Museum store. Food service**: Full service restaurant in Museum. **For people with disabilities**: Accessible.

Figure 55. Abraham Lincoln Presidential Library and Museum, Springfield, Illinois. Photograph by Patricia L. Newcomb.

FOR ADDITIONAL INFORMATION: Contact: The Abraham Lincoln Presidential Library and Museum, 212 North Sixth Street, Springfield, Illinois 62701, (217) 558-8844. **Web site**: *www.alplm.org.* **Read**: David Herbert Donald. 1996. *Lincoln.*

Andrew Johnson

Seventeenth President — 1865–1869

Born December 29, 1808, Raleigh, North Carolina
Died July 31, 1875, Carter Station, Tennessee

> *When I die, I desire no better winding sheet than the Stars and Stripes, and no softer pillow than the Constitution of my country.*

— Andrew Johnson

Andrew Johnson was a quintessential self-made man who represented the most desirable traits of the American character. He was born into poor circumstances that were made even more difficult by the death of his father when Andrew was only four. Lacking education and opportunity, Andrew was indentured to a tailor at the age of thirteen and became highly skilled at the craft.

At eighteen, Johnson moved to Greeneville, Tennessee, where he opened his own tailor shop and became successful enough to afford marriage and the purchase of a small house. Success as a tailor was not enough, however, for he had an overwhelming desire to advance further in life. He knew that advancement required education, so his wife read to him for hour after hour while he worked with needle and thread. When child-rearing demanded more of her time, Johnson hired local men to carry on the lessons. After work, he practiced public speaking and entered local debates. Within a few years, Johnson had become so respected for his industry, intelligence, and ability that he was elected alderman, then mayor of Greeneville.

Johnson's ambition, energy, dedication, and remarkable solicitude for his fellow citizens carried him far beyond Greeneville — to the Tennessee statehouse as governor, the United States Congress as congressman and senator, the vice presidency, and the White House.

While serving as a senator in the months preceding the Civil War, Johnson pleaded with his fellow southern senators for national unity while asserting his belief that the South would not secede from the Union. In one speech he said, "I voted against him [Lincoln]; I spoke against him; I spent my money to defeat him; but I still love my country; I love the Constitution; I intend to insist upon its guarantees."

Eastern Tennessee supported Johnson's position, but the state as a whole voted to secede. Johnson was the only southern senator who refused to secede with his state. In 1862, after Union armies had gained a foothold in western Tennessee, President Lincoln appointed Johnson military governor of the state. This position of influence led to Johnson's nomination and successful election as Lincoln's vice president in 1864.

Johnson assumed the presidency upon Lincoln's assassination in April, 1865, and immediately was plunged into political tumult. He attempted to implement Lincoln's reconstruction plans, to "bind the nation's wounds" with lenient policies toward the South, but he faced a hostile, radical congress that viewed the South as a conquered nation. In 1868, after many bruising political battles, presidential vetoes, and congressional overrides, the House of Representatives drew up articles of impeachment after Johnson vetoed the Tenure of Office Act. A trial in the senate resulted in his acquittal by a margin of one vote.

Johnson completed his term of office in 1869 and went back to Tennessee, but he returned to Washington in 1875 as United States Senator, the only ex-president to serve in that capacity. He died later that year, and his body was sent back to Greeneville for burial. In honor of his wishes, he was interred wrapped in Old Glory, with a copy of the Constitution placed beneath his head.

I intend to stand by the Constitution as it is, insisting upon compliance with all its guarantees . . . . it is the last hope of human freedom.

— Andrew Johnson

Andrew Johnson Birthplace

RALEIGH, NORTH CAROLINA

Raleigh, the capital of North Carolina, had a population of less than one thousand in 1808. Many visitors to Raleigh lodged at Casso's Inn where the hostler, Jacob Johnson, cared for their horses while his wife, Mary, known as "Polly the Weaver," did weaving for the inn. The Johnsons lived in a small kitchen-dwelling (Plate 6) behind the inn, and it was here that their son Andrew was born.

The Johnsons were poor and uneducated, but possessed qualities of character that earned them the respect and friendship of the townspeople. Andrew inherited their positive traits.

In 1904, the Wake County Committee of the Colonial Dames of America purchased the tiny house in which Johnson was born and presented it to the City of Raleigh. In 1975, the building was moved to Mordecai Historic Park and restored. The park contains several other buildings of local historic interest in addition to the Johnson house, including the Mordecai plantation house that dates to 1785. Mordecai Historic Park is managed by the City of Raleigh, Parks and Recreation Department.

DIRECTIONS: From I 440, exit onto Capital Boulevard toward downtown and proceed southbound to Old Louisburg Road, turn left at light onto Old Louisburg Road (which becomes Wake Forest Road) to Mordecai Park (Figure 56).

PUBLIC USE: Season and hours: One-hour guided tours of Mordecai Park, which includes the Johnson Birthplace, are conducted Tuesday-Saturday, 10 AM-4 PM, and Sunday, 1 PM-4 PM. The last tour leaves at 3 PM. **Admission fee. Gift shop. For people with disabilities:** Most attractions in the park are accessible, but the birthplace is not.

FOR ADDITIONAL INFORMATION: Contact: Mordecai Historic Park, 1 Mimosa Street, Raleigh, North Carolina 27604, (919) 857-4364. **Web site:** *www.raleighnc.gov/mordecai.* **Read:** Hans L. Trefousse. 1989. *Andrew Johnson.*

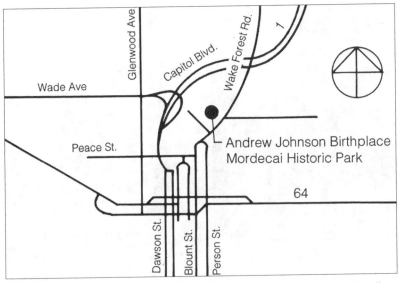

Figure 56. Location of Andrew Johnson Birthplace, Raleigh, North Carolina.

Andrew Johnson National Historic Site

GREENEVILLE, TENNESSEE

The charming town of Greeneville, proud of its Johnson heritage, hosts a number of attractions associated with the former president. One, open to the public, is a replica of Johnson's birthplace in Raleigh, presented to the city by Mrs. Margaret Johnson Patterson Bartlett, President Johnson's great-granddaughter. A city park near the home features a statue of President Johnson.

The Andrew Johnson National Historic Site encompasses several other important Johnson remembrances, the most moving being Johnson's tiny tailor shop where he worked at his trade and listened to his readers. The shop is protected from the elements, housed within the walls of a National Park Service visitor center that also contains exhibits, letters, and displays that trace the career of one of America's most unusual presidents. Just across the street from the visitor center is a small two-story brick house in which the

Figure 57. Andrew Johnson National Historic Site, Greeneville, Tennessee. Photograph courtesy of National Park Service.

Johnsons lived during their early days in Greeneville. The house contains exhibits about Andrew Johnson's life.

A larger brick house, the Johnson Homestead (Figure 57), which they purchased in 1851, is only a few blocks away. It features many mementos of Johnson's presidential years, including a handsome tilt-top table inlaid with five hundred pieces of wood, a gift from the people of Ireland.

The Andrew Johnson National Cemetery is a mile farther up Main Street. The former president's resting place is marked by a tall marble shaft topped by an American eagle. On one side is a scroll depicting the United States Constitution, which Johnson valiantly defended. His epitaph reads:

His faith in the people never wavered.

DIRECTIONS: Andrew Johnson National Historic Site is located in central Greeneville (Figure 58).

PUBLIC USE: Season and hours: 9 AM-5 PM. Closed Thanksgiving Day, Christmas Day, New Year's Day. Tours of the homestead are conducted in groups of 12 at every hour on the half-hour. **Book store. For people with disabilities:** The visitor center and early home are accessible. The Homestead is not.

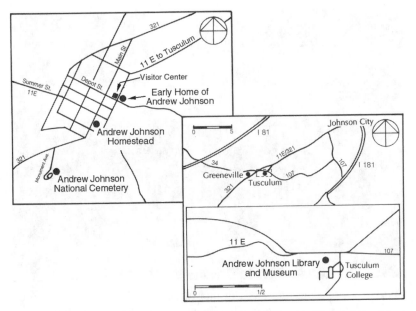

Figure 58. Location of Andrew Johnson National Historic Site and President Andrew Johnson Museum and Library, Greeneville, Tennessee.

FOR ADDITIONAL INFORMATION: Contact: Andrew Johnson National Historic Site, 121 Monument Avenue, Greeneville, Tennessee 37743, (423) 638-3551. **Web site:** *www.nps.gov/anjo.* **Read:** Hugh Lawing. 1962. "Andrew Johnson National Historic Site."

President Andrew Johnson Museum and Library

GREENEVILLE, TENNESSEE

Andrew Johnson developed and honed his rhetorical and oratorical skills at debates held on the campus of Tusculum College, although he did not matriculate there. He remained grateful to Tusculum and was interested in its affairs throughout his life, serving as a trustee of the college for thirty-five years.

Figure 59. President Andrew Johnson Museum and Library on the campus of Tusculum College, Greeneville, Tennessee. Photograph by William G. Clotworthy.

The library and museum (Figure 59) devoted to Johnson is located in a building called "Old College" on the campus of Tusculum. Completed in 1841, it is the home of the Tusculum College Archives, the Tusculum College Museum Studies program, and the President Andrew Johnson Collection. This collection consists of approximately 100 three-dimensional artifacts, ranging from the former president's top hat and political memorabilia to a copy of President Lincoln's life-mask, and over 800 volumes from Johnson's personal library. Much of the collection was presented to the college in 1980 by Johnson's great-granddaughter, Mrs. Margaret Johnson Patterson Bartlett.

"Old College" is an appropriate repository for the collection. In 1841, several hundred citizens including then-state legislator Andrew Johnson, subscribed a total of $4,245.62 in cash and in-kind, for construction and equipping of the new building.

The President Andrew Johnson Museum is one of ten buildings located on the campus of Tusculum College that are on the National Register of Historic Places. Tusculum is the "oldest college in Tennessee" and the twenty-third oldest in continuous operation in the country.

DIRECTIONS: Tusculum College is located on SR 107 (Erwin Highway). The museum is the second building on the left after entering the campus on Gilland Street (Figure 58).

PUBLIC USE: Season and hours: Monday-Friday, 9 AM-5 PM. Closed national and college holidays. **For people with disabilities:** Fully accessible.

FOR ADDITIONAL INFORMATION: Contact: President Andrew Johnson Museum and Library, Tusculum College, Box 5026, Greeneville, Tennessee 37743, (423) 636-7348. **Web site:** *http://ajmuseum.tusculum.edu.* **Read**: Robert W. Winston. 1928. *Andrew Johnson: Plebian and Patriot.*

Ulysses Simpson Grant

Eighteenth President — 1869–1877

Born April 27, 1822, Point Pleasant, Ohio
Died July 23, 1885, Saratoga Springs, New York

> *Whoever hears of me in ten years, will hear of a well-to-do old Missouri farmer!*

> — U. S. Grant, 1853

Jesse Grant owned a tannery and a small farm in rural southwestern Ohio where son Ulysses became familiar with hard times and harder work at an early age. Ulysses was ambitious and often thought of college, but mean circumstances seemed to preclude any chance for higher education. Father Jesse, too, dreamed of college for Ulysses, but his thoughts were on West Point where the education would be free. When a neighbor's son failed his examinations and left the Military Academy, Jesse asked United States Senator Thomas Morris for the open appointment for Ulysses. Morris replied that he had filled his quota, but he suggested that Congressman Thomas Hamer still might have an opening. Jesse Grant and Congressman Hamer had once had political differences, but Jesse swallowed his pride and made the request. His letter arrived at Hamer's office on the last day of the congressman's term, just in time for the appointment to be made, an appointment that changed young Ulysses's life and influenced the course of the nation.

Grant was a dogged, determined cadet and young officer, but he left the army in 1854, depressed by prolonged absences from his family. Subsequent careers in farming, real estate, and storekeeping were similarly unsuccessful and Grant lived for much of a decade in quiet obscurity — a military genius in need of a war to fulfill his destiny.

The right man met the right war at the right time as the Civil War provided an opportunity for Grant to return to the military where his strategy, tactics, determination, and leadership skills culminated in victory after victory. Military success made Grant a popular hero and the inevitable choice to lead the nation as president.

Success in battle was no guarantee of success in political office, however, and Grant's administration was rife with fraud, dishonesty, and scandal. Leaving the presidency after two terms, Ulysses and Mrs. Grant toured the world where they were received everywhere with honor and respect. Grant returned home with some of his popularity restored and made a feeble attempt to regain the White House, but was soundly defeated at his party's convention.

A financial swindle wiped out Grant's fortune, so at the urging of Mark Twain and others, he began to write his memoirs in hopes of replenishing his fortune and keeping his family financially stable. Stricken with cancer of the throat and in constant pain, he struggled with characteristic courage to complete the task. He died only a few days after completing the manuscript, never able to enjoy the critical acclaim and monetary success that followed publication of his memoirs.

Grant Birthplace

Point Pleasant, Ohio

Ulysses S. Grant was born in the bedroom of a tiny frame house of Allegheny white pine that consisted only of a kitchen, living room, and bedroom (Figure 60). The house was set high on the banks of the Ohio River in the village of Point Pleasant. The house, now owned by the Ohio Historical Society, has been restored and furnished with historic memorabilia and authentic furniture that includes the cradle in which the infant Ulysses slept.

DIRECTIONS: Grant Birthplace is on US 52E at its intersection with SR 232 (Figure 61).

Figure 60. Grant Birthplace, Point Pleasant, Ohio. Photograph by William G. Clotworthy.

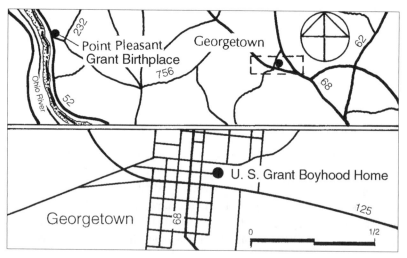

Figure 61. Location of Grant Birthplace, Point Pleasant, Ohio, and U. S. Grant Boyhood Home, Georgetown, Ohio.

PUBLIC USE: Season and hours: April 1-October 31, Wednesday-Saturday, 9:30 AM-12 M and 1 PM-5 PM; Sunday, 12 M-5 PM. Closed major holidays. **Admission fee. For people with disabilities:** Partially accessible.

FOR ADDITIONAL INFORMATION: Contact: Grant Birthplace, Box 2, New Richmond, Ohio 45157, (513) 553-4911. **Web site:** *www.ohiohistory.org/ places/grantbir/.* **Read:** U. S. Grant. 1885. *Personal Memoirs of U. S. Grant.*

U. S. Grant Boyhood Home

GEORGETOWN, OHIO

In 1823, when Ulysses was an infant, the Grant family moved from Point Pleasant to Georgetown, thirty miles to the southeast. Father Jesse established a tannery and built a two-story brick house with one room downstairs and one upstairs (Figure 62). As family fortunes improved over the next five years, he added a kitchen, hall, parlor, and two additional bedrooms. Ulysses lived in this house longer than any home in his lifetime until he left for West Point in 1839.

Figure 62. U. S. Grant Boyhood Home, Georgetown, Ohio. Photograph courtesy of Mr. and Mrs. John Ruthven.

The Grant home was owned for many years by Mr. and Mrs. John Ruthven, who completed a restoration in 1982. In 2002, in a gracious gesture of generosity, the Ruthvens presented the house to the State of Ohio to be administered by the Ohio Historical Society. The house is also a National Historic Landmark.

Mr. Ruthven, a noted wildlife artist, is the proprietor of the Thompson House Art Gallery, located just north of the Grant house. The gallery serves as a visitor center where a curator presents a short orientation lecture before leading a tour of the Grant home, and then leads a five-block walk to a schoolhouse once attended by Ulysses.

A computer kiosk in the house shows pictures of the second floor for those visitors unable to go upstairs, plus a section of the basement not open for touring. The house also features a display with stories and artifacts delineating Ulysses's military career, an animatronic figure of Grant at age fifteen telling childhood stories, other personal family artifacts, and several pieces of Grant furniture.

Visitors also may enjoy a walking tour of Georgetown that leads past Jesse Grant's tannery, a second school house attended by Ulysses, the Brown County Courthouse, and other buildings of historic interest.

DIRECTIONS: U. S. Grant Boyhood Home is located at 219 East Grant Avenue in Georgetown, 1 block north of SR 125 (Figure 61).

PUBLIC USE: Season and hours: Memorial Day-Labor Day, Wednesday-Sunday, 12 M-5 PM; September-October, weekends only, 12 M-5 PM. Tours by appointment throughout the year. **Admission fee.** For the house and school house. **For people with disabilities:** No special facilities.

FOR ADDITIONAL INFORMATION: Contact: U. S. Grant Boyhood Home and Schoolhouse, 219 E. Grant Avenue, Box 59, Georgetown, Ohio 45121. Telephone, Selma Brittingham, (937) 378-4222. **Web site:** *www.usgrantboyhoodhome.org.* **Read:** Jean Edward Smith. 2001. *Grant.*

Ulysses S. Grant National Historic Site

SAINT LOUIS, MISSOURI

In 1820, Frederick Dent, a Saint Louis businessman, purchased a two-story frame house and farm in the country as an escape from the city's summer heat. He named this property White Haven (Plate 7). Dent's son, Fred, roomed with Ulysses Grant at West Point and Grant, stationed near Saint Louis in 1843, visited White Haven. Once Fred's sister Julia returned home from boarding school, Grant visited often. Friendship developed into romance, and when Grant's company was transferred from Saint Louis in 1844, he asked Mr. Dent for Julia's hand in marriage.

White Haven remained a focal point in the lives of the Grants for over forty years. Their first child was born in the house in 1850, and when Lieutenant Grant was posted to California, Julia waited for him at White Haven. They lived on the estate from 1849 to 1859 before purchasing the land from Julia's family during the Civil War, with plans to retire there to raise and breed thoroughbred horses. The Grants owned the property until 1884.

Ten acres of the White Haven property on the north side of Grant Road is managed by the National Park Service as the Ulysses S. Grant National Historic Site. The site contains a modern visitor center plus five historic

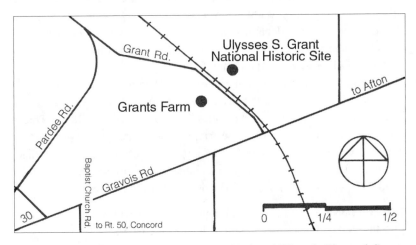

Figure 63. Location of Ulysses S. Grant National Historic Site and Grants Farm, Saint Louis, Missouri.

structures — the original White Haven house, a chicken house, a stone building, an ice house, and a stable that opened as a museum early in 2007.

DIRECTIONS: From I 270, go northbound on Gravois Road to Grant Road, then go north on Grant Road to the site (Figure 63).

PUBLIC USE: Season and hours: 9 AM-5 PM, with guided house tours on the half-hour beginning at 9:30 AM. The last tour is at 4 PM. Closed Thanksgiving Day, Christmas Day, New Year's Day. **For people with disabilities:** Accessible.

FOR ADDITIONAL INFORMATION: Contact: Ulysses S. Grant National Historic Site, 7400 Grant Road, Saint Louis, Missouri 63123, (314) 842-3298. **Web site:** *www.nps.gov/ulsg.* **Read:** (1) Julia Dent Grant. 1975. *The Personal Memoirs of Julia Dent Grant.* (2) William S. McFeely. 1981. *Grant: A Biography.*

Grant's Farm

SAINT LOUIS, MISSOURI

After Grant resigned from the army in 1854, he returned to White Haven to farm one hundred acres of the property that his father-in-law, Frederick Dent, had given to Julia. The Grants hand-built a log cabin on the property and facetiously named it Hardscrabble, not only for the land itself but for the difficulties of the times. Within six years the farming venture had failed, so the Grants moved to Galena, Illinois, where they experienced further disappointment and financial hardship before the Civil War brought Ulysses opportunity, military success, fame, and fortune.

Hardscrabble Cabin is now part of Grant's Farm, a 281-acre entertainment and educational complex operated by Anheuser-Busch. Grant's Farm is located south of Grant Road just minutes from downtown Saint Louis. Trackless trams transport visitors past the original Hardscrabble cabin (Figure 64), a carefully preserved symbol of an important part of our national heritage. Bordering the farm, like a sentry, is a dramatic memorial to veterans of the Civil War — a fence built from 2563 rifle barrels from the great conflict.

DIRECTIONS: From I 270, go northbound on Gravois Road to Grant Road, then turn left on Grant Road to Grants Farm (Figure 63).

PUBLIC USE: Season and hours: Spring (mid-April to mid-May): Wednesday-Friday, 9 AM-3 PM; Saturday, 9 AM-3:30 PM; Sunday, 9:30 AM-3:30

Figure 64. Hardscrabble, Grant's Farm, Saint Louis, Missouri. Photograph copyright © 2005 Anheuser-Busch Cos., Inc. Used with permission of Anheuser-Busch Cos., Inc. All rights reserved.

PM. **Summer** (mid-May to mid-August): Tuesday-Friday, 9 AM-3:30 PM; Saturday, 9 AM-4 PM; Sunday, 9:30 AM-4 PM; Holiday Mondays, 9 AM-4 PM. **Fall** (mid-August to October 31): Wednesday-Friday, 9:30 AM-2:30 PM; Saturday, Sunday, 9:30 AM-3:30 PM. Special seasonal celebrations are held November and December. Call ahead for exact dates. Closed November-April. **Admission fee:** There is a parking charge, but none for admission. **Food service:** The full-service Bauernhof Restaurant is on the grounds and there are snack kiosks throughout the park. **Gift shop. For people with disabilities:** Fully accessible.

FOR ADDITIONAL INFORMATION: Contact: Grant's Farm, 10501 Gravois Road, Saint Louis, Missouri 63123, (314) 843-1700. **Web site:** *www.grantsfarm.com.*

Ulysses S. Grant Home State Historic Site

GALENA, ILLINOIS

In 1860, Grant and his family moved to Galena, Illinois, where he hoped to reverse his financial misfortunes by working in a leather store owned by his father and managed by his brothers. Only a year later, however, he left to rejoin the US Army as colonel of the Twenty-First Illinois Volunteer Infantry Regiment.

On August 18, 1865, Grant returned to Galena as a conquering hero. After a jubilant parade and patriotic speeches, the citizens of Galena presented General and Mrs. Grant with a handsome, fully furnished house (Figure 65), typical of the Italianate bracketed style, as a symbol of their pride, respect, and gratitude. Julia Grant recalled, "after a glorious triumphal ride around the hills and valleys, so brilliant with smiles and flowers, we were conducted to a lovely villa exquisitely furnished with everything good taste could desire."

General Grant was not destined to enjoy the new home for long, as he was called to further service as President of the United States. The Grants returned to Galena following his second term as president, but soon embarked

Figure 65. Ulysses S. Grant Home State Historic Site, Galena, Illinois. Photograph by Jim Quick; use courtesy of Illinois Historic Preservation Agency, Galena State Historic Sites.

on an extensive world tour. When they returned to the United States in 1879, they were treated to another welcome-home celebration in Galena before settling into permanent residency in New York City.

The Galena house remained in the Grant family until 1904, when the Grant children presented it to the City of Galena, "with the understanding that the property is to be kept as a memorial to the late General Ulysses S. Grant, and for no other purpose." In 1931, Galena deeded the property to the State of Illinois, which maintains it under the management of the Illinois Historic Preservation Agency.

Restoration and modernization activities have continued without destroying the charm and ambience of the period. Most of the furnishings are original Grant pieces which makes the house an excellent example of mid-nineteenth century taste in exterior design and interior décor.

DIRECTIONS: Galena is in the northwestern corner of Illinois on US 20 and SR 84. There are historical site markers leading visitors to the Grant house (Figure 66).

PUBLIC USE: Season and hours: April-October, Wednesday-Sunday, 9 AM-5 PM; November-March, Wednesday-Sunday, 9 AM-4 PM. Closed Thanksgiving Day, Christmas Day, New Year's Day, Martin Luther King's Birthday,

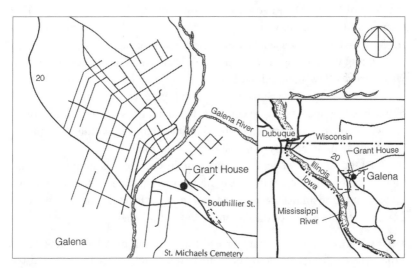

Figure 66. Location of Ulysses S. Grant Home State Historic Site, Galena, Illinois.

159

Presidents' Day, Veterans' Day, Election Day. **For people with disabilities:** Accessibility is limited to the first floor but photographs of the second floor are displayed for those unable to reach the upstairs.

FOR ADDITIONAL INFORMATION: Contact: Grant Home State Historic Site, 500 Bouthillier Street, Box 333, Galena, Illinois 61036, (815) 777-3310. **Web site:** *www.granthome.com.* **Read:** (1) Kenneth N. Owens. 1963. *Galena, Grant and the Fortunes of War: A History of Galena, Illinois during the Civil War.* (2) Thomas A. Campbell, Jr. 1979. "The U. S. Grant Home State Historic Site."

Grant Cottage State Historic Site

MOUNT MCGREGOR, NEW YORK

Man proposes, God disposes.

— Ulysses S. Grant

In June, 1885, General Ulysses S. Grant and his family journeyed from New York City to a simple vacation cottage owned by Joseph W. Drexel, on the slope of Mount McGregor near Saratoga Springs, New York (Figure 67). Grant was terminally ill with painful throat cancer, and it was hoped that the fresh air and beautiful scenery would ease his suffering.

Grant went to the Drexel cabin to finish his memoirs. Occasionally he was carried a few hundred yards to a scenic overlook above the Hudson Valley, but he dared not spend much time enjoying the surroundings as most of his time was spent racing to complete his memoirs which he hoped would sell well enough to replenish a fortune lost in a financial swindle. The manuscript was completed only a few days before he died.

At the moment of death, the clock in the cottage was stopped, a spontaneous and symbolic act to freeze the moment in time — to preserve the cottage, its furnishings, decorations, and other effects just as they were, a dramatic tribute to one of the nation's great military heroes.

DIRECTIONS: Mount McGregor is 40 miles north of Albany, New York. From Albany, take I 87 northbound to Exit 16 and proceed westbound on Ballard Road. At the intersection with US 9, there are historical markers directing visitors to the cottage that is on the grounds of the Mount McGregor

PLATE 1

Top: Mount Vernon, George Washington's plantation home situated along the south side of the Potomac River in Virginia, as seen from the northwest. **Bottom:** Peacefield, or the "Old House," in Quincy, Massachusetts, home of John and Abigail Adams and several generations of their descendants.

PLATE 2

Poplar Forest, Thomas Jefferson's octagon-shaped "retreat" in the foothills of the Blue Ridge Mountains near Forest, Virginia.

PLATE 3

Top: Montpelier, lying upon the rolling Piedmont near Orange, Virginia, was the boyhood home of James Madison and, later, the residence for he and wife Dolley. **Middle:** Ash Lawn-Highland, the working farm home of James and Elizabeth Monroe, is situated only a mountain top away from friend Thomas Jefferson's Monticello. **Bottom:** The Hermitage, near Nashville, Tennessee, was home and sanctuary for Andrew and Rachel Jackson.

PLATE 4

Top: Martin Van Buren retired to his home town of Kinderhook in the Hudson Valley and purchased the gracious Lindenwald mansion. **Middle:** Berkeley, one of the great James River plantation homes, was the birthplace of President William Henry Harrison. **Bottom:** Sherwood Forest, another James River plantation home, was the retirement estate of John and Julia Tyler and remains a working farm and home of their direct descendants.

PLATE 5

Top: The James K. Polk house in Columbia, Tennessee, is representative of success and fine living in the early nineteenth century. **Middle:** The Millard Fillmore House Museum in East Aurora, New York, was hand-built by Fillmore as a residence for he and wife Abigail. **Bottom:** The Pierce Manse in Concord, New Hampshire, was the home of Franklin and Jane Pierce when he was plucked from political obscurity and elected president of the United States.

PLATE 6

Top: Wheatland, in Lancaster, Pennsylvania, was purchased by Secretary of State James Buchanan in 1848 as a country estate. It became his political headquarters, then his retirement home following his presidency. **Middle Right:** Abraham Lincoln's Boyhood Home alongside Knob Creek is near Hodgenville, Kentucky. **Bottom:** Andrew Johnson's Birthplace was a kitchen/residence located in the yard of Casso's Inn in Raleigh, North Carolina.

PLATE 7

Top: The Grants lived briefly at White Haven in Saint Louis, Missouri, following their marriage, and Julia waited here for him when he was posted to the west coast. **Middle:** Spiegel Grove in Fremont, Ohio, was an important place in the lives of Rutherford and Lucy Hayes. **Bottom:** Lawnfield, in Mentor, Ohio, was the home of James and Lucretia Garfield from the time of his congressional service until his assassination in 1881.

PLATE 8

Top: The President Chester A. Arthur Historic Site in Fairfield, Vermont, contains a small church and a reconstruction of Arthur's birth house, shown here. **Middle:** The Grover Cleveland Birthplace in Caldwell, New Jersey, was the manse of the Caldwell First Presbyterian Church served by Cleveland's father. **Bottom:** The President Benjamin Harrison House in Indianapolis, Indiana, was Harrison's home before and after his presidency.

PLATE 9

Top: The reconstructed William McKinley birthplace is part of the McKinley Memorial Library, Museum, and Birthplace Home complex in Niles, Ohio. **Middle:** Sagamore Hill is located on the Theodore Roosevelt estate overlooking Oyster Bay and Long Island Sound in Oyster Bay, New York. **Bottom:** The William Howard Taft National Historic Site in Cincinnati, Ohio, features the Taft family home in which the president was born and raised.

PLATE 10

Top: The Woodrow Wilson House in an upscale neighborhood of Washington, DC, was the residence to which the president retired and where he died in 1921. **Middle:** Warren and Florence Harding lived in this home in Marion, Ohio, following their marriage in its parlor in 1891. **Bottom:** The Calvin Coolidge Homestead in Plymouth, Vermont, is where Coolidge was sworn in as president of the United States by his notary father in 1923.

PLATE 11

Top: The Herbert Hoover Presidential Library and Museum, West Branch, Iowa, is located alongside the Herbert Hoover National Historic Site, a preserved village complex that includes Hoover's Birthplace cottage. **Bottom:** The Roosevelt Vacation Cottage at Campobello Island is located in New Brunswick, immediately east of the Maine border, as part of the Roosevelt Campobello International Park.

PLATE 12

Top: The home of Harry and Bess Truman in Independence, Missouri, is the centerpiece of the Harry S Truman National Historic Site. **Bottom:** The Dwight D. Eisenhower boyhood home is located on the grounds of the Eisenhower Presidential Center in Abilene, Kansas.

PLATE 13

Top: John F. Kennedy was born in this modest frame house in Brookline, Massachusetts; it is now the John Fitzgerald Kennedy National Historic Site. **Middle:** This farm home in the rugged Texas Hill Country is a reconstruction of the Lyndon B. Johnson birthplace. **Bottom:** Richard M. Nixon was born in 1913 in a small farm house that has been reconstructed on its exact location in Yorba Linda, California.

PLATE 14

Top: The Gerald R. Ford Presidential Museum in Grand Rapids, Michigan, is located in the area Ford served as a congressman for many years. **Bottom:** The Carter Presidential Center in Atlanta, Georgia, is an architecturally integrated complex of buildings, including the Jimmy Carter Library and Museum shown here, set in a beautifully landscaped tract of rolling hills.

PLATE 15

Top: The Ronald Reagan Boyhood Home is a modest, two-story frame building in the lively community of Dixon, Illinois. **Bottom:** The George Bush Presidential Library and Museum is located on the campus of Texas A&M University in College Station, Texas.

PLATE 16

Top: The Clinton Presidential Center is situated on the south side of the Arkansas River in Little Rock, Arkansas. **Bottom:** The George W. Bush Childhood Home Museum is located in Midland, Texas.

Figure 67. Grant Cottage State Historic Site, Mount McGregor, Saratoga Springs, New York. Photograph courtesy of The Friends of the Ulysses S. Grant Cottage.

Correctional Facility (Figure 68). Visitors will be stopped briefly for identification before driving to the cottage.

PUBLIC USE: Season and hours: Memorial Day-Labor Day, Wednesday-Sunday, 10 AM-4 PM. Each weekend in September and the first two weekends in October, 10 AM-4 PM. **Admission fee. Food service:** Picnics are allowed at Grant's Overlook. **For people with disabilities:** Fully accessible.

FOR ADDITIONAL INFORMATION: Contact: The Friends of the Ulysses S. Grant Cottage, Box 2294, Wilton, New York 12831, (518) 587-8277. **Web site:** *www.nysparks.state.ny.us.* **Read:** Thomas M. Pitkin. 1973. *The Captain Departs: Ulysses S. Grant's Last Campaign.*

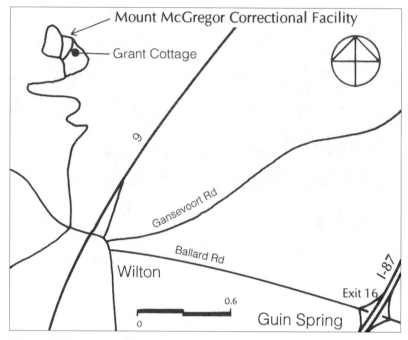

Figure 68. Location of Grant Cottage State Historic Site, Mount McGregor, Saratoga Springs, New York.

Rutherford Birchard Hayes

Nineteenth President — 1877–1881

Born October 4, 1822, Delaware, Ohio
Died January 17, 1893, Fremont, Ohio

> *He serves his party best who serves his country best.*

> — Rutherford B. Hayes

Just as Abraham Lincoln was known as "Honest Abe," our nineteenth president could have been called "Honest Rud," for it was his reproachless reputation that made Rutherford Birchard Hayes a candidate for president in 1876. Following the scandals of the Grant administration, which had been tainted by fraud, spoils, and political chicanery, the electorate would accept nothing less than a man of proven honesty and unswerving devotion to truth and honor. Rutherford B. Hayes was such a man.

Hayes's father died shortly before Rud's birth, and Rud was reared by his mother and her brother, Sardis Birchard, who became Hayes's guardian. Birchard was a flinty, transplanted Vermonter who made sure that young Hayes had a proper education. He and Rud's mother Sophia, an overly protective mother, instilled in the future president, and his sister Fanny, strong convictions with an expectation of exemplary behavior.

In 1852, Hayes married Lucy Ware Webb, a graduate of Cincinnati Wesleyan Women's College. Although Lucy shared Rutherford's belief in temperance, it was he, not Lucy, who, years later, would not allow alcohol in the White House, not even on state occasions. Because of her husband's politically motivated stricture, it was Lucy who took the blame for the policy and became unfairly known to future generations as "Lemonade Lucy."

Hayes's path to the White House was through the law and distinguished military service. He entered the Civil War as a major and emerged a brevet major general — popular with his men and brave in battle. Stories of his heroism drifted back to Ohio, where he was urged to run for congress but Hayes refused to leave active service even if elected, remarking, "An officer fit for duty who at this crisis would abandon his post to electioneer for a seat in congress ought to be scalped."

Such feelings were the genesis of his future political attitude, one of absolute integrity and devotion to duty. That strength was destined to carry the former congressman and three-term governor of Ohio to the White House.

Rutherford B. Hayes Presidential Center

FREMONT, OHIO

I'd rather die in Spiegel Grove than anywhere else.

— Rutherford B. Hayes

Spiegel Grove (Plate 7) is a pleasant, restful wooded estate of twenty-five acres located in northern Ohio. It is crowned by a stately red brick house whose thirty-one rooms are filled with precious antiques and mementos of the president who lived there. Hayes's Uncle Sardis built the original structure around 1860, and it was he who named the place Spiegel Grove, using the German word for "mirror" to describe the reflection of pools of sparkling water that formed following rains. Birchard died in 1874 and bequeathed Spiegel Grove to his nephew, already in residence. Spiegel Grove was Hayes's permanent home between his second and third terms as Governor of Ohio. Hayes also enlarged the house in 1880 and 1889, additions that brought the three-story Victorian home to its present size. The imposing residence represents the glory days of Victorian architecture and interior décor in the American Midwest. Hayes loved the serene beauty of Spiegel Grove and returned often during his terms as governor and later as president.

Sometime between 1909 and 1914, Hayes's descendants presented Spiegel Grove to the State of Ohio, under the condition that the state erect a separate library and museum building to house the late president's books and other belongings. Thus, in 1916, the nation's first presidential library and museum came into being, housed in a building of classic architecture and constructed of Ohio sandstone. Over the years, the Hayes family established several organizations that were combined in the mid-1980s to create the Rutherford B. Hayes Presidential Center with the purpose and mandate to administer the center in conjunction with the Ohio Historical Society.

The museum section contains two floors of exhibits chronicling Hayes's life and political career. Among the more popular artifacts are the president's carriage, two dollhouses belonging to the president's daughter Fanny and a set of the Hayes's unique White House china. The library section, a major research collection of items from the post-Civil War period, contains 75,000 volumes and 3500 linear feet of manuscript and photographic material, including the personal papers of President and Mrs. Hayes.

The peaceful, flower- and tree-filled estate is enclosed by a decorated wrought-iron fence with six gates, all brought from the White House grounds. Winding paths allow visitors to enjoy and appreciate the quiet grandeur of a particularly restful presidential retreat. President and Mrs. Hayes are buried on a wooded knoll near an old Indian trail that winds through the serenity of Spiegel Grove.

DIRECTIONS: Fremont is just off I 80/90 (Ohio Turnpike). Take Exit 91 (Fremont) and follow the historical markers to the Center (Figure 69).

PUBLIC USE: Season and hours: Monday-Saturday, 9 AM-5 PM; Sundays and holidays, 12 M-5 PM. The library is closed on Sundays and holidays. Tours of the house are guided. Tours of the Museum are self-guided. All attractions are closed Thanksgiving Day, Christmas Day, New Year's Day, Easter Sunday. **Admission fee.** Yes, for access to the house and the museum. The library is open without charge. **Museum shop. For people with disabilities:** The museum is accessible. The first floor of the home is accessible with a videotape tour of the second floor available.

FOR ADDITIONAL INFORMATION: Contact: Rutherford B. Hayes Presidential Center, Spiegel Grove, Fremont, Ohio 43420-2796, (419) 332-2081. **Web site:** *www.rbhayes.org.* **Read:** (1) Watt P. Marchman. 1988. *The Story of a President: Rutherford B. Hayes and Spiegel Grove.* (2) Ari Hoogenboom. 1995. *Rutherford B. Hayes: Warrior and President.*

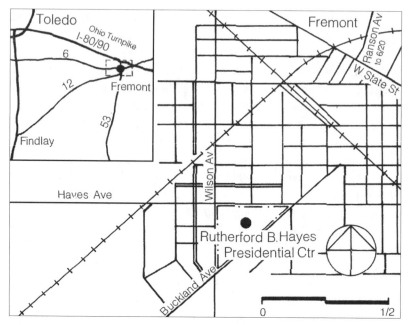

Figure 69. Location of Rutherford B. Hayes Presidential Center, Fremont, Ohio.

James Abram Garfield

Twentieth President — March 1881–September 1881

Born November 19, 1831, Orange Township (Moreland Hills), Ohio
Died September 19, 1881, Elberon, New Jersey

No man ever started so low that accomplished so much in all our history. . . . not Franklin or Lincoln even.

— Rutherford B. Hayes, speaking of Garfield

Hayes's reflection on Garfield might have been exaggerated, but James A. Garfield, the last president of the United States to have been born in a log cabin, was nonetheless quite a man. His father died when he was two; he was reared by a tenacious frontier mother who lived long enough to attend his inauguration as President of the United States.

Early in life, Garfield was forced to work hard, as a mule driver, farmer, and carpenter. A rough exterior belied a precocious, retentive mind and a rare gift for public speaking. At the outbreak of the Civil War, he joined the Union Army where he served with distinction and rose to the rank of major general. After the war, he represented his home district as congressman for nine terms before the Ohio Legislature elected him to the United States Senate in 1880. Before taking the oath of office as a senator, however, a divided Republican national convention nominated him for president on the thirty-sixth ballot.

On July 2, 1881, only four months into his term, as Garfield prepared to leave Washington for a vacation, he was shot by Charles Guiteau, a deranged, frustrated office seeker. The critically wounded president lingered in the capital for two months before he was moved to the Garfield vacation home on the New Jersey shore where he died on September 19, 1881.

James A. Garfield National Historic Site

MENTOR, OHIO

> .... *where my boys can learn to work and where I can get some exercise, where I can touch the earth and get some strength from it.*

— James A. Garfield

In 1876, Congressman James A. Garfield bought a farm and rundown 1½-story house in Mentor, Ohio. The house became the nucleus of what would evolve into a twenty-nine-room Victorian mansion with gables and bay windows (Plate 7). The property was named Lawnfield by reporters who camped out on Garfield's farm during the 1880 presidential campaign, although Garfield himself preferred to call it simply his Mentor farm. Garfield was to enjoy his home only briefly.

Following Garfield's assassination, thousands of grief-stricken citizens, concerned for Mrs. Garfield's welfare, sent donations of money. Moved by emotion and their generosity, she decided that a library would be an appropriate tribute to the president who had held such a deep appreciation of education and love for books. The Library, completed in 1886, is filled with the president's books, as well as mementos, souvenirs, gifts, and other remembrances. Included are the desk Garfield used when serving in Congress, a funeral wreath sent by Queen Victoria, and a Wooton desk with its 110 filing compartments. Garfield's correspondence and other papers are preserved in the Library of Congress.

The Garfield family remained at Lawnfield until the 1930s, when the house and furnishings were donated to the Western Reserve Historical Society. Today the National Park Service owns and operates the site while the Western Reserve Historical Society owns the collections. An extensive restoration project that involved structural repair and refurbishing of Lawnfield was completed in 1998. An 1893 carriage house was converted to a visitor center which houses a gift shop, exhibits, and an eighteen-minute video presentation dealing with President Garfield's life from cradle to grave.

DIRECTIONS: From I 90, take the SR 615/Center Street Exit and proceed northbound for 2 miles to US 20 (Mentor Avenue), then go west on Mentor Avenue 1 mile to Lawnfield (Figure 70). From SR 2, take the SR 615/Center Street Exit and proceed southbound for 2 miles to US 20 (Mentor Avenue), then go westbound on Mentor Avenue 1 mile to Lawnfield.

PUBLIC USE: Season and hours: May 1-October 31, Monday-Saturday, 10 AM-5 PM; Sunday, 12 M-5 PM. November-April, Saturday and Sunday, 12 M-5 PM. Closed New Year's Day, Thanksgiving Day, Christmas Eve Day and Christmas Day. **Admission fee. Gift shop. For people with disabilities:** Most of the site is accessible. The exception is a small section of the house tour. This area may be viewed by video.

FOR ADDITIONAL INFORMATION: Contact: James A. Garfield National Historic Site, 8095 Mentor Avenue, Mentor, Ohio 44606, (440) 255-8722. **Web site:** *www.nps.gov/jaga.* **Read:** (1) Allen Peskin. 1978. *Garfield.* (2) Ken Ackerman. 2003. *Dark Horse.*

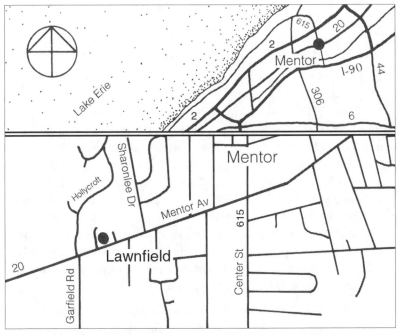

Figure 70. Location of James A. Garfield National Historic Site, Mentor, Ohio.

Chester Alan Arthur

Twenty-First President — 1881–1885

Born October 5, 1829, Fairfield, Vermont
Died November 18, 1886, New York City, New York

> *Chet Arthur, President of the United States? Good God!*

— Unknown politician

> *The people and the politicians will find that Vice President Arthur and President Arthur are different men.*

— Governor Foote of Ohio

Governor Foote was correct. When James A. Garfield was nominated for president by the Republican Party in 1880, Chester A. Arthur of New York was chosen as his running mate in an effort to "balance the ticket" and as a sop to New York's political bosses. Arthur was considered a political hack, a common politico with neither national nor foreign policy experience. But, by one of those dramatic flukes of history, he was destined to become the twenty-first President of the United States.

When President Garfield was assassinated, the nation was traumatized. Most were appalled by the thought of Chester Arthur as president. Some politicians suggested that he should reject the office, although others were more sanguine. One young woman wrote:

> *Rise to the emergency. Disappoint our fears. Force the nation to have faith in you. Show from the first that you have none but the purest aims. It may be difficult at once to inspire confidence, but*

persevere. In time . . . when you have given reason for it . . . the country will love and trust you. Your name is now on the annals of history . . . . it is for you to choose whether your record shall be written in black or in gold. For the sake of your country, for your own sake and for the sake of all who have ever loved you, let it be pure and bright.

The words were taken to heart. Chester A. Arthur, like other vice presidents, rose to the challenge.

Chester Alan Arthur, the son of a Baptist minister; was born in a parsonage near his father's church in rural Vermont. He was brought up in Schenectady, New York, where he attended Union College and earned a law degree. In his early twenties, ambitious to a fault, he traveled to New York seeking fame and fortune, gaining both beyond his wildest dreams. As a member of the New York bar, he distinguished himself as a champion of civil rights for African Americans. Active in Republican politics, he fell under the control of Senator Roscoe Conkling, who became Arthur's political mentor.

During the Civil War, Arthur accepted an appointment as a general in the New York Militia and served as Quartermaster General of the Port of New York, a position of great importance and influence. He conducted the assignment with skill, and it led to his post-war appointment as Collector of Customs of New York, a lucrative and blatantly political post, as the Customs House was a dumping ground of political patronage. Once in office, however, President Arthur defied the existing system by striking an early blow at the spoils system that had been endemic to all government affairs.

Arthur may have come to the presidency by a path of political expediency, but once in office he was capable and incorruptible.

President Chester A. Arthur Historic Site

Fairfield, Vermont

William Arthur was a well-educated, albeit destitute Irish immigrant who arrived in Fairfield, Vermont, as a Baptist minister. His son, Chester, destined to become President of the United States, was born in a tiny, temporary parsonage just down the rocky hill from the Reverend Arthur's church.

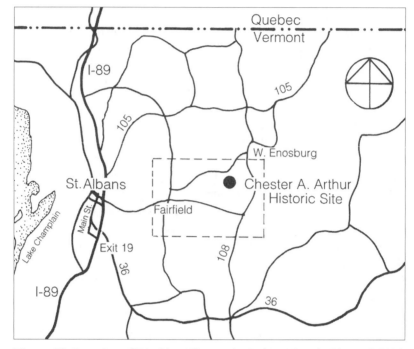

Figure 71. Location of President Chester A. Arthur Historic Site, Fairfield, Vermont.

The present brick church, which dates from 1830 and was constructed on the site of the original church, is open for visitation, and a building was constructed by the State of Vermont in 1953 to represent the original house to which the Arthur family moved in 1830 (Plate 8). The home has two downstairs rooms and an attic or sleeping loft above. It is not furnished as the cramped living space it must have been, but offers instead a pictorial exhibit of President Arthur's life and political career.

DIRECTIONS: Fairfield is in the northwest corner of Vermont, close to the Canadian border. It can be reached by either SR 36 or SR 108. The Arthur Historic Site is 3.5 miles east of Fairfield Station (Figure 71).

PUBLIC USE: Season and hours: Late May through mid-October, Wednesday-Sunday, 11 AM-5 PM. **Picnic area. For people with disabilities:** Accessible.

FOR ADDITIONAL INFORMATION: Contact: Vermont Division for Historic Preservation, National Life Building, Drawer 20, Montpelier, Vermont 05620-1501, (802) 828-3211. **Web site:** *www.historicvermont.org.* **Read**. (1) George Frederick Howe. 1934. *Chester A. Arthur: A Quarter Century of Machine Politics.* (2) Thomas Reeves. 1975. *Gentleman Boss: The Life of Chester Alan Arthur.*

Stephen Grover Cleveland

Twenty-Second President — 1885–1889
Twenty-Fourth President — 1893–1897

Born March 18, 1837, Caldwell, New Jersey
Died June 24, 1908, Princeton, New Jersey

I have tried so hard to do right.

— Grover Cleveland's dying words

Grover Cleveland is the only president to serve a term, lose a bid for reelection, and then win a second term. He is also the only president to hang a man (that happened while he was sheriff of Buffalo, New York), the only president to be married in the White House and his daughter Esther was the first child of a president to have been born in the White House. Grover Cleveland was an ordinary man of common sense, determined and honest — traits he acquired from his pious, devoted parents in the strict atmosphere of Presbyterian parsonages.

Cleveland brought to the White House a breath of fresh air after twenty-five years of rule by the opposition party and the political shenanigans and congressional malfeasance that took place during Reconstruction. He fought New York's Tammany Hall and other special interests who had subverted and manipulated the nation's political system for personal gain. One way he accomplished his goals was to exercise his power of presidential veto, which he did more times than had his twenty-one predecessors combined!

Grover Cleveland Birthplace

CALDWELL, NEW JERSEY

Grover Cleveland was born in the manse of the Caldwell First Presbyterian Church (Plate 8) in which his father served as pastor. The simple frame building of 2½ stories was built in 1832 for the sum of $1490. With its gabled roof and clapboard siding, it is similar to many houses of the period.

The Clevelands moved a few years later to a calling in Fayetteville, New York. The Caldwell manse served the church through many successors until it was purchased and restored as a house-museum memorial to the president who had been born within its walls.

Today the house looks as it appeared in the mid-nineteenth century, with artifacts and furniture dating to the Cleveland occupancy. A resident curator is on hand to show visitors the downstairs rooms and to answer questions about Grover Cleveland and his times.

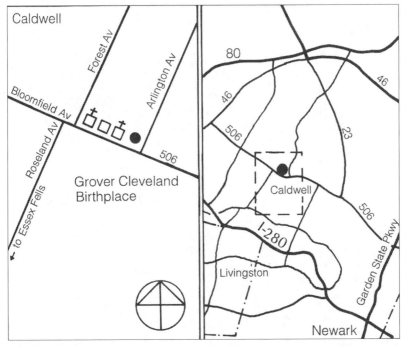

Figure 72. Location of Grover Cleveland Birthplace, Caldwell, New Jersey.

DIRECTIONS: The Cleveland House is located on the north side of SR 506 (Bloomfield Avenue) between Arlington and Forest avenues in Caldwell (Figure 72).

PUBLIC USE: Season and hours: Wednesday-Friday, 9 AM-6 PM; Saturday, 9 AM-5 PM; Sunday, 1 PM-6 PM. Closed 12 M-1 PM each day. Closed holidays. **For people with disabilities:** Fully accessible.

FOR ADDITIONAL INFORMATION: Contact: Grover Cleveland Birthplace, 207 Bloomfield Avenue, Caldwell, New Jersey 07006, (973) 226-0001. **Web site:** *www.caldwellnj.com/grover.htm.* **Read:** Richard E. Welch, Jr. 1988. *The Presidencies of Grover Cleveland.*

Benjamin Harrison

Twenty-Third President — 1889–1893

Born August 20, 1833, North Bend, Ohio
Died March 13, 1901, Indianapolis, Indiana

> *When a man receives the approbation of his neighbors, he is
> indeed blessed.*

— Benjamin Harrison

Benjamin Harrison was the grandson of the ninth president and the great-grandson of a signer of the Declaration of Independence. Harrison brought to the White House a family heritage of commitment to service and public responsibility. His father was a farmer who served two terms in the United States Congress. More important, he provided son Benjamin with a wholesome Midwestern upbringing and a solid education.

Benjamin served with distinction as a brevet brigadier general during the Civil War, then returned to Indiana to resume his law practice. He was elected to the United States Senate in 1881, and from that powerful political seat was nominated in 1888 as the Republican presidential candidate. Evincing little interest in the honor, Harrison ran a quiet campaign from his home. He surprised everyone, including himself, by winning the presidency in the Electoral College, although he polled fewer popular votes than his rival, Grover Cleveland. Four years later, Harrison was defeated by Cleveland.

Benjamin Harrison was a devout and vocal patriot. As president, he declared that the nation's flag should fly from every school and public building, a tradition still honored. He rejoiced when, in 1892, Francis Bellamy of Boston wrote:

I pledge allegiance to my flag and the Republic for which it stands; one nation indivisible, with Liberty and Justice for all.

After he left office, Harrison commented:

I did try to make the administration thoroughly American and hope that something was done to develop an increased love of the flag at home and an increased respect for it abroad.

President Benjamin Harrison Home

INDIANAPOLIS, INDIANA

Great lives do not go out, they go on.

— Benjamin Harrison

General Benjamin Harrison returned to Indianapolis after a distinguished Civil War career. He opened a law office and began construction of a sixteen-room mansion which was completed in 1875 (Plate 8). The house was of the brick Italianate style, although the addition of a spacious porch reflected the Colonial Revival style that became popular in the 1890s.

Except for his terms as senator and president, Harrison lived in Indianapolis until he died in 1901. In 1913, his second wife, Mary, and his daughter Elizabeth moved to New York and leased the house to private tenants, and in 1937, they sold it to the Jordan Conservatory of Music to be used as a dormitory. In 1965, the President Benjamin Harrison Foundation was formed, assumed control of the house, and converted it to its original state. Family members contributed papers, furniture, and memorabilia to the memorial effort.

Harrison's first wife, Caroline, was a talented, professionally trained artist who had filled the house with colorful work, including the Harrison White House china of her design: corn tassels on the border, forty-four stars to symbolize the states, and an American eagle representing strength and unity. Ten rooms have been fully restored, the third floor serving as a museum gallery for Harrison's personal artifacts and other exhibits.

The Harrison Home is the center for an interactive educational program, including activities designed for all grade levels. A special first-person interpretation, *Live from Delaware Street*, is presented four times a year.

DIRECTIONS: The Harrison home is 1 block from I 65. Southbound on I 65, take the Meridian Street exit to 11th Street and continue straight on 11th Street to Delaware Street, turning left to the home. From I 65 northbound, exit at Pennsylvania Street, immediately turning left for 1 block to 11th Street, then turning left for 1 block to Delaware Street, and left again to the home (Figure 73). Parking is in the rear of the home or on the street.

PUBLIC USE: Season and hours: Monday-Saturday, 10 AM-3:30 PM. Sundays in June and July, 12:30 PM-3:30 PM. Guided tours are conducted every 30 minutes; the last tour is at 3:30 PM. Closed major holidays, Indianapolis 500 Race Day and the first three weeks in January. **Admission fee. Gift shop. For people with disabilities:** There is a ramp to the first floor and an elevator to the second and third floors. A videotaped tour of those floors is also available.

FOR ADDITIONAL INFORMATION: Contact: President Benjamin Harrison Home, 1230 North Delaware Street, Indianapolis, Indiana 46202-2531, (317) 631-1888. **Web site:** *www.pbhh.org.* **Read:** (1) Harry J. Sievers, 1952. *Benjamin Harrison, Hoosier Warrior, 1833–1865.* (2) Harry J. Sievers, 1959. *Benjamin Harrison: Hoosier Statesman. From the Civil War to the White House, 1865–1888.* (3) Harry J. Sievers, 1968. *Benjamin Harrison: Hoosier President. The White House and After.* (4) Homer E Socolofsky and Allan B. Spetter. 1987. *Presidency of Benjamin Harrison.* (5) Charles W. Calhoun. 2005. *Benjamin Harrison.*

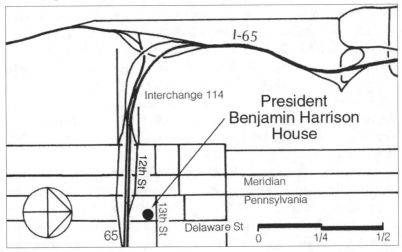

Figure 73. Location of President Benjamin Harrison Home, Indianapolis, Indiana.

William McKinley

Twenty-Fifth President — 1897–1901

Born January 29, 1843, Niles, Ohio
Died September 14, 1901, Buffalo, New York

> *Up to this time, I'd never really believed that a man could be*
> *a good Christian and a good politician.*

— Attending physician at McKinley's death

William McKinley, the son of an iron foundry owner, was raised in Niles, Ohio. Forced to leave Allegheny College because of illness and a financial downturn that affected his father's business, the young man volunteered for the Ohio Twenty-Third Volunteer Infantry as a private, but his leadership qualities soon surfaced. By the time of the Battle of Antietam he was a commissary lieutenant. Mustered out of the Union army as brevet major, he was revered by the troops he had led in engagements that included the Valley campaign of 1864 and he was respected by his commanding officer, General Rutherford B. Hayes, who he was destined to follow into the White House.

After leaving the Army, McKinley continued his education, turned to the law, and eventually began to practice in the growing city of Canton, Ohio. His progress through elected offices was steady: Stark County Prosecutor, United States Congressman for seven terms, and Governor of Ohio for two terms. From the latter lofty and influential position, he proved a formidable national political figure. In 1896, the Republican party nominated him to face William Jennings Bryan for the presidency.

The presidential campaign posed an awkward personal problem for McKinley as his wife, Ida, suffered from epilepsy and emotional difficulties that had developed after the deaths of their two daughters in the 1870s. Therefore, he and his advisors developed the famous "front-porch" campaign in which politicians and private citizens trekked to Canton to call on the candidate. These campaigns were held at another property owned by the McKinleys which was located on North Market Street and has since been razed. It was reported that over a half-million people traveled there to see and hear him. The campaign proved successful, as McKinley won with an electoral advantage of 271 to 176.

In 1900, McKinley and Bryan faced one another again. The prosperity of the nation led voters to sweep McKinley into a second term. McKinley was inaugurated in March, 1901, with many initiatives planned for his second term. After an extended southern and western tour, President and Mrs. McKinley spent August in Canton, then ended their vacation with a visit to the opening of the Pan-American Exposition in Buffalo, New York, before returning to Washington. There in Buffalo, on September 6, 1901, William McKinley was shot by anarchist, Leon Czolgosz. The president died eight days later, with the words of the song *Nearer, My God, to Thee* on his lips.

Saxton McKinley House

CANTON, OHIO

The Saxton McKinley House (Figure 74), the family home of Ida Saxton, William McKinley's wife, became the McKinleys's Canton residence when McKinley served in the United States Congress, 1878–1891.

In 1998, the Saxton McKinley House was dedicated as the home of the National First Ladies' Library — the first facility to honor and celebrate the lives and accomplishments of America's first ladies and where visitors learn about the contributions of these women through permanent and changing exhibits. The only collection of portraits to include all of the first ladies, and others who served as White House hostesses, is on display in the third-floor ballroom. All publicly accessible rooms have been restored to their original splendor, complete with ornate historical wallpaper and period furniture,

Figure 74. Saxton McKinley House, Canton, Ohio. Photograph courtesy of National First Ladies' Library.

the restorations being based in part on the study of early photographs for design elements. For example, furnishings in President McKinley's study were duplicated from the photographs as were the furnishings and wallpaper in Ida McKinley's sitting room and bedroom, and in the family parlor.

The front entry and stair hall feature recreated wallpaper of a dense fruit, flower, and foliage design. The library and parlor are decorated in the opulent Italianate style and the first floor area is decorated with twenty-three different wallpaper patterns in subtle shades of tan, grayish green, rose, and warm beige. The Wilton carpet chrysanthemum pattern was loomed in the mill that was used by Dolley Madison when she ordered the same carpet for the White House.

In 2003, First Lady Laura Bush dedicated the National First Ladies' Library Education and Research Center, located in a seven-story building only a block north of the Saxton McKinley House which remains open as a museum. The Education Center hosts the largest archive of writings, artifacts, and resources associated with first ladies, provides educational programs and curricular enrichment materials, and has a constantly expanding electronic bibliography of over 50,000 entries — manuscripts and publications — about first ladies, all available from any Internet-accessible personal computer. The Saxton McKinley House has been designated by the federal government as the First Ladies National Historic Site.

DIRECTIONS: The First Ladies National Historic Site is in downtown Canton. From I 77, take Exit 105 (Tuscarawas Street, SR 172) and proceed eastbound to South Market Avenue. Turn right (south) to the corner of 4th Street, SW, and the Saxton McKinley House on the right (Figure 75). The Education and Research Center, one block north, is at 205 South Market Avenue.

PUBLIC USE: Season and hours: Historical tours are conducted Tuesday-Saturday, 9:30 AM, 10:30 AM, 12:30 PM, 1:30 PM, 2:30 PM. During June, July and August; tours also are conducted on Sunday, 12:30 PM, 1:30 PM, 2:30 PM. Tours, which take 1½ hours, begin at the Education and Research Center and continue at the Saxton McKinley House. Reservations are required for groups of six or more. For less than six, reservations are recommended but not required. **Admission fee.** Yes, with discounts for students and seniors. **Gift shop. For people with disabilities**: Accessible.

FOR ADDITIONAL INFORMATION: Contact: First Ladies' National Historic Site, Saxton McKinley House, 331 South Market Avenue, Canton, Ohio 44702, (330) 452-0876. **Web site**: *www.firstladies.org/SaxtonMcKinley House.htm*. **Read**: Carl Sferrazza Anthony, ed. 2003. *The National First Ladies' Library and the Importance of First Lady History.*

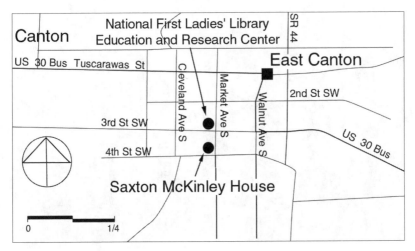

Figure 75. Location of the Saxton McKinley House and the National First Ladies' Library Education and Research Center, Canton, Ohio.

Wm. McKinley Presidential Library and Museum

CANTON, OHIO

One of the most impressive and imposing presidential resting places is the McKinley Tomb in Canton, Ohio (Figure 76). One-hundred-eight broad granite steps lead up to a magnificent mausoleum high above the city that McKinley served with devotion and love. President and Mrs. McKinley and their two infant daughters are entombed in a handsome double-domed building

Figure 76. The Memorial, Wm. McKinley Presidential Library and Museum. Photograph by William G. Clotworthy.

of pink Milford granite. The exterior dome is seventy-five feet in diameter and ninety-five feet high.

Near the foot of the steps is a living memorial, a museum that serves the cultural needs of Stark County and the City of Canton with displays and educational programs for all grade levels. One gallery is devoted exclusively to McKinley; the clothing, furniture, photographs, and personal mementos representing his private and public life constitute the largest collection of McKinley memorabilia in the country. The gallery is dramatized by a tableau of the McKinley living room, fully decorated and featuring life-like animatronic figures of the McKinleys in full evening dress as they welcome good friends to their cheery home.

The McKinley Room is only part of the eclectic charm of the museum. A "Street of Shops" contains full-sized reproductions of stores representative of an Ohio town of the 1880s, and an eighty-two-foot HO-gauge model train complex follows the Pennsylvania Railroad's route through Canton, Massillon, and points west. Industrial Hall, Discover World — devoted to

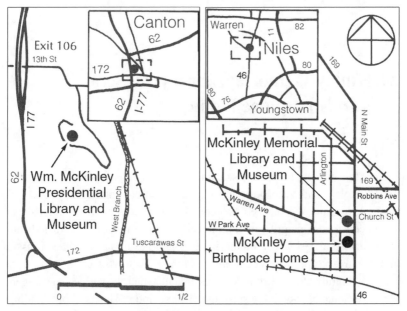

Figure 77. Location of Wm. McKinley Presidential Library and Museum, Canton, Ohio, and McKinley Memorial Library, Museum, and Birthplace Home in Niles, Ohio.

hands-on science — and a planetarium are three of the other attractions dedicated to the spirit of the great American lying at peace at the top of the nearby hill.

DIRECTIONS: From I 77, use Canton Exit 106 that leads to 13th Street, NW. Proceed eastbound on 13th Street to the bottom of the hill and turn right on Park Drive. Proceed to the stop sign and turn right to the parking area (Figure 77).

PUBLIC USE: Season and hours: Monday-Saturday, 9 AM-5 PM; Sunday, 12 M-5 PM. Closed major holidays. The monument may be closed December-April. **Admission fee. Picnic area. Gift shop. For people with disabilities:** Fully accessible.

FOR ADDITIONAL INFORMATION: Contact: Wm. McKinley Presidential Library and Museum. 800 McKinley Monument Drive, NW, Canton, Ohio 44708, (330) 455-7043. **Web site:** *www.mckinleymuseum.org.* **Read:** (1) H. Wayne Morgan. 1963. *William McKinley and his America.* (2) Edward T. Heald. 1992. *The Condensed Biography of William McKinley.* (3) Richard L. McElroy. 1996. *William McKinley and Our America.* (4) Christopher Kenney. 2006. *The McKinley Monument: A Tribute to a Fallen President.*

McKinley Memorial Library, Museum, and Birthplace Home

NILES, OHIO

After William McKinley's death, the City of Niles wished to honor the president who had been born and reared in the community. A successful public subscription campaign exceeded its modest goal which enabled the city to construct a magnificent marble edifice as its memorial and to dedicate the structure in 1917. The memorial, a notable example of Greek Classic architecture, has become a centerpiece of the downtown area.

A central outdoor atrium features an Italian marble garden and a larger-than-life statue of McKinley surrounded by sculptured busts of outstanding national and local political figures. The enclosed south side of the structure houses the modern Niles Public Library while the enclosed north wing is a spacious civic auditorium and hall of statuary. On the mezzanine of the auditorium is a collection of McKinley memorabilia and a photographic history of the construction of the memorial.

In 2003, the Birthplace Memorial added to its complex by constructing the McKinley Birthplace Home and Research Center (Plate 9). It is an exact reconstruction of the place where William McKinley was born and is located on the exact site of the original McKinley home, only 1½ blocks from the Library/Museum. The comfortable eight-room house has been furnished to represent the interior of a typical home of the period. A research center attached to the rear features information on McKinley's life in Ohio and other presidential-related material.

DIRECTIONS: Niles is 10 miles northwest of Youngstown, Ohio. From I 80, exit to SR 46 and proceed northbound 4 miles to Niles and the Memorial (Figure 77).

PUBLIC USE: Season and hours: *Library/Museum:* Monday-Thursday, 9 AM-8 PM; Friday-Saturday, 9 AM-5:30 PM; Sunday, 1 PM-5 PM. Closed Sundays during the summer. ***Birthplace Home and Research Center***: Memorial Day-Labor Day, Wednesday-Saturday, 9 AM-5 PM; First Sunday of each month, 1 PM-5 PM. Rest of year, First weekend each month, Saturday, 9 AM-5 PM; Sunday, 1 PM-5 PM. Closed Easter, Memorial Day, July Fourth, and Labor Day. **For people with disabilities:** Ramp and restroom facilities in the library only.

FOR ADDITIONAL INFORMATION: Contact: McKinley Memorial Library, 40 N. Main Street, Niles, Ohio 44446, (330) 652-1704. McKinley Birthplace Home and Research Center, 40 South Main Street, Niles Ohio 44446, (330) 652-1774. **Web site:** *www.mckinley.lib.oh.us.* **Read:** (1) Joseph G. Butler. 1924. *Life of William McKinley and History of the National McKinley Birthplace Memorial.* (2) Anonymous. 1990. "McKinley Birthplace Memorial." *Ohio Libraries.* July/August: 12.

Theodore Roosevelt

Twenty-Sixth President — 1901–1909

Born October 27, 1858, New York City, New York
Died January 6, 1919, Sagamore Hill, Oyster Bay, New York

> *At Sagamore Hill we love a great many things...birds and trees and books, and all things beautiful, and horses and rifles and children and hard work and the joy of life.*

— Theodore Roosevelt

For many years after the death of Abraham Lincoln, America drifted. Presidential power had eroded in an era of bossism, and often vice presidents were to be seen and not heard. If they succeeded to the presidency they often became caretakers, their role in office solely to continue existing policies and to tend the country on a temporary basis until the next election.

That attitude changed with the unexpected presidency of Theodore Roosevelt, one of those "Accidencies" who turned out to be a man of substance and principle, indebted to no one save himself and the citizens of the United States.

Theodore Roosevelt, born in New York City into a family of wealth and social position, suffered from asthma as a child and was confined to home and schooled by private tutors. He was blessed, however, with an active mind that sponged up knowledge, especially in natural history.

Roosevelt, in his autobiography, wrote reverently of his father who, night after night, walked the floor carrying the pale and suffering young Theodore, tending him with love and concern. He also recalled his father's admonition, "You have the mind, but you haven't got the body. To do all you can with your mind, you must make your body to match it." It was that strong, forceful, and loving advice that compelled Teddy to start a vigorous program of physical exercise and outdoor activity that turned the frail boy into a robust man.

Roosevelt graduated from Harvard, then turned his attention and activities to politics and served from 1882 until 1884 in the New York State Assembly. In 1880, he married Alice Lee, who gave birth to a baby girl, Alice, in 1884. Roosevelt experienced a double tragedy when his mother and his young wife both died on February 14, 1884. Distraught, he fled to Dakota Territory, where he purchased a ranch and attempted to ease his despondency with hard outdoor living. The ranching venture failed, however, and Roosevelt returned to New York, never again to stray far from the political arena.

Roosevelt held a number of elected and appointed positions, including those of New York City Police Commissioner, from 1895 until 1897, and of Assistant Secretary of the Navy, from 1897 until 1898. He resigned the latter post to organize and lead the Rough Riders to fame in the War with Spain — fame that became a springboard to Roosevelt's 1898–1901 governorship of New York and then to second spot on the Republican presidential ticket with William McKinley. He assumed the presidency September 14, 1901, upon McKinley's death; at forty-two, he had become the youngest man to hold the office.

Theodore Roosevelt is considered by historians to have been the first modern chief executive. He was certainly the most active, packing many careers into one lifetime: President of the United States; prolific writer; naturalist; conservationist; cowboy; big-game hunter; soldier; Nobel Prize winner; loving husband, and caring father.

Theodore Roosevelt Birthplace National Historic Site

New York, New York

Theodore Roosevelt was born in a narrow, four-story brownstone (Figure 78) in midtown New York City, just west of Gramercy Park, a prosperous neighborhood where the Roosevelts lived until they moved to a more prestigious address on West 57th Street when Theodore was fourteen.

Figure 78. Theodore Roosevelt Birthplace National Historic Site, New York, New York. Photograph courtesy National Park Service.

The brownstone house at 28 East 20th Street was demolished in 1916 to make room for a commercial building, but after Roosevelt's death in 1919, a group of women formed an association with the purpose of preserving the memory and spirit of the president who had passionately and vigorously moved the nation forward. Their archives describe those efforts:

Devotion to a single individual prompted the formation of many early preservation groups, as in the case of the Womens' Roosevelt Memorial Association. This organization's intriguing effort is earmarked by several unusual twists. Although the house where he lived between 1858 and 1872 had been torn down in 1916, the Association was undaunted. In 1919 these concerned women purchased the commercial structure which occupied the site and demolished it. The female architect Theodate Pope Riddle designed a replica brownstone based on adjacent rowhouses and family reminiscences. The Theodore Roosevelt Association administered the reconstructed house museum from its opening in 1923 until its donation to the National Park Service in 1963.

Thanks to that group of dedicated women, we can enjoy a visit to the replicated Roosevelt House, a vivid representation of prosperous city living in the mid-nineteenth century. Over forty percent of the furnishings are original Roosevelt pieces; the others are of the period. It was in rooms like those of this house that Theodore Roosevelt began his life-long love affair with mental and physical exertion and with the discipline that would make him such an outstanding American leader.

DIRECTIONS: Lexington Avenue #6 subway trains stop at the 23rd Street station on Park Avenue South. N and R trains stop at the East 23rd Street station on Broadway and there is frequent bus service. All are within easy walking distance of the Roosevelt house (Figure 79).

PUBLIC USE: Season and hours: Tuesday-Saturday, 9 AM-5 PM. House tours are conducted on the hour with the last tour at 4 PM. Closed all federal holidays. **Admission fee.** Yes. Under 16, free. **For people with disabilities:** Limited accessibility to people with extreme mobility impairment.

FOR ADDITIONAL INFORMATION: Contact: Theodore Roosevelt Birthplace National Historic Site, 28 East 20th Street, New York, New York 10003, (212) 260-1616. **Web site:** *www.nps.gov/thrb.* **Read:** (1) Theodore Roosevelt. 1913. *The Autobiography of Theodore Roosevelt.* (2) Edmund Morris. 1979. *The Rise of Theodore Roosevelt.* (3) Edmund Morris. 2001. *Theodore Rex.*

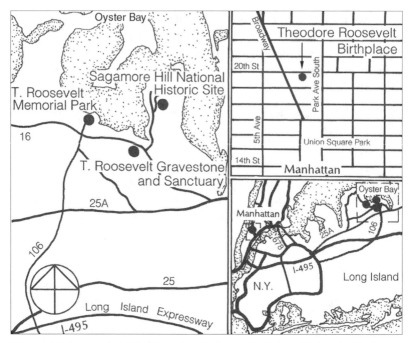

Figure 79. Location of the Theodore Roosevelt National Historic Site, New York, New York, and Sagamore Hill National Historic Site, Oyster Bay, New York.

Sagamore Hill National Historic Site

OYSTER BAY, NEW YORK

I wonder if you will ever know how I love Sagamore Hill?

— Theodore Roosevelt, the night he died at Sagamore Hill

In 1880, two months before he married Alice Lee, Theodore Roosevelt began to acquire acreage on a promontory overlooking Oyster Bay, on the northern shore of Long Island. Plans were drawn up for a house, which was to be named Leeholm, after Alice. Before construction of the house had begun, however, Alice died.

At the urging of his sister, who convinced him that he needed a home for his infant daughter, Roosevelt went ahead with plans for the house. By 1885, he had built a rambling Victorian structure of frame and brick, its wide, sweeping verandah providing a panoramic view of Oyster Bay and Long Island Sound. Roosevelt renamed the property Sagamore Hill (Plate 9) after the Indian Chief Sagamore Mohannis, who had signed the land away two hundred years earlier.

In December 1886, Roosevelt married Edith Kermit Carow; they moved to Sagamore Hill the following spring. Eventually the house resounded with the sounds of more children, a fact that Roosevelt acknowledged as a source of delight:

> *For unflagging interest and enjoyment, a household of children, if things go reasonably well, certainly makes all of the forms of success and achievement lose their importance by comparison.*

As Roosevelt progressed politically, the house also became a mecca for public figures: potentates, prize fighters, politicians, and professors — all associates of the gregarious, inquisitive Roosevelt. In 1905, Roosevelt added the North Room to the house in order to provide a formal and roomy space for receiving his guests. The room, popular with today's visitors, was finished with exotic Philippine and American woods and is filled with Roosevelt's books, paintings, flags, and hunting trophies, as well as souvenirs of his public career and world travels.

An adjunct to the mansion is the Roosevelt Museum at Old Orchard, part of the Sagamore Hill property. Built as a family home by General Theodore Roosevelt, Jr., it is a popular museum that houses exhibits and movies that tell the story of President Roosevelt's early and public life and provides today's visitors with a feel for what Sagamore Hill was like a century ago.

Edith Roosevelt died in 1948. Sagamore Hill and its treasures were acquired by the Theodore Roosevelt Association that year. In 1963, the association, which also owned the birthplace brownstone in New York City, donated both properties to the federal government for the enjoyment and edification of the American people. These properties are now administered by the National Park Service.

DIRECTIONS: Take I 495 (Long Island Expressway) to Exit 41 N, or the Northern State Parkway to Exit 35 N, and proceed northbound on SR 106 to Oyster Bay, then follow the historical markers to Sagamore Hill (Figure 79).

PUBLIC USE: Season and hours: September-May, Wednesday-Sunday, 10 AM-4 PM. June-August, daily, 10 AM-4 PM. Grounds are open dawn to dusk. The house is open by guided tour only. Closed Thanksgiving Day, Christmas Day, New Year's Day. **Admission fee:** For the house tour only. **Book store. For people with disabilities:** The first floor of the mansion is accessible, the second floor is not. The visitor center and museum in Old Orchard are fully accessible.

FOR ADDITIONAL INFORMATION: Contact: Sagamore Hill National Historic Site, 20 Sagamore Hill Road, Oyster Bay, New York 11771, (516) 922-4788 **Web site:** *www.nps.gov/sahi.* **Read:** (1) Hermann Hagedorn. 1953. *A Guide to Sagamore Hill.* (2) Hermann Hagedorn. 1954. *The Roosevelt Family of Sagamore Hill.* (3) John A. Gable. 1977. *Sagamore Hill: A Historic Guide.*

Maltese Cross Cabin

THEODORE ROOSEVELT NATIONAL PARK
MEDORA, NORTH DAKOTA

Roosevelt visited the North Dakota badlands in 1883 to hunt buffalo, and he returned in 1884 following the deaths of his mother and his young wife. There he hoped to ease his grief by indulging in the rugged outdoor life of a cowboy.

He became alarmed when he observed the damage being inflicted on the land and wildlife by human intrusion; thus, conservation became an important part of his personal and political agenda. As president he established the National Forest Service, set aside eighteen national monuments, and was instrumental in persuading congress to establish five national parks and fifty-five wildlife refuges.

As Theodore Roosevelt was the first "Conservation President," it was appropriate that a national park bearing his name be established in the rugged land that had inspired his efforts. The Maltese Cross Cabin (Figure 80), named for the ranch where he lived, is simply a rough, shingle-roofed 1½-story cottage of pine logs, with three downstairs rooms and a sleeping loft. It was acquired by the State of North Dakota shortly after Roosevelt's inauguration as president, and was transferred to the federal government in 1959.

Figure 80. Maltese Cross Cabin in Theodore Roosevelt National Park, Medora, North Dakota. Photograph courtesy National Park Service.

DIRECTIONS: Theodore Roosevelt National Park is 135 miles west of Bismarck, North Dakota, on I 94. The cabin is located next to the South Unit visitor center in Medora (Figure 81).

PUBLIC USE: Season and hours: The park is open year-round. Tours of the cabin from mid-June to Labor Day are guided, those during the rest of the year are self guided. Closed Thanksgiving Day, Christmas Day, New Year's Day. **Admission fee. Food service:** Picnic and camp areas are close by. **For people with disabilities:** Accessible.

FOR ADDITIONAL INFORMATION: Contact: Theodore Roosevelt National Park, Box 7, Medora, North Dakota 58645, (701) 623-4466. **Web site:** *www.nps.gov/thro*. **Read:** (1) A. M. Christianson. 1955. "The Roosevelt Cabin." (2) Chester L. Brooks and Ray H. Matison. 1983. *Theodore Roosevelt and the Dakota Badlands.* (3) Hermann Hagedorn. 1987. *Roosevelt in the Badlands.*

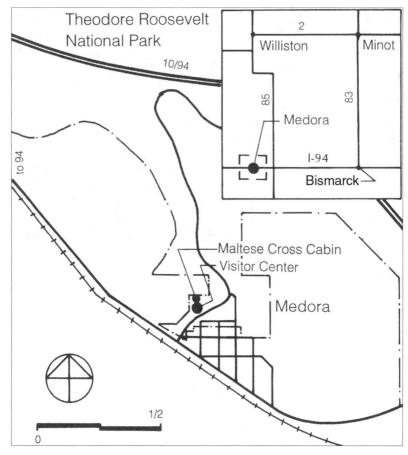

Figure 81. Location of Maltese Cross Cabin, Theodore Roosevelt National Park, Medora, North Dakota.

Pine Knot

KEENE, VIRGINIA

Shortly after Theodore Roosevelt began his first full term in office, his wife Edith wanted a place where she and the president might occasionally escape the pressure (or perhaps the stifling heat) of Washington, DC. In 1905, as a surprise to her husband, she purchased fifteen acres in the deep woods of Albemarle County, Virginia (for only $280) that contained only a small twelve-by-thirty-two-foot two-floored farm worker's cabin which lacked electricity, indoor plumbing, or other modern facilities. She christened it "Pine Knot," reflecting the trees surrounding the property. It was a month before the president visited, but Edith felt confident that the rustic retreat fit his style and character as he relished strenuous living and close contact with nature. In a letter to his son Kermit, Theodore wrote it "was perfectly delight-ful" and "the nicest little place of the kind you could imagine" where "it was lovely to sit there in the rocking chairs and hear all the birds by daytime and at night the whippoorwills and little forest folk." Pine Knot's curator, Paula Beazley, said, "Pine Knot very much provides a window into their souls." In 1911, Edith added seventy-five acres to their retreat in anticipation that Theodore would win the presidency in 1912. During the time that the Roosevelts owned the cabin, Mrs. Roosevelt added only the outdoor piazza, but they opened the three-room downstairs into one larger room and moved the stairs from the center to the side to create a tiny room upstairs for their daughter.

The Roosevelts are known to have made nine trips to Pine Knot, generally staying four or five days each visit. Their daily routine rarely var-ied; in the daytime they traipsed the woods, observed birds, rode horses, and enjoyed the plant life. At dusk they relaxed on the piazza to watch the sun disappear behind the foothills of the Blue Ridge and in the fall or winter they passed long evenings reading or doing needlework by lamplight beside a log fire.

The tiny cabin (Figure 82) is owned by the Theodore Roosevelt Association and operated by a local nonprofit organization, the Edith and Theodore Roosevelt Pine Knot Foundation. The association has developed interpretive materials and facilities and has restored the cottage as a historic site. Chimneys have been repaired, foundations reinforced, holes made by nocturnal animals have been sealed and caulked, and a vehicular bridge and

Figure 82. Pine Knot, Keene, Virginia. Photograph courtesy The Edith and Theodore Roosevelt Pine Knot Foundation.

fences have been created at the entrance. The work is ongoing, although at present (2008) Pine Knot is open for educational events in May and October and daily from April through November for visitation by previously arranged appointment.

DIRECTIONS: Pine Knot is on Coles Rolling Road in Keene, Virginia, 15 miles southeast of Charlottesville near the intersection of SR 20 and CR 712 (Figure 10).

PUBLIC USE: Season and hours: Pine Knot is open year-round by appointment. **For people with disabilities**: Accessible.

FOR ADDITIONAL INFORMATION: Contact: Pine Knot, Box 213, Keene, Virginia 22946, (434) 286-6054. **Web site**: *www.pineknot.org* or *www.theodoreroosevelt.org/modern/pineknot.htm*. **Read**: (1) Sylvia Jukes Morris. 1980. *Edith Kermit Roosevelt, Portrait of a First Lady.* (2) William Harbaugh. 1993. *The Theodore Roosevelts' Retreat in Southern Albemarle: Pine Knot 1905–1908.*

William Howard Taft

Twenty-Seventh President — 1909–1913

Born September 15, 1857, Cincinnati, Ohio
Died March 8, 1930, Washington, DC

> *It's great to be great, but it's greater to be human. He was our*
> *great fellow because there was more of him to be human. We are*
> *parting with three hundred pounds of solid charity to everyone,*
> *and love and affection for all his fellow men.*

> — Will Rogers, eulogizing Taft

One must hark back to the early days of the republic to find a family as
devoted to public service as have been the Tafts of Cincinnati. Only the
Adamses, the Harrisons, and the Kennedys have spawned as many influential activists — both elected and appointed officials in the highest levels of
government. Alphonso Taft sat on the federal bench, was twice a member of
President Grant's cabinet and served as minister to Vienna and Saint Petersburg. His son, William Howard Taft, became president, and his grandson,
Robert, became famous as "Mr. Republican," representing Ohio in the United
States Senate for many years. Great-great-grandson Bob Taft served as governor of Ohio in the early years of the twenty-first century.

William Howard Taft is best remembered for his hefty physique and for
being the first president to throw out the first ball at the start of the baseball
season. His real accomplishments transcended such superficiality, for he
had a fine legal mind, a sense of fair play, and unparalleled skill at mediation.
A brilliant young attorney, he was appointed Solicitor General of the United

States at just thirty-three, then progressed to influential positions as Governor of the Philippines and as Theodore Roosevelt's Secretary of War.

As president, Taft was uncharacteristically indecisive, irritable, and procrastinating. Political differences between Taft and Theodore Roosevelt, his predecessor and mentor, split the Republican party in 1912 which enabled Woodrow Wilson and the Democrats to win the White House.

Following his defeat, Taft was named Professor of Constitutional Law at his alma mater, Yale University. He enjoyed academia and the chance to work with young people, but he was not reluctant to leave in 1921 when President Harding offered him the one appointment he coveted more than any other — Chief Justice of the United States Supreme Court. He accepted, and filled the post with distinction until shortly before his death.

William Howard Taft National Historic Site

CINCINNATI, OHIO

In the mid-nineteenth century, Cincinnati was a thriving metropolis of 200,000 people scattered among hills and valleys along the north side of the Ohio River in extreme southwestern Ohio. The arrangement was one that suggested many small towns, rather than one large city. In 1851, attorney Alphonso Taft bought a two-story brick house on Auburn Street (Plate 9) to accommodate his growing family, soon to include a future president. Will Taft was born in a first floor bedroom, and his mother wrote her sister, "He is perfectly healthy and hearty, and I take real comfort in taking care of him. He is very large for his age, and grows fat everyday."

The Taft house was sturdy and roomy, with Victorian scroll-trimmed eaves and a New England captain's walk. There was a wide verandah and a large, sweeping lawn, a perfect playground for active boys who swam, skated, fought — and loved each other. Will's favorite game was baseball, an interest that continued through his life.

The Taft home had several owners over the years until 1961 when it was bought by the Taft Memorial Association. The association turned the property over to the federal government as a National Historic Site in 1969. The ground floor is fully furnished and appears as it did during the Taft residency. The upper floor contains museum galleries with displays high-lighting Taft's career as attorney, diplomat, chief executive, professor, and Chief Justice of the Supreme Court.

In 1999, the National Park Service opened The Taft Education Center, a multi-functional educational facility on three floors of a building adjacent to the Taft home. The center houses exhibits and sponsors educational pro-grams for local school groups and an extensive outreach program for adults — all highlighting the Taft family, their values, and their contributions to Cincinnati and the nation. The signature exhibit is an animatronic figure of the president's son, Charlie, telling stories about different family members.

DIRECTIONS: Southbound on I 71, exit at William Howard Taft Road (Exit 3) and proceed westbound to Auburn Avenue. Turn left and drive 0.5 mile to the house. Northbound, take the left-side exit at Reading Road-Eden Park Drive (Exit 2). Upon exiting, the exit ramp divides. Stay to the right side of the off-ramp. At the first stoplight, turn left onto Dorchester Street and proceed up the hill to Auburn Avenue (Figure 83).

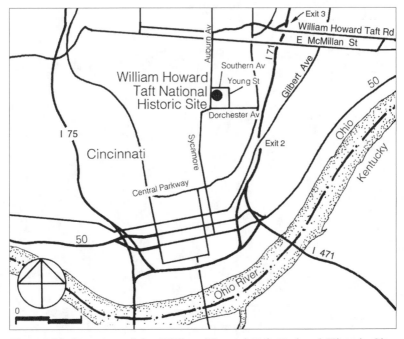

Figure 83. Location of the William Howard Taft National Historic Site, Cincinnati, Ohio.

PUBLIC USE: Season and hours: Guided tours every 30 minutes, 8 AM-4 PM. Last tour at 3:30 PM. Closed Thanksgiving Day, Christmas Day, New Year's Day. **Gift shop. For people with disabilities:** Fully accessible, with an interior elevator to the upper floors.

FOR ADDITIONAL INFORMATION: Contact: Superintendent, William Howard Taft National Historic Site, 2038 Auburn Avenue, Cincinnati, Ohio 45219, (513) 684-3262. **Web site***: www.nps.gov/wiho.* **Read:** (1) Henry Fowles Pringle. 1939. *The Life and Times of William Howard Taft.* (2) Ishbel Ross. 1964. *An American Family. The Tafts.* (3) Judith Icke Anderson. 1981. *William Howard Taft: An Intimate History.*

Thomas Woodrow Wilson

Twenty-Eighth President — 1913–1921

Born December 28, 1856, Staunton, Virginia
Died February 3, 1924, Washington, DC

> *I am not one of those that have the least anxiety about the triumph of the principles I have stood for — that we shall prevail is as sure as God reigns.*

> — Woodrow Wilson

"Tommy" Wilson was the son of a Presbyterian minister. The family moved often, but always under pleasant and congenial circumstances. When Wilson graduated from Princeton University, he left with the intention of pursuing a career in law until he realized that "law and justice have little to do with one another." He switched to the study of history, especially political history, and earned his doctorate with a brilliant dissertation that ensured him an early yet solid reputation in academia.

Wilson had discovered his true calling, teaching and scholarship, and held a number of college teaching posts on his way to becoming president of his alma mater, Princeton, the first non-clergyman named to that honor. He developed an outstanding record as an administrator, which brought him to the attention of New Jersey's political hierarchy. They urged him to run for the governorship, and he agreed, but only after extracting a commitment of non-interference from the bosses. In 1912, Governor Wilson was nominated for the presidency of the United States and easily defeated the candidate of the deeply divided Republicans.

During Wilson's first term, many domestic programs were enacted, and the nation prospered under his vigorous leadership. Wilson had hoped to stay out of the war in Europe, but failed. In April, 1917, he proclaimed the joint resolution that enjoined the United States in World War I.

In January, 1918, Woodrow Wilson announced his famous Fourteen Points as a basis for world peace; he hoped that they would be written into the peace treaty at the end of the war. When Armistice was declared on November 11, 1918, he immediately embarked for Europe, where he toured triumphantly before attending the Paris Peace Conference.

In Paris, Wilson pressed for a League of Nations, but was forced to sail home to face questioning from the Senate regarding the terms of the treaty as any treaty entered into by the United States must be ratified by the Senate. Opposition by that body was growing but, nevertheless, Wilson confidently returned to Europe and signed the Versailles Treaty, which included the Covenant of the League of Nations.

Wilson returned home to begin a grueling whistle-stop railroad tour in an attempt to elicit enough public support to force senate compliance with the treaty. The controversy and rigors of travel exhausted him, however, and he was forced to return to Washington where, on October 26, 1919, he suffered the paralytic stroke that disabled him for the remainder of his life.

The next year encompassed both the lowest and highest points of Woodrow Wilson's career. In March, 1920, the United States Senate rejected the Versailles Treaty, effectively killing Wilson's beloved concept of a League of Nations. In December, ironically, Wilson was awarded the Nobel Peace Prize in recognition of his extensive efforts to bring about a just and lasting peace for all mankind.

Wilson attended the inauguration of Warren G. Harding in 1921, then retired to a comfortable townhouse in an exclusive Washington neighborhood. White-haired and shrunken, he lived until 1924, loved and respected by his neighbors, by every American, and by the citizens of the world.

Woodrow Wilson Presidential Library

STAUNTON, VIRGINIA

In 2004, the Woodrow Wilson Birthplace changed its name designation to properly reflect the importance of what is actually a multi-faceted campus that includes a Woodrow Wilson Museum, his Birthplace Manse, and a presidential library, currently housed in the Dolores Lescure Center building. The Woodrow Wilson Presidential Library is designed primarily for use by scholars and researchers, further communicating the life, work and impact on the world of our twenty-eighth president. A fund-raising campaign is currently (2008) in progress to construct an additional library building that will be a major addition to the present campus.

Figure 84 Woodrow Wilson Birthplace at Woodrow Wilson Presidential Library, Staunton, Virginia. Photograph by Tommy Thompson; use courtesy of Woodrow Wilson Presidential Library.

The Woodrow Wilson Birthplace was the manse of the Presbyterian Church where his father served as pastor (Figure 84). It was not a simple parsonage, but a large and imposing townhouse built in the Greek Revival style — a rectangular, brick structure with a two-story, pillared portico reminiscent of Jefferson's Monticello, a particularly attractive exterior. It is framed by sculptured lawns and an unusual rear garden that features boxwoods planted in a distinctive bowknot design, interlaced with brick walks and a staircase leading to the house.

The twelve spacious rooms in the house are filled with original Wilson furniture and memorabilia such as the crib in which infant Tommy slept and

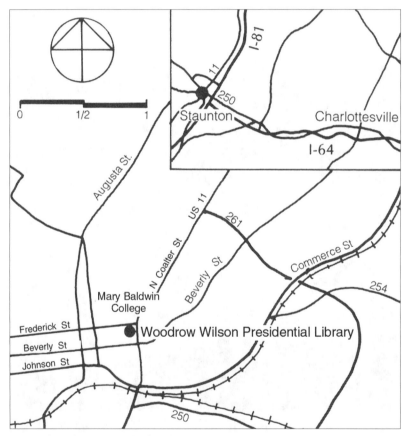

Figure 85. Location of Woodrow Wilson Presidential Library, Staunton, Virginia.

the family Bible that records his birth in 1856. The Wilsons were in residence for only three years before the Reverend Wilson was transferred to Augusta, Georgia. The house remained a church manse until 1929 when it was deeded to neighboring Mary Baldwin College. Since 1938, it has been maintained by the Woodrow Wilson Birthplace Foundation, which has been responsible for its refurbishing and decoration.

Some years ago the Foundation purchased an imposing chateau-style mansion two doors away from the manse and converted it into a museum with exhibit galleries that graphically represent Wilson's life as student, teacher, university president, governor, president, and world statesman. An attached garage contains President Wilson's Pierce-Arrow touring car in mint condition, one of the first presidential limousines.

DIRECTIONS: From I 81, take Exit 222 and go westbound on US 250 to US 11 in Staunton, then go northbound on US 11 that becomes Coalter Street. The Wilson Birthplace is on the left (Figure 85).

PUBLIC USE: Season and hours: March-October, Monday-Saturday, 9 AM-5 PM; Sunday, 12 M-5 PM. November-February, Monday-Saturday, 10 AM-4 PM; Sunday, 12 M-4 PM. Closed Thanksgiving Day, Christmas Day, New Year's Day, Easter Sunday. **Admission fee. Gift shop. For people with disabilities:** The museum is accessible, and two of the three floors in the birthplace are accessible.

FOR ADDITIONAL INFORMATION: Contact: Woodrow Wilson Presidential Library, 18–24 North Coalter Street, Staunton, Virginia 24402, (540) 885-0897. **Web site:** *www.woodrowwilson.org.* **Read:** Katherine L. Brown. 1991. *The Woodrow Wilson Birthplace.*

Boyhood Home of President Woodrow Wilson

AUGUSTA, GEORGIA

The Reverend Joseph R. Wilson accepted the pulpit of the First Presbyterian Church of Augusta in 1858, and moved into an old parsonage with his wife, two daughters and infant son Tommy. Two years later, the church purchased a new house in order to provide more suitable and spacious accommodations for its pastor. The Wilsons lived in the new manse at 7th and Telfair streets for ten years.

Figure 86. Boyhood Home of President Woodrow Wilson, Augusta, Georgia. Photograph courtesy of Historic Augusta, Inc.

The house (Figure 86) was not fancy, an ordinary brick building of 2½ stories, with a separate outside structure used both as kitchen and servants' quarters. A rear porch extended the full width of the house, and a stable was located in the northwest corner of the property.

Woodrow Wilson once recalled that his earliest memory was of an event that took place when he was living in Augusta: while playing outside, he heard that Abraham Lincoln had been elected president and that there was to be war. He ran inside to ask his father what the news meant.

The Civil War began when Wilson was four years old and ended when he was eight, and it made an important impression on him. Augusta was a crossroads and a major urban center of 20,000 people. Although the city was never invaded, much war-related activity, including constant troop movement, took place there. A United States arsenal, the Confederate Powderworks, and factories for cotton goods, arms, munitions, shoes, camp equipment, and scores of other products were located in Augusta, then second only to Richmond in southern manufacturing capability. Joseph Wilson's church was used for a time as a stockade for federal prisoners and, like many other public buildings, it was used as a hospital.

In later years, Wilson remembered many of these events and circumstances, including the hardships stemming from the scarcity of food and other essentials. Surely these experiences influenced the undeveloped psyche of the person who was destined, many years later, to lead his nation through "the war to end all wars."

In 1870, Joseph Wilson was called to Columbia, South Carolina, and a new pastor moved into the Augusta manse. Changes and renovations were effected over the years — additional water closets were installed, decayed woodwork was overhauled, painting was done, and mantels were added to the dining and living rooms. Significant repairs were necessary following a tornado in 1911. Later, the house was sold by the church to a private party, after which it changed hands one more time. In 1979, the home was listed on the National Register of Historic Places, but its preservation was uncertain until 1991 when it was bought at auction by Historic Augusta, Inc., a non-profit organization whose mandate is to preserve historically and architecturally significant sites and structures in Augusta.

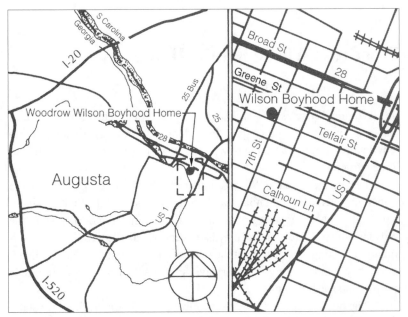

Figure 87. Location of the Boyhood Home of President Woodrow Wilson, Augusta, Georgia.

They have done a superb job of restoration, furnishing the home with pieces from the 1860s period, including furniture, carpets and flooring, window treatments, light fixtures, upholstery, and linens. There are thirteen original Wilson furniture items on display, plus a silver butter dish and a book of Indian Club exercises owned by teenager Woodrow Wilson.

DIRECTIONS: Exit I 20 at Washington Road and proceed eastbound (Washington Road becomes Calhoun Expressway, then Greene Street). Turn right on 7th Street; the house is at the end of the block on the right (Figure 87). The visitor center and parking lot are next door at 415 Seventh Street.

PUBLIC USE: Season and hours: Tours are conducted Tuesday-Saturday, 10 AM-5 PM on the hour. Last tour starts at 4 PM. Groups are accommodated by appointment. Closed major holidays. **Admission fee. For people with disabilities:** The first floor is accessible, the second is not.

FOR ADDITIONAL INFORMATION: Contact: Boyhood Home of President Woodrow Wilson, 419 Seventh Street, Augusta, Georgia 30901, (706) 722-9828. **Web site:** *www.wilsonboyhoodhome.org.* **Read:** August Heckscher. 1991. *Woodrow Wilson.*

Woodrow Wilson Family Home

COLUMBIA, SOUTH CAROLINA

Tommy Wilson spent three important years during his teens in Columbia — a southern town occupied by federal troops, a town attempting to rebuild after the conflagration of war, a town trying to survive the trauma of Reconstruction.

During those years, Wilson's father was Professor of Theology at the Columbia Theological Seminary and served as pastor of the First Presbyterian Church. Neither post provided housing. Being financially able, the Wilsons built a house, the first they had ever owned. The building is conservative, reflecting the lifestyle of the owners and the era in which they lived; it had bay windows, arched doorways, iron mantels painted to resemble marble, and gas lighting.

The house (Figure 88) was saved from demolition in 1928 by a statewide fundraising drive conducted by the American Legion. It was open to the public for many years, but again fell into decline until its most recent

Figure 88. The Woodrow Wilson Family Home, Columbia, South Carolina. Photograph courtesy of Historic Columbia Foundation.

rescue by the Historic Columbia Foundation. Under the Foundation's direction, the Wilson house has been restored to the spirit of the 1870s — the clapboard siding repainted and the interior restored, according to the curator, "to the flair the Wilsons and their contemporaries loved. Sentimental clutter mingles in the rooms with trademarks of the age: the antimacassar, the lambrequin, the ottoman." The house also contains the bed in which Wilson was born in Staunton, as well as his mother's four-volume set of the Bible, a gift from her husband. The pretty little front garden is graced by a large tea olive tree and several magnolias planted by Mrs. Wilson.

During their stay in Columbia, Woodrow joined his father's church, and he often remarked on his affection for South Carolina. It was apparent that the faith he accepted and the political and human chaos he witnessed there contributed to his developing philosophy and his compassionate attitude.

DIRECTIONS: From I 26, take Exit 108 to I 126/US 76 which becomes Elmwood Avenue in Columbia. At the end of Elmwood, turn right on Bull Street and proceed 4 blocks to Blanding Street. Turn left on Blanding to Henderson Street, then right on Henderson for 0.5 block to the parking area of Historic

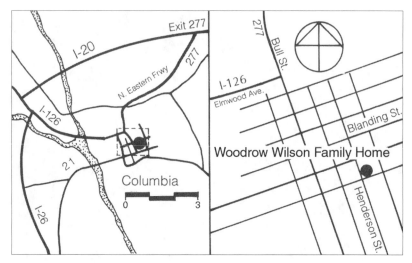

Figure 89. Location of the Woodrow Wilson Family Home, Columbia, South Carolina.

Columbia Foundation's museum shop to purchase admission tickets for any of four house museums — Hampton-Preston Mansion, Robert Mills House, Mann-Simons Cottage and the Woodrow Wilson Family Home. From I 20, take Exit 73 and from I 77, take Exit 18, both marked "277" to Columbia where SR 277 becomes Bull Street. From there follow the above directions (Figure 89).

PUBLIC USE: Season and hours: The Wilson Home is closed for major renovation. It is not scheduled for completion until at least 2009.

FOR ADDITIONAL INFORMATION: Contact: Historic Columbia Foundation, 1601 Richland Street, Columbia, South Carolina 29201, (803) 252-7742. **Web site:** *www.historiccolumbia.org/history/wilson.htm.*

Woodrow Wilson House Museum

Washington, DC

Upon the end of his presidency, Woodrow Wilson moved from the White House to a handsome, four-story red brick townhouse (Plate 10) in an exclusive neighborhood of Washington, DC. There he passed away in 1924.

His widow, Edith Bolling Wilson, remained in the house until 1961 and carefully preserved its furnishings and ambience. Upon her death, the house was bequeathed to the National Trust for Historic Preservation which converted it to a house museum dedicated to the life and career of one of America's greatest leaders and one of the great internationalists.

Each room, from the fully stocked kitchen to the cheery solarium overlooking a formal walled garden, reflects the variety of Wilson's life and the honesty and simplicity of his values. Large and light, the rooms are rich with souvenirs, gifts, and other possessions that highlight Wilson's career as professor, administrator, governor, president, and international statesman. Visitors are intrigued by the collection of presidential memorabilia: his inaugural Bible, his typewriter, a framed mosaic presented by the Pope, and many others. Visitors can see a closet where his clothes still hang, the bed made to copy the famous "Lincoln Bed" in the White House, and the fully equipped nurse's room. In this house one gains an intimate understanding of how difficult Wilson's last months were, both on him and on those who loved and cared for him. Yet, the house is not unhappy. It is pleasant testimony to the indomitable spirit of the man who led his nation through a great world war and into the modern era of international responsibility.

DIRECTIONS: From downtown Washington, DC, take the Metro Red Line subway to Dupont Circle and use the Q Street exit. Follow Q Street to Massachusetts Avenue and bear right. Proceed northwest on Massachusetts Avenue for 4 blocks to 24th Street. Turn right on 24th, then right on S Street to the Wilson house (Figure 15).

PUBLIC USE: Season and hours: Tuesday-Sunday, 10 AM-4 PM. Closed major holidays. **Admission fee. For people with disabilities:** The first floor is fully accessible and there is a small elevator that can accommodate some disabled visitors, although those requiring assistance should call ahead.

FOR ADDITIONAL INFORMATION: Contact: Woodrow Wilson House Museum, 2340 S Street, NW, Washington, DC 20008, (202) 387-4062. **Web site:** *www.woodrowwilsonhouse.org.* **Read:** (1) Eugene Smith. 1964. *When the Cheering Stopped.* (2) Henry Bragdon. 1967. *Woodrow Wilson: The Academic Years.*

Warren Gamaliel Harding

Twenty-Ninth President — 1921–1923

Born November 2, 1865, Corsica (Blooming Grove), Ohio
Died August 2, 1923, San Francisco, California

> *Government is not of super-men, but of normal men, very much like you and me.*

> — Warren G. Harding

> *Here was a man whose soul was seared by a great disillusionment. We saw him gradually weaken, not only from physical exhaustion but also from mental anxiety. Warren Harding had a dim realization that he had been betrayed by a few of the men who he believed were his devoted friends. That was the tragedy of Warren Harding.*

> — Herbert Hoover, 1931

Harding's tragedy was, of course, the nation's. Both were bruised and damaged by Teapot Dome, one of the greatest financial scandals in the country's history.

It has been said that any president, insulated as he is, is often the worst-informed man in Washington. Such may well have been the case with Harding, who was not a "hands-on" executive to begin with. In addition, at the time of Teapot Dome, Harding was distracted by his wife's illness, as well as an illness of his own which ultimately claimed his life before his first term of office had ended.

Harding's friendly, gregarious nature and trusting character brought fatal consequences. Yet his accomplishments were varied and contributed positively to adjustments following World War I as America entered a new era of world influence and cooperation.

President Harding's Home

MARION, OHIO

Warren G. Harding was born in the tiny hamlet of Corsica, Ohio, now called Blooming Grove. He was reared and schooled in nearby Caledonia, then went to Ohio Central College in Iberia. His father was a country doctor and farmer who worked hard to support his family of eight children. The family moved to the larger community of Marion when Warren was in his teens and where, with his father's help, he purchased the *Marion Star*. He remained as editor and publisher until he left Marion for the White House. He sold the newspaper in June, 1923.

Harding was a gregarious booster, joiner, and backslapper who drifted into local politics with no thoughts of where his sunny personality and innate speaking ability would lead. There are some who have said that neither his personality nor his speaking ability were the biggest influences on his career, but rather that it was his wife, Florence. She worked with Harding at the *Star* and was unquestionably important to his career — personally, professionally, and politically.

The Hardings were married in a new Victorian house (Plate 10) and took up residence immediately after their honeymoon. The house remained their home until they moved to the White House in 1921. The house, typically Midwestern and contemporary, reflected the popular architecture and styling of the day — 2½ stories, painted red with dark red trim. In 1903, the house was painted green and white, and a rotunda porch was added, the latter often decorated with pots of petunias and geraniums. The house gained fame in 1920 as the site of Harding's front-porch presidential campaign when 600,000 people visited Marion to see and hear the candidate. His was a campaign reminiscent of William McKinley's two decades earlier, and James Garfield's even before that.

Mrs. Harding bequeathed the home and furnishings to the Harding Memorial Association, and four rooms were opened to the public in 1926. In 1965, the association renovated the house to appear as it had at the time of the Harding residency. Electric light fixtures were replaced by the original gas fixtures, the Harding wallpaper was duplicated and hung and furniture was returned to its original arrangement. Personal effects were left as found, creating the feeling that Warren Harding has just stepped out for a stroll, leaving his straw hat and cane in the hall. President Harding's Home is owned by the State of Ohio and operated by the Ohio Historical Society.

In 1920, Harding bought a small outbuilding picked from the Sears and Roebuck catalog, placed it behind the house, and used it as headquarters for the national press corps covering the presidential campaign. The building has been converted to a visitor center that includes a small museum. Just outside, in a neatly trimmed garden, is a sundial mounted on a granite base. Inscribed in the granite are words spoken by Warren Harding in 1916 that were paraphrased by another president almost fifty years later:

> *In this great fulfillment we must have a citizenship less concerned about what the government can do for it and more anxious about what it can do for the nation.*

Ironic words from a president with a tarnished reputation whose administration was heedless to those words of wisdom.

President and Mrs. Harding are entombed in a circular monument of white Georgian marble situated in the center of ten acres of landscaped parkland adjacent to the Marion Cemetery, immediately east of SR 423, about a mile south of President Harding's Home.

DIRECTIONS: From US 23, exit westbound onto SR 95 that becomes Mount Vernon Avenue in Marion. Follow the historical markers to the house (Figure 90).

PUBLIC USE: Season and hours: Tours are conducted Memorial Day-Labor Day, Wednesday-Saturday, 9:30 AM-5 PM; Sunday and holidays, 12 M-5 PM. Mid-September-October and early April-mid-May, Saturday, 9:30 AM-5 PM; Sunday, 12 M-5 PM. The last tour begins one hour before closing. Closed November-March. **Admission fee. Gift shop. For people with disabilities:** Not accessible.

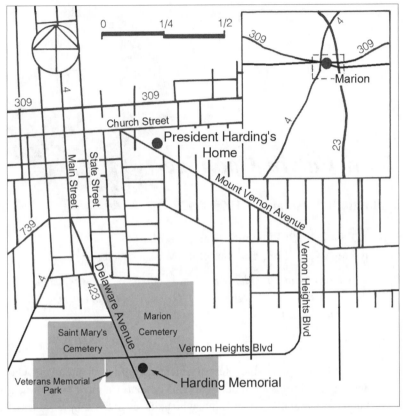

Figure 90. Location of President Harding's Home and Harding Memorial, Marion, Ohio.

FOR ADDITIONAL INFORMATION: Contact: President Harding's Home, 380 Mount Vernon Avenue, Marion, Ohio 43302, (740) 387-9630.**Web site**: *www.ohiohistory.org/places/harding.* **Read:** (1) Robert K. Murray. 1969. *The Harding Era.* (2) Randolph Downes. 1970. *The Rise of Warren Gamaliel Harding, 1865–1920.* (3) Robert Ferrell. 1996. *The Strange Deaths of President Harding.*

John Calvin Coolidge

Thirtieth President — 1923–1929

Born July 4, 1872, Plymouth Notch, Vermont
Died January 5, 1933, Northampton, Massachusetts

> *We draw our Presidents from the people. It is a wholesome thing for them to return to the people. I came from them. I wish to be one of them again.*

— Calvin Coolidge

Calvin Coolidge was the latest in generations of family members who lived and worked in tiny Plymouth Notch, Vermont. Calvin's father was a farmer and the owner of a general store who believed in the simple values of hard work, public service, and love of God and family. Calvin came to share those values and carried them through his own career and into the White House.

Upon the death of President Harding, Coolidge became another of our vice presidents who rose to the occasion and fulfilled the high office of the presidency with competence, diligence, and probity. Coolidge had not been tarnished by the scandals of the Harding administration; the country responded favorably to his native honesty and taciturn personality, and he rode their best wishes and a robust post-war economy to his own election for a full term in 1924.

Coolidge was known as "Silent Cal," a sobriquet that stereotyped him as ineffective and indecisive. His demeanor is well exemplified by the often-told story of the Washington hostess who gushed at dinner that she had bet that she could get more than two words out of him. When she tried, Coolidge coolly replied, "You lose!"

President Calvin Coolidge State Historic Site

PLYMOUTH NOTCH, VERMONT

> *It was here that I first saw the light of day; here I received my bride; here my dead lie, pillowed on the loving breast of our everlasting hills.*

— Calvin Coolidge

Calvin Coolidge was the only president born on the fourth of July. The event took place in a tiny bedroom in the back of his father's general store. The house in which he was raised is just across the street, a house made famous early one August morning in 1923 when Vice President Coolidge was sworn in by his notary public father as the thirtieth President of the United States.

The Coolidge Homestead remains as it was on that early morning in August, as does the hamlet of Plymouth Notch — a rural village in a perfect state of preservation (Plate 10). In 1947, the State of Vermont made a strong commitment to preserve the late-nineteenth-, early-twentieth-century characteristics of the town by forming a Division for Historic Preservation which now owns and maintains nearly the entire historic village — some two dozen buildings and 550 acres of land — as the President Calvin Coolidge State Historic Site. In 1970, the entire Plymouth Notch Historic District, which includes the state historic site, became a registered National Historic Landmark.

The state historic site contains the Coolidge Birthplace, the Coolidge Homestead, the homes of Coolidge's family and neighbors, the community dance hall that served as the 1924 Summer White House office, the Plymouth Cheese Factory (still using the original 1890 recipe to make the traditional granular curd "Plymouth Cheese"), and other buildings, all preserved as they were in the early part of the twentieth century. Two Wilder family barns, for example, display and interpret a fine collection of agricultural equipment from the late nineteenth and early twentieth centuries. The Plymouth Notch Historic District also includes the Union Christian Church owned by the Calvin Coolidge Memorial Foundation, and the Plymouth Notch Cemetery, owned by the town.

Calvin Coolidge left Vermont to seek his fortune in neighboring Massachusetts, where he worked as an attorney and became interested in politics. He served as mayor of Northampton, state senator, lieutenant governor, and

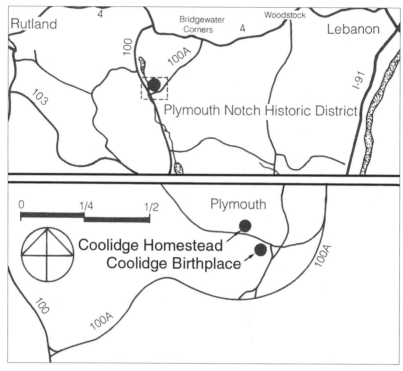

Figure 91. Location of President Calvin Coolidge State Historic Site, Plymouth Notch, Vermont.

governor before entering the national political arena as Warren Harding's vice presidential running mate.

Coolidge may have left Vermont physically but in his heart Plymouth Notch remained home. He returned to visit and vacation often and, in 1933, he returned for eternity. The president and Mrs. Coolidge lie in the village cemetery along with seven generations of family members. His grave noble in its simplicity, Calvin Coolidge is pillowed forever on the loving breast of the everlasting hills.

DIRECTIONS: Plymouth Notch is on SR 100A, 6 miles south of US 4, midway across the state (Figure 91).

PUBLIC USE: Season and hours: Late May-mid-October, 9:30 AM-5 PM. The site's office in the Aldrich House is open most weekdays year-round and contains exhibits especially designed for winter visitors. **Admission fee.**

Food service: The Wilder House restaurant is open for lunch. **Gift shops. For people with disabilities:** The visitor center and most of the village are wheelchair accessible.

FOR ADDITIONAL INFORMATION: Contact: President Calvin Coolidge State Historic Site, Box 247, Plymouth, Vermont 05056, (802) 672-3773. **Web site:** *www.HistoricVermont.org/Coolidge.* **Read:** (1) Calvin Coolidge. 1929. *The Autobiography of Calvin Coolidge.* (2) Jane Curtis, Will Curtis, and Frank Lieberman. 1985. *Return To These Hills: The Vermont Years of Calvin Coolidge.* (3) Robert Sobel. 1998. *Coolidge: An American Enigma.*

Calvin Coolidge Presidential Library and Museum

NORTHAMPTON, MASSACHUSETTS

Upon his graduation from Amherst College, Calvin Coolidge read law with a prominent Northampton firm and was admitted to the bar in 1897. He began a long and successful political career, first as a city councilman, and later as state legislator, mayor of Northampton, state senator, lieutenant governor, Governor of Massachusetts, vice president, and finally President of the United States. Throughout his career, even as president, the Coolidges retained their home at 21 Massasoit Street in Northampton and returned there after leaving Washington. They later purchased a more private home, "The Beeches," and it was there that Calvin Coolidge passed away in 1933.

Following Coolidge's nomination for vice president in 1920, librarian Joseph Harrison of Northampton's Forbes Library (Figure 92) began to collect photographs, articles, and other memorabilia associated with the nominee. Over the years the president, family members, staffers, and others contributed personal and governmental files and other material to the Forbes collection. These donations included Coolidge's papers as governor and vice president, as well as speech texts, proclamations, and scores of news clippings. In 1985, the Coolidge presidential papers, found by son John Coolidge in the family homestead in Plymouth, Vermont, were presented to the Forbes Library by Mr. Coolidge.

Figure 92. Calvin Coolidge Presidential Library and Museum, Forbes Library, Northampton, Massachusetts. Figure by Joanne Marion Goding; use courtesy of Forbes Library.

The Forbes Library is unique in being the only public library in the United States that houses a presidential collection. The Calvin Coolidge Presidential Library and Museum's auditorium is dominated by the official White House portraits of Calvin and Grace Coolidge, likenesses painted by the famed illustrator Howard Chandler Christy.

DIRECTIONS: From US 91, exit westbound onto SR 9, go south on Main Street to West Street, then go south on West Street to the library on the east side of the road (Figure 93).

PUBLIC USE: Season and hours: Monday, 3 PM-8 PM; Tuesday, 1 PM-5 PM; Wednesday, 3 PM-8 PM; Thursday, 1 PM-5 PM; Friday, closed; Saturday, 9 AM-12 M; Sunday, closed. Closed on all federal and state holidays. **For people with disabilities:** Fully accessible.

FOR ADDITIONAL INFORMATION: Contact: Calvin Coolidge Presidential Library and Museum, Forbes Library, 20 West Street, Northampton, Massachusetts 01060, (413) 587-1014. **Web site:** *www.forbeslibrary.org/coolidge/ coolidge.shtml.* **Read:** (1) Sally Thompson. 1972. *Growing Up in Plymouth Notch, Vermont, 1872–1895. The Boyhood of Calvin Coolidge.* (2) J. R. Green. 1997. *Calvin Coolidge's Plymouth, Vermont.*

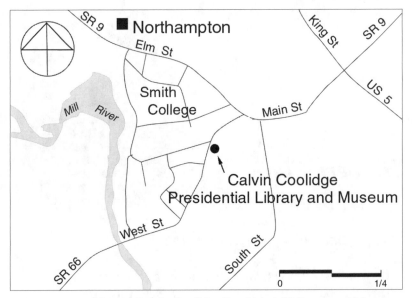

Figure 93. Location of Calvin Coolidge Presidential Library and Museum, Northampton, Massachusetts.

Herbert Clark Hoover

Thirty-First President — 1929–1933

Born August 10, 1874, West Branch, Iowa
Died October 20, 1964, New York City, New York

> *But I prefer to think of Iowa as I saw it through the eyes of a ten year-old boy . . . and the eyes of all ten year-old Iowa boys are or should be filled with the wonders of Iowa's streams and woods, of the mystery of growing crops. His days should be filled with adventure and great undertakings, with participation in good and comforting things.*

> — Herbert Hoover

"Bert" Hoover, born in the tiny Quaker town of West Branch, Iowa, was the first president born west of the Mississippi River. Quakers live by principles of hard work, honesty, and responsibility to the less fortunate, and Herbert Hoover grew to exemplify those noble characteristics.

Herbert's father, a blacksmith, died when the boy was six, and his mother passed away only three years later. Herbert was sent to live with his Uncle Henry and Aunt Laura Minthorn in Newberg, Oregon, when he was eleven. The Minthorns had recently lost their own son and welcomed the young Iowan with love and enthusiasm.

At fifteen, he started to work for the Oregon Land Company, then worked his way through Stanford University as a member of its first graduating class in 1895. Degree in hand, he launched an industrial and business career in mining that sent him around the globe. America's entry into World War I found him in London, where the American ambassador asked him to assist thousands of stranded Americans to return home.

When the United States entered the war in April, 1917, Hoover returned to the United States to join President Wilson's war cabinet as United States Food Administrator. Hoover used public relations and ingenuity to control food supplies and feed both civilian and military populations in the Allied countries, without rationing. The job was so well-conducted that it earned him a post-war appointment as Director General of Post War Relief and Rehabilitation. That monumental effort saved hundreds of thousands of lives and became the model for the Marshall Plan that followed World War II.

Hoover's successes in humanitarian efforts led President Harding to appoint him Secretary of Commerce. He was retained in that position by President Coolidge, and when Coolidge declined to run for reelection as president in 1928, the Republicans nominated Herbert Hoover as their candidate for president.

Hoover's successful business and political careers, as well as his positive contributions to the nation and world, were noteworthy and exemplary, but they will always be overshadowed by the fact he was in office at the time of the 1929 stock market crash — the beginning of the Great Depression. Hoover was, however, a unique and talented man. He lived another thirty-one years after leaving the White House, time that he made productive by his service on important governmental commissions and by his prolific writing — he was the author of forty books. He also provided invaluable advice to those who followed him into the White House.

Herbert Hoover National Historic Site and Herbert Hoover Presidential Library and Museum

WEST BRANCH, IOWA

The Herbert Hoover National Historic Site comprises almost two hundred acres of the small, mid-nineteenth-century town of West Branch and its environs. The visitor center provides an introduction to the site, which includes the Hoover birthplace cottage (Figure 94) and other buildings that were part of West Branch when Hoover was growing up, the graves of President and Mrs. Hoover, and an eighty-one-acre tract of tallgrass prairie.

Hoover's birthplace cottage, a tiny fourteen-by-twenty-foot frame house built by father Jesse Hoover in 1871, consists of a single bedroom and a kitchen-living room flanking a central chimney. The bedroom contains a rope bed with feather ticking and a trundle bed pulled from beneath for the children. When it was cold, the living room served as the kitchen; the stove was utilized for both cooking and heating. In warmer weather the stove was moved to the back porch. Other nearby buildings dating from Hoover's childhood include the town's first schoolhouse, the Quaker meeting house, and a blacksmith shop similar to the one operated by Hoover's father.

The memorial, where the graves of President and Mrs. Hoover are marked by simple marble slabs, is on a grassy knoll that overlooks the village of West Branch.

The Herbert Hoover Presidential Library and Museum (Plate 11), one of twelve presidential libraries administered by the National Archives and Records Administration, is also located on the grounds of the Herbert Hoover National Historic Site (Figure 94). The library is archival, serving as a research center for scholars and historians interested in studying Hoover's extraordinary and often unappreciated role in the political history of the United States. The museum contains exhibits, displays, documents, photographs, and other memorabilia covering Hoover's ninety years of life and decades of service to the public welfare. Visitors are charmed by the reproduction of his retirement office in New York's Waldorf Towers, amused by an exhibit of Roaring 20s souvenirs, and moved by a display chronicling Hoover's monumental work in feeding Europe after World War I, the effort that earned him the sobriquet "The Great Humanitarian." The Library-Museum also has a regular rotation of changing exhibits. Among the themes featured in recent years were the Civil War, the 1950s, Iowa's Frontier Heritage, and American Presidents and Their Families.

DIRECTIONS: Exit I 80 at Exit 254 and go northbound 0.5 mile to the visitor center (Figure 95).

PUBLIC USE: Season and hours: 9 AM-5 PM. Closed Thanksgiving Day, Christmas Day, New Year's Day. **Admission fee. Museum shops. For people with disabilities:** Fully accessible with the exception of the schoolhouse.

Figure 94. Herbert Hoover birthplace, West Branch, Iowa.

FOR ADDITIONAL INFORMATION: Contact: Herbert Hoover National Historic Site, Box 607, West Branch, Iowa 52358, (319) 643-2541. **Web site:** *www.nps.gov/heho.* Herbert Hoover Presidential Library and Museum, Box 488, West Branch, Iowa 52358, (319) 643-5301. **Web site:** *www.hoover.archives.gov.* **Read.** (1) Herbert Hoover. 1931. *A Boyhood in Iowa.* (2) David Burner. 1979. *Herbert Hoover: A Public Life.*

Hoover-Minthorn House

NEWBERG, OREGON

After the untimely deaths of his parents, eleven-year-old Herbert Hoover moved to Oregon to live with his maternal uncle, Dr. Henry John Minthorn, and his wife Laura. The Minthorn House (Figure 96) was ordinary: a white two-story frame building with a big cellar that Hoover called "Aunt Laura's social security," filled as it was with preserved fruits, vegetables, jams, and jellies. The house had been constructed in 1881 by Jesse Edwards,

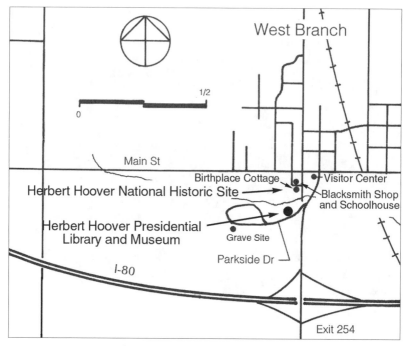

Figure 95. Location of Herbert Hoover National Historic Site and Herbert Hoover Presidential Library and Museum, West Branch, Iowa.

the Quaker founder of Newberg. The Minthorns purchased it in 1885 when they moved to town, he to become superintendent of the Friends Pacific Academy and to act as physician to the pioneer farming community. Laura joined him at the academy as school administrator and teacher. Young Hoover found himself in a loving, intellectual home surrounded by a community of other people devoted to high principles, a living experience that augured well for the lifetime of service that lay ahead. Even today, a visit to the Minthorn house and a walk through the streets and quiet neighborhoods of small-town Newberg engender admiration for the solid Quaker values imbued in our nation's thirty-first president.

In 1947, the Minthorn house was purchased by the Herbert Hoover Foundation, friends, and colleagues of President Hoover, and opened as a museum in 1955 on Hoover's eighty-first birthday. In 1982, the home, then owned by George Fox College in Newberg, was presented to the National

Figure 96. The Hoover-Minthorn House, Newberg, Oregon. Photograph courtesy Hoover-Minthorn House.

Society of Colonial Dames of Oregon. Restoration efforts have followed the room plans associated with the time when young "Bert" Hoover lived there. Most of the furnishings are of the period, although the furniture in Hoover's bedroom is the actual set he used as a boy.

DIRECTIONS: Exit SR 99W onto South River Street and go 1 block south to the house (Figure 97).

PUBLIC USE: Season and hours: March-November, Wednesday-Sunday, 1 PM-4 PM; December and February, Saturday-Sunday, 1 PM-4 PM. Closed in January and major holidays. **Admission fee. Picnic area.**

FOR ADDITIONAL INFORMATION: Contact: Hoover-Minthorn House, 115 South River Street, Newberg, Oregon 97132, (503) 538-6629. **Web site:** *www.viamagazine.com/weekenders/berts04.asp.* **Read:** Herbert Hoover. 1951–1952. *The Memoirs of Herbert Hoover.*

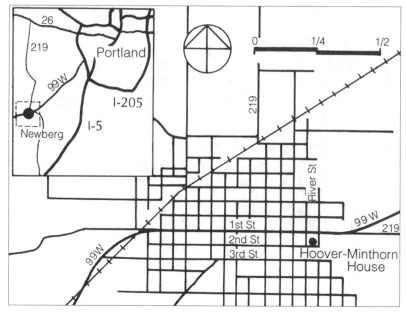

Figure 97. Location of the Hoover-Minthorn House, Newberg, Oregon.

Franklin Delano Roosevelt

Thirty-Second President — 1933–1945

Born January 30, 1882, Hyde Park, New York
Died April 12, 1945, Warm Springs, Georgia

> *The only limit to our realization of tomorrow will be our doubts*
> *of today. Let us move forward with strong and active faith.*

> — Franklin D. Roosevelt's last written words

On March 4, 1933, Franklin Delano Roosevelt was sworn in as the thirty-second President of the United States. The country was in desperate financial straits. Millions of citizens were unemployed; banks were either failing or foreclosing on family homes and farms. The future was uncertain.

The nation had wisely chosen the right man for the hard times. Roosevelt's strong and confident voice rallied the country with words of hope tempered with a dose of common sense and sacrifice:

> *Let me assert my firm belief that the only thing we have to fear*
> *is fear itself . . . terror which paralyzes needed efforts to convert*
> *retreat into advances . . . .*

The people responded as Roosevelt, by personal and moral persuasion, increased the power of the presidency by using it, but not abusing it, for the well-being of all citizens.

Roosevelt, like a few other modern presidents, was akin to our first presidents, those Virginia aristocrats with private educations and inner mandates to serve and protect their fellows. Roosevelt, too, was born to the gentry. He was educated abroad and by tutor at home, and he matriculated at Groton. Although Roosevelt wished to go to Annapolis, he attended Harvard's law school at his father's urging, but he did not receive his degree from Harvard. He did receive a law degree from Columbia University, was admitted to the bar in 1902, but was a less-than-avid attorney as he was more interested in politics than in practicing law. He enjoyed an almost casual career in both elected and appointive offices until 1921, the year in which he was stricken with infantile paralysis. He used a wheelchair for the rest of his life. Somehow galvanized by the adversity, Roosevelt willed himself to greater efforts and accomplishments. Martin Tupper's words challenged him:

> *Never give up . . . if adversity presses, Providence wisely has mingled the cup, and the best counsel in all your distresses, is the stout watchword of "Never Give Up!"*

Roosevelt's greatest successes lay ahead, in his roles as Governor of New York and President of the United States. To Americans everywhere he was a modern George Washington — beloved in both war and peace, content in the love and approbation of his countrymen.

Home of Franklin D. Roosevelt National Historic Site and Franklin D. Roosevelt Presidential Library and Museum

HYDE PARK, NEW YORK

> *This is the house in which my husband was born and brought up . . . . He always felt that this was his home, and he loved the house and the view, the woods, special trees . . .*

— Eleanor Roosevelt

Franklin Roosevelt was born in 1882 in a seventeen-room clapboard house (Figure 98) built between 1800 and 1826. When his father purchased the house in 1867, it was called Brierstone; the name was changed later to

Figure 98. Springwood Mansion, Home of Franklin D. Roosevelt National Historic Site, Hyde Park, New York. Photograph by W. D. Urbin; use courtesy of National Park Service.

Springwood. Roosevelt spent much of his life at Springwood, now more commonly known by Hyde Park, the name of the town in which the estate is situated. Here Roosevelt was shaped into a man; here he brought his bride; here he recuperated from the psychological, physical, and emotional trauma of infantile paralysis.

In 1915, with an eye to the future, Roosevelt initiated extensive alterations and renovations at Springwood. A small tower was removed to make room for a complete third floor of bedrooms, nurseries, and maids' quarters. Stucco was added to the clapboard siding, two wings of native blue fieldstone were built, and the exterior blossomed with a classic columned portico.

The heavy Victorian décor of the interior remained unchanged, although seven more bathrooms were installed, and the addition of a paneled living room and library lent a dignity to the house that it had not enjoyed previously. The library, featuring a portrait of Roosevelt's great-great-grandfather, opens to a screened porch overlooking the lawn and a dramatic view of the Hudson Valley. It is a scene that makes visitors reflect, as did Frances Perkins in her book, *The Roosevelt I Knew:*

> *He particularly admired the beautiful view, as did everyone. . . . . Roosevelt looking off down the river at the view he admired, with a book, often unopened, in one hand, and a walking stick in the other; dogs playing nearby, and the children romping a little further down the lawn. The scene was like a Currier and Ives print of Life along the Hudson.*

Until 1939, presidential papers were considered private property to be retained by the president after leaving office — sometimes saved, but often lost forever. Franklin Roosevelt, ever cognizant of his place in history, arranged to perpetuate his legacy by building the Franklin D. Roosevelt Library. The library was built with private funds, then turned over to the National Archives. His action ensured that his records would become the property of the people, a decision honored by subsequent chief executives.

The Roosevelt Library is a building of Dutchess County native blue fieldstone. A museum section was opened to the public in 1941 and the library portion was opened to research scholars in 1946. The original arrangement of displays in the museum was personally supervised by the president. The exhibits provide an intimate glimpse into Roosevelt's life and the historical period that he dominated. Most visitors smile when they see Roosevelt's specially equipped Ford roadster, which he loved to drive over the country roads around Hyde Park. His White House desk and many other artifacts are on display.

Another part of the Hyde Park experience is Top Cottage, located just past the easternmost end of the estate. Opened to the public in 2001, it was designed and built by President Roosevelt in 1939, imagined as a place he could use as a retreat when he returned to private life after his second term in office. When he was elected to a third term, the little retreat became a temporary haven of relaxation, a place to escape the influx of visitors and constant pressure at Springwood.

The Roosevelt story moved further into the twenty-first century with the opening of the Henry A. Wallace Visitor and Education Center in 2003. The Center is a public-private project designed to serve students, teachers, and the visiting public with expanded facilities to enhance their experiences in Hyde Park. The architectural design is based on the simple lines of

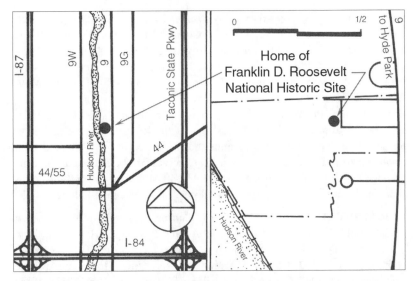

Figure 99. Location of the Home of Franklin D. Roosevelt National Historic Site and Franklin D. Roosevelt Presidential Library and Museum, Hyde Park, New York.

other Dutch buildings on the estate and elsewhere in the Hudson River Valley. FDR loved that style as is evidenced by the buildings that he personally designed — the FDR Presidential Library, Top Cottage, and wife Eleanor's hideaway, Val-Kill. Val-Kill, at the time located on the estate, is now a separate National Historic Site about two miles away.

The Hyde Park experience — the Library, the Springwood mansion, Top Cottage, the Henry A. Wallace Education Center and the spacious grounds — creates an atmosphere of relaxation and nostalgia. Guests contemplate Roosevelt's historical contributions when visiting the museum, reflect on his background and lifestyle in the mansion and may be touched by viewing the exquisite Rose Garden situated between the house and library. There the President and Mrs. Roosevelt lie at rest, their graves as simple as the president had specified: "a plain white monument — no carving or decoration . . . ."

DIRECTIONS: Hyde Park is on US 9, 5 miles north of Poughkeepsie, New York. Historical markers guide visitors to the National Historic Site (Figure 99).

PUBLIC USE: Season and hours: Home of Franklin D. Roosevelt National Historic Site is open daily, 9 AM-5 PM. All facilities are closed Thanksgiving

Homes and Libraries of the Presidents

Day, Christmas Day, New Year's Day. **Home:** Guided tours of the Roosevelt Home begin at the Henry A. Wallace Visitor and Education Center with the last tour leaving at 4 PM. **Museum:** November-April, 9 AM-5 PM; May-October, 9 AM-6 PM. **Library:** Reserved for research, it is open Monday-Friday, 8:45 AM-5 PM. Closed all national holidays. **Top Cottage:** May-October, Thursday-Monday. Access is by shuttle bus (additional fee) available in front of the Wallace Visitor Center. Reservations (845-229-5320) are suggested. **Admission:** Fee includes tour of the Roosevelt home and entry to the Library and Museum. **Museum shop:** Located in the Wallace Center. **Food Service:** The Henrietta Nesbitt Cafe serves breakfast and lunch at the Wallace Visitor Center April-October, 10 AM-4 PM. **For people with disabilities:** The library, museum, home and Wallace Visitor Center are fully accessible.

FOR ADDITIONAL INFORMATION: Contact: (1) Franklin D. Roosevelt Presidential Library and Museum, 4079 Albany Post Road, Hyde Park, New York 12538, 1-800-FDR-VISIT. **Web site:** *www.fdrlibrary.marist.edu.* **or** (2) Home of Franklin D. Roosevelt National Historic Site (Home and Wallace Visitor Center), 4097 Albany Post Road, Hyde Park, New York 12538, (845) 229-9115. **Web site:** *www.nps.gov/hofr.* **Read:** (1) Geoffrey C. Ward. 1985. *Before the Trumpet.* (2) Franklin D. Mares and Richard Cheek. 1993. *Springwood.*

Roosevelt Campobello International Park

CAMPOBELLO ISLAND, NEW BRUNSWICK

It is most fitting that the memory of so gallant and illustrious an American should be so honored on the Canadian Island which he loved.

— England's Queen Mother, at dedication, 1967

Campobello Island, located immediately east of the Maine-New Brunswick border, was purchased by a group of American investors late in the nineteenth century and promoted as a summer resort for the wealthy. Franklin Roosevelt's father bought four acres and an unfinished house in 1883 and completed the house in 1885. The family enjoyed summers of sailing, hiking, swimming, and picnicking at Campobello (Plate 11).

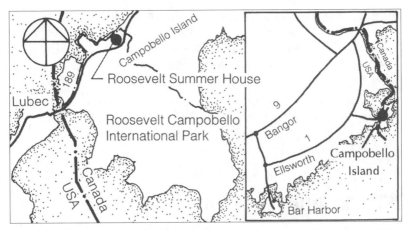

Figure 100. Location of Roosevelt Campobello International Park, Campobello Island, New Brunswick, Canada.

In 1910, Roosevelt's mother purchased a Dutch Colonial cottage nearby for the use of Franklin and Eleanor, who visited the island regularly with their active children, to enjoy its isolation, bracing climate, and relaxing atmosphere. It was at Campobello in 1921, after a cold swim, that Franklin Roosevelt was stricken with infantile paralysis — polio.

The Roosevelt Campobello International Park was established by agreement between the governments of the United States and Canada, and the Roosevelt cottage opened in 1964 with Mrs. Lester Pearson, wife of Canada's prime minister, and Mrs. Lyndon B. Johnson officiating. The visitor center was dedicated by England's Queen Mother in 1967. The Roosevelt cottage is maintained as it was during the family's visit in 1921, the rooms furnished with original Roosevelt possessions and reminders of the vigorous personality who vacationed there; these mementos include a family telescope, Franklin Junior's crib, the large frame chair used to carry the disabled president, even a megaphone used to hail boats — and to call children home to dinner. The park itself contains landscaped gardens and manicured paths that lead to woods, fields, and glorious views of the islands and shores of Passamaquoddy and Cobscook bays in Canada and Maine.

DIRECTIONS: Take US 1 northbound to Maine SR 189 that crosses the Roosevelt Memorial Bridge at Lubec, Maine, and becomes New Brunswick Route 774. The park is 1.5 miles past the Canadian Customs station (Figure 100).

PUBLIC USE: Season and hours: From the Saturday preceding Memorial Day through Columbus Day, 10 AM-6 PM ADT (9 AM-5 PM Eastern Daylight Time). **Gift shop**. **Picnic areas**. **For people with disabilities:** The first floor of the cottage is accessible, with a film presentation of the second floor exhibits available.

FOR ADDITIONAL INFORMATION: Contact: Roosevelt Campobello Park Commission, Box 129, Lubec, Maine 04652, (506) 752-2922. **Web site:** *www.fdr.net.* **Read:** Jonas Klein. 2000. *Franklin and Eleanor and the Legacy of Campobello.*

FDR's Little White House

WARM SPRINGS, GEORGIA

Franklin Roosevelt, searching for relief from the debilitating physical effects of polio, first traveled to Warm Springs in 1924. Delighted with the rejuvenating waters and relaxing atmosphere, he returned again and again, eventually building his own six-room bungalow among the whispering Georgia pines and surrounded by azaleas, dogwoods, and mountain laurels (Figure 101).

The bucolic aura encouraged contemplation and Warm Springs was the crucible for ideas manifested in Roosevelt's activities as president, especially in those social programs affecting the weak, poor, and disenfranchised. It was his experience in Warm Springs and his interaction with other patients, for example, that inspired the organization of the March of Dimes, the premier charitable group devoted to stamping out polio.

Millions have visited Roosevelt's Little White House since it opened as a national shrine in 1947. In order to improve accessibility while providing a state-of-the-art exhibit, the Georgia Department of Natural Resources built the new FDR Memorial Museum, which was completed in 2005. This 11,000-square-foot stone building is a LEEDS certified "Green" structure, recognized for its environmentally friendly construction standards. The exhibitions within provide a combination of experiences for visitors including multimedia displays, rich graphical images, and storyboards. Visitors are also treated to the award-winning fourteen-minute film, *Presidential Portrait: FDR at Warm Springs.* Other exhibits include FDR's 1938 Ford with hand controls, presidential gifts, official documents, and personal belongings.

Figure 101. FDR's Little White House, Warm Springs, Georgia. Photograph courtesy of State of Georgia.

Guests then proceed onto the grounds where they may view the "Walk of Flags and Stones" or sit at the Memorial Fountain. All fifty states, as well as the District of Columbia, contributed a specimen of native stone; the stones are embedded along the sides of the path, each marked by a brass plate with the flag of each state flying above its respective stone.

The tour next leads to the historic grounds where the Little White House and the Guest and Servants' Quarters are located. The six-room, clapboard house reflects FDR's desire and need for privacy, comfort, and the restorative environment Warm Springs provided. The Little White House has been preserved as it was in 1945 when he passed away while having his portrait painted.

Mme. Shoumatoff's famous painting, the "Unfinished Portrait," is displayed in the Legacy Exhibit of the museum. Also featured is Jack Benny's Vault for the March of Dimes and other paintings capturing the spirit of Franklin D. Roosevelt.

Visitors to Warm Springs are encouraged to visit the historic Pools and Springs Museum where FDR had his polio therapy. It is just under a mile away and there is no additional admission fee.

DIRECTIONS: From Atlanta, Georgia, take I 85 southbound to the second Newnan Exit (Exit 41) and proceed southbound on US 27A to Warm Springs. Follow the historical markers to the Little White House (Figure102).

PUBLIC USE: Season and hours: 9 AM-4:45 PM. The last admission ticket is sold at 4:45 PM. Closed Thanksgiving Day, Christmas Day, New Year's Day. **Admission fee. Food service:** Snack bar. **Gift shop. For people with disabilities:** The house and museum are fully accessible. Tour Mates for the visually impaired are available along with pictorial tours for the Guest and Servants' Quarters.

FOR ADDITIONAL INFORMATION: Contact: Little White House State Historic Site, 401 Little White House Road, Georgia Highway 85 Alt., Warm Springs, Georgia 31830, (706) 655-5870. **Web site:** *www.fdr-littlewhitehouse.org.* **Read:** (1) Turnley Walker. 1953. *Roosevelt and the Warm Springs Story.* (2) Hugh Gregory Gallagher. 1985. *FDR's Splendid Deception.*

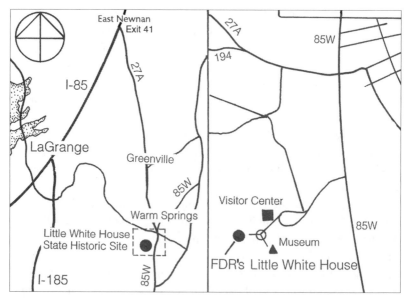

Figure 102. Location of FDR's Little White House, Warm Springs, Georgia.

Harry S Truman

Thirty-Third President — 1945–1953

Born May 8, 1884, Lamar, Missouri
Died December 26, 1972, Kansas City, Missouri

> *My definition of a leader in a free country is a man who can persuade people to do what they don't want to do, or what they're too lazy to do, and like it.*

> — Harry S Truman

Where does America find men who, in times of national trauma, can step into one of the most difficult jobs in the world and perform with such aplomb, intelligence, and force of character? Where does America find men like Harry Truman?

Harry Truman was Franklin Roosevelt's third vice president. He inherited the presidency when the country, deeply traumatized by Roosevelt's death and still fighting a war, needed a man of strength, experience, and vision. Hence the nation wondered — the entire world wondered — how an obscure, Midwestern machine politician could successfully terminate World War II and simultaneously prepare his country for difficult post-war adjustments at home and abroad.

Truman often remarked that he got his strength from the people. Perhaps that's so, but it's more likely he inherited his common sense from his parents and learned the values of hard work and honesty in a hard Missouri boyhood. Faced with horrendous problems as president, this common man from the heartland of America made his decisions with courage and determination. He was a man of the people who called him "Mr. Citizen," a nickname he loved and appreciated more than any worldly honor.

Harry S Truman Birthplace State Historic Site

LAMAR, MISSOURI

On May 8, 1884, Mrs. Martha Ellen Truman gave birth to a healthy boy in the downstairs bedroom of a 1½-story farmhouse in Lamar, Missouri. The baby was christened just plain "Harry." Truman added the "S" later in life as he felt it appeared more dignified. He claimed it did not stand for any one name but was a compromise between names of his grandfathers that began with an "S," Anderson Shipp Truman and Solomon Young. Truman, perhaps joking, once told newspaper reporters that there should not be a period after the S. There is still controversy over the use of the period, even though many surviving documents reveal that Truman used it himself on occasion.

John and Martha Truman had purchased the tiny house and lot for $685 in 1883. It had four rooms downstairs and two upstairs; a smokehouse

Figure 103. Harry S Truman Birthplace State Historic Site, Lamar, Missouri. Photograph by Rita Embry.

and a well were other improvements on the property (Figure 103). The family lived in Lamar only briefly; then finally settled in Independence in 1890.

The United Auto Workers of America purchased the Lamar house in 1957. They restored it, decorated it with furnishings from the period of the Truman occupancy, and turned it over to the State of Missouri as a State Historic Site to be maintained by the Missouri Department of Natural Resources, Division of Parks and Recreation. President Truman was present at the dedication in 1959 and remarked:

> *They don't do this for a former President until he's been dead fifty years. I feel like I've been buried and dug up while I'm alive and I'm glad they've done it to me today.*

DIRECTIONS: The house is located on Truman Street, off of US 160, just east of the US 71/160 intersection in Lamar (Figure 104).

PUBLIC USE: Season and hours: Monday-Saturday, 10 AM-4 PM; Sunday, 12 M-4 PM. Closed Thanksgiving Day, Christmas Day, New Year's Day, Easter Sunday. **Gift shop. For people with disabilities:** Accessible.

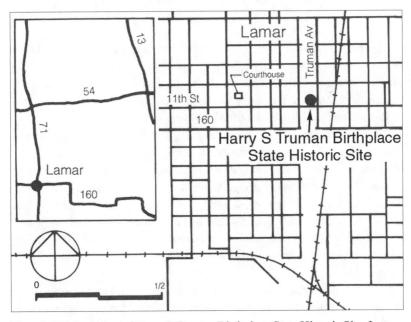

Figure 104. Location of Harry S Truman Birthplace State Historic Site, Lamar, Missouri.

FOR ADDITIONAL INFORMATION: Contact: Harry S Truman Birthplace, 1009 Truman Avenue, Lamar, Missouri 64759, (417) 682-2279. **Web site:** *www.mostateparks.com/trumansite.htm.* **Read:** (1) Harry S. Truman. 1960. *Mr. Citizen.* (2) Robert Ferrell. 1991. *Harry S. Truman: His Life on the Family Farms.* (3) David McCullough. 1992. *Truman.*

Harry S Truman National Historic Site

INDEPENDENCE, MISSOURI

I always came back to Independence every chance I got because the people in Independence, the people in Missouri had been responsible for sending me to Washington. And that's why I ended up in the White House, after I had finished the job, I came back here. This is where I belong.

— Harry S Truman

Harry Truman not only belonged to Independence, he *was* Independence — as he represented the basic, good, honest values nurtured in Independence and all of the other small towns, neighborhoods, and farms of midwestern America. The Harry S Truman National Historic Site commemorates and interprets Truman's life in and near Independence.

Shortly after Harry Truman's birth, the family moved to Independence, where they resided in a succession of houses as their fortunes ebbed and flowed. They were living on Waldo Street when Harry graduated from high school, but his dream of college was not to be, as his father had made a disastrous investment that wiped out the family's savings. Most of the family moved to grandfather Young's farm in nearby Grandview, but Harry stayed in Independence where he worked at a variety of jobs — bank clerk, theater usher, and piano player until his father asked him to help manage the farm in Grandview.

Truman lived and worked on the farm (Figure 105) for ten years before joining the military in World War I. Later he described the farming experience as "the best years of my life." Days on the farm were filled with physical activity and nights with public life as a soldier, mason, postmaster, and school

Figure 105. Farm Home, Harry S Truman National Historic Site, Grandview, Missouri. Photograph courtesy of Harry S Truman National Historic Site.

board member — a life of hard work and community service that established a pattern for his future political career. And somehow in this busy schedule he found time to travel to Independence to court and eventually win the heart of Bess Wallace.

Harry Truman commanded an artillery battery in France during World War I and was mustered out of the army as a major. He did not return to Grandview, although the farmhouse and land remained in the family until 1981 when it was purchased by the Truman Farm Home Foundation. The Foundation restored the house and furnished it with period furniture as a tribute to the "grass roots boy" who had left Grandview as an ordinary farmer and went on to become one of the world's most influential and beloved leaders. On May 8, 1994, the Truman Farm Home became part of the Harry S Truman National Historic Site. The house, the central feature of the historic site, is a two-story frame structure with six rooms and an outside well. It dates to before World War I.

Harry Truman married Bess Wallace in 1919. The couple returned from their honeymoon to live with Bess's widowed mother at 219 North Delaware Street. The Truman home on Delaware Street (Plate 12) is the center of a historic district with a distinctive assortment of architectural styles that represent every decade since the mid-nineteenth century. This was the neighborhood where President Truman took his famous constitutionals — a neighborhood of solid citizens proud of, but not intimidated by, their famous neighbor. Except for their years in Washington, the house in Independence was the Truman home until Mrs. Truman's death in 1982.

Truman biographer Jonathan Daniels commented:

> *Truman the man matches the sturdy Midwestern character of North Delaware Street and the neighborhood which, more than any other, suggests the life and career of the former Chief Executive.*

The house is a fourteen-room Victorian built in 1885 by Mrs. Truman's grandparents. It has seven bedrooms, a high-ceilinged parlor, a music room, and a large dining room. The interior reflects prosperity — tile fireplaces, heavy mahogany and walnut furniture, windows with colored glass borders, and a pleasant screened porch which leads outside to a small, heavily bordered rear yard and a two-car garage. The exterior is decorated with the exaggerated jigsaw trim typical of the late-nineteenth century.

Harry Truman was not a man for change, and the house received minimal modernization over the years, although central heating, electricity, telephone, and radio were brought into the house. Thus the house has remained, as one visitor remarked, "Harry Truman comfortable," a home in the best sense, warm and charming, and a true reflection of the folks who lived within its walls. During Truman's presidency, the house hosted world leaders, and afterwards it became a popular tourist attraction while the ex-president resided there. President Truman once said:

> *In all the years since I left the White House, I have wondered why so many people come from so far away and take so much trouble to look at the house where I live. Perhaps it's because once a man has been President he becomes an object of curiosity like those other notorious Missouri characters, Mark Twain and Jesse James.*

It is more likely that they came, and still come, in tribute to the humble little man who led the country with dignity and courage through days of peril and turmoil.

Mrs. Truman bequeathed the home to the nation, and 219 North Delaware Street was declared a National Historic Site to be maintained by the

National Park Service. A visitor center is located at 223 North Main Street, just five blocks away, where tickets are available for guided tours of the home. Of course, the Truman home is only one of many attractions in Independence that are associated with President Truman. Maps are available for those who wish to take a Truman neighborhood walking tour, and the Jackson County Courthouse is nearby, as is the Missouri-Pacific Railroad station where Truman's famous "whistle-stop" campaign of 1948 came to its end.

DIRECTIONS – *Truman Farm Home*: Grandview is just south of Kansas City, Missouri. Take I 435 southbound to US 71, then continue southbound on US 71. Exit US 71 at Blue Ridge Boulevard. Turn right and continue 0.5 mile to the farm on the left, just past the Truman Corners Shopping Center (Figure 108). *219 Delaware Street*: From Kansas City, Missouri, take I 70 eastbound to I 435 and proceed northbound on I 435 to the Truman Road Exit. Proceed 3 miles east on Truman Road to Main Street. The visitor center is on the southeastern corner, with parking across the street. The home itself, at 219 North Delaware Street, is 5 blocks west of the visitor center (Figure 106).

PUBLIC USE – *Truman Farm Home*: **Season and hours:** The Truman Farm Home grounds are open every day for self-guided tours. Guided tours of the

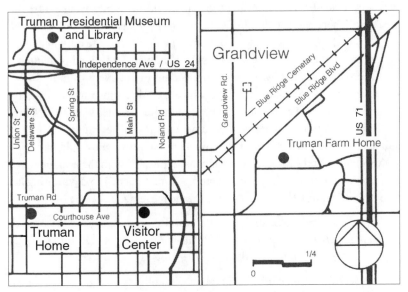

Figure 106. Location of Harry S Truman National Historic Site and Truman Presidential Museum and Library in Independence and Grandview, Missouri.

farmhouse are available from May through August. ***219 Delaware Street*:**
Season and hours: Visitor center is open 8:30 AM-5 PM with tours of the
home during the summer beginning at 9 AM conducted on a first-come, first-
served basis. No tours are offered on Mondays, September-May. Closed
Thanksgiving Day, Christmas Day, New Year's Day. **Admission fee. Gift shop.**
For people with disabilities: Accessible.

FOR ADDITIONAL INFORMATION: Contact: Harry S Truman National
Historic Site, 223 North Main Street, Independence, Missouri 64050, (816)
254-9929. **Web site:** *www.nps.gov/hstr.* **Read:** (1) Harry Truman and Merle
Miller. 1973. *Plain Speaking.* (2) Robert H. Ferrell. 1991. *Harry S. Truman:
His Life on the Family Farms.*

Harry S. Truman Little White House Museum

KEY WEST, FLORIDA

Before Camp David, there was no official presidential retreat, and it
was not unusual for the president to remain in the White House over the
weekend. There were no "flights to the ranch" as Johnson and Reagan made,
or "hops to the Cape" as made by John Kennedy. There were only long trips
by train, car, buggy, or horseback to isolated homes, farms, and plantations.

Harry S. Truman was the only president to get away from it all at a
naval base. In 1946, unable to shake a severe cold, Truman was ordered by
his physician to take a vacation in the sun. Admiral Chester W. Nimitz, Chief
of Naval Operations, suggested the Commandant's home (Figure 107) at the
submarine base in Key West, Florida, where the president would have privacy, security, and sunshine. Truman was so pleased with the arrangements
that he would return to Key West ten times, for a total of 175 days during his
terms in office. In 1949, he had written home to Bess:

> *Dear Bess, you should see the house! . . . . the place is all
> redecorated, new furniture and everything. I've got a notion to
> move the capital to Key West and just stay.*

It wasn't until his fifth visit that he was able to persuade Mrs. Truman
to join him. Daughter Margaret said that Mrs. Truman felt that "it was a stag
place and that he would have a better time beyond her critical eye." Mrs.

Truman enjoyed her infrequent visits, but her point was well taken. The president and his cronies, lubricated with bourbon and branch water, relaxed over nightly poker sessions.

The submarine base closed in 1974 and the property was sold in 1986 to a real estate investor who transferred the title to the State of Florida. Careful study of naval records and redecoration sketches from 1949 enabled restorers to replicate the look of the house during the time President Truman worked, played, and rested there. Most of the furniture is original, including the famous poker table with its mahogany top that folded down to hide the evidence of cards and chips from the press and public during the day.

The Little White House Museum provides the public with an opportunity to discover a personal side of Harry Truman and to understand how his no-nonsense personality was balanced with an ability to shake off the tremendous pressure of high office away from Washington.

Figure 107. Harry S. Truman Little White House Museum, Key West, Florida. Photograph by Oscar Thompson.

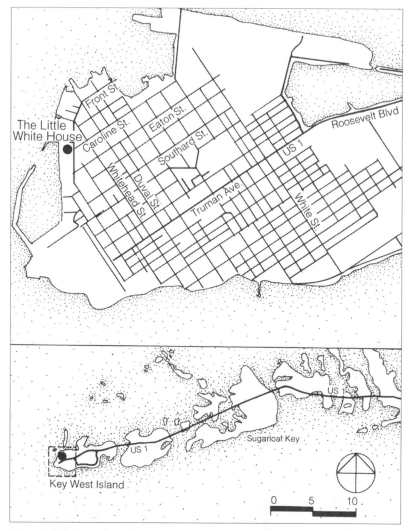

Figure 108. Location of Harry S. Truman Little White House Museum, Key West, Florida.

DIRECTIONS: Key West, Florida, is the southern terminus of US 1, 150 miles south of Miami. Follow US 1 to Whitehead Street, then turn right and proceed several blocks to Caroline Street. Walk 1 block through the Presidential Gates to the Little White House Museum (Figure 108).

PUBLIC USE: Season and hours: 9 AM-5 PM. **Admission fee. Gift shop. For people with disabilities:** First floor fully accessible.

FOR ADDITIONAL INFORMATION: Contact: Harry S. Truman Little White House Museum, 111 Front Street, Key West, Florida 33040, (305) 294-9911. **Web site:** *www.trumanlittlewhitehouse.com.* **Read:** (1) Margaret Truman. 1972. *Harry S. Truman.* (2) Arva Moore Parks. 1991. *Harry Truman and the Little White House in Key West.* (3) Robert Wolz and Barbara Hayo. 2004. *The Legacy of the Harry S. Truman Little White House Key West: Presidents in Paradise.*

Truman Presidential Museum and Library

INDEPENDENCE, MISSOURI

The pride and joy of President Truman's retirement was the Truman Presidential Museum and Library (Figure 109), administered by the National Archives and Records Administration. He spent many hours in its planning,

Figure 109. The Truman Presidential Museum and Library, Independence, Missouri. Photograph courtesy of Truman Presidential Museum and Library.

and maintained an office in the library after it became a reality. The building is noble in simplicity, a reflection of the sincerity and common sense of "a most uncommon man."

In December, 2001, a ceremony celebrated the grand rededication of the library and museum following structural renovation and expansion. Particularly important were the openings of a new White House Decision Center and "Harry S. Truman: The Presidential Years," an interactive exhibit chronicling Truman's presidency.

The retrospective on Truman's years in the presidency covers the monumental issues he dealt with as president — the Atom Bomb, the Korean conflict, the Marshall Plan, the formation of the United Nations, the Berlin Airlift, and the Truman Doctrine. The White House Decision Center in the new Ed and Beth Smith Education Wing is set in an area reminiscent of the West Wing of the White House. Students assume the roles of President Truman and his staff as they face real-life historic decisions. According to the museum, the "program engages students in research, analysis, decision making, leadership, and communications. Students understand the role of the president and his advisors, how presidential decisions are made, models for decision making, and a historical perspective in which decisions are made."

The museum's more familiar features remain in place — the replication of the Oval Office as it appeared in the early 1950s, the Thomas Hart Benton mural in the main lobby and a documentary film *Harry S. Truman: 1884–1972*. A large picture window enables visitors to stand in the courtyard to look into President Truman's office, kept as it was at the time of his death.

The courtyard holds the plain graves where Harry and Bess Truman rest peacefully in the soil of the town, state, and nation they loved and served with dedication.

> *The president — whoever he is — has to decide. He can't pass the buck to anyone. No one else can do the deciding for him. That's his job.*

> — Harry S Truman

DIRECTIONS: From Kansas City, Missouri, take I 70 eastbound to I 435 northbound to US 24 (Independence Avenue) and the Winner Road Exit. Proceed eastbound for 3 miles on US 24 to the Truman Library Exit (Figure 106).

PUBLIC USE: Season and hours: Monday-Saturday, 9 AM-5 PM; Sunday, 12 M-5 PM. Open until 9 PM on Thursdays. Closed Thanksgiving Day, Christmas Day, New Year's Day. Tours are self-guided. **Admission fee. Museum shop. For people with disabilities:** Fully accessible.

FOR ADDITIONAL INFORMATION: Contact: Truman Presidential Museum and Library, 500 West US Highway 24, Independence, Missouri 64050, 1-800-833-1225. **Web site:** *www.trumanlibrary.org.* **Read:** (1) Jonathan Daniels. 1950. *The Man of Independence.* (2) Alonzo L. Hamby. 1995. *Man of the People.*

Dwight David Eisenhower

Thirty-Fourth President — 1953–1961

Born October 14, 1890, Denison, Texas
Died March 28, 1969, Washington, DC

> *The mission of this Allied Force was fulfilled at 0241, local time, May 7, 1945.*

> — Eisenhower's first report noting the end of World War II in Europe.

Dwight Eisenhower, like Truman, was a product of the great American Midwest. He was raised by strong parents who struggled, but never lost sight of the homely values of hard work and honesty tempered by faith. Eisenhower once remarked:

> *I have found out in later years we were very poor, but the glory of America is that we didn't know it then . . . if each of us in his own mind would dwell more upon those simple virtues — integrity, courage, self-confidence and unshakable belief in his Bible — would not some of [our] problems tend to simplify themselves?*

Eisenhower's decision to enter the United States Military Academy was based on the family's financial situation as much as Dwight's youthful exuberance and combative nature. Through his army career, he was assigned to many posts, including a stint as Douglas MacArthur's aide in the Philippines. At the beginning of World War II, when he was a staff colonel in Texas, his organizational skills caught the eye of General George C. Marshall, Army Chief of Staff. Marshall picked Eisenhower to lead the Allied invasion of North Africa. Eisenhower's success at this assignment led to his promotion to Supreme Allied Commander for the Allied invasion of Europe.

Following the end of World War II, Eisenhower returned to the United States in triumph and served a term as Army Chief of Staff before resigning to accept the presidency of Columbia University. The nation, however, called again for his military and diplomatic skills when President Truman appointed him Commander of NATO forces in Europe. While fulfilling that commitment, the Republican Party nominated him to be their candidate for president. He returned to the United States in 1952 to successfully campaign against, and defeat, Adlai E. Stevenson in the general election.

Eisenhower had much in common with President Ulysses S. Grant. Both were commanders of victorious armies and the only two graduates of West Point to achieve the presidency, yet neither had political experience before assuming office. Eisenhower, unlike Grant, however, used his military command skills effectively as president and prevented the rampant fraud that was endemic to the Grant administration.

Eisenhower Birthplace State Historic Site

Denison, Texas

I am the most religious man I know. Nobody goes through six years of war without faith.

— Dwight D. Eisenhower

When Dwight Eisenhower entered West Point, he claimed Tyler, Texas, as his birthplace. Fifty years later, at the height of his military fame, an elderly schoolteacher in Denison, Texas, recalled the Eisenhower family and the baby boy she had rocked to sleep in 1890. A call to General Eisenhower's mother confirmed that Dwight had indeed been born in Denison, where his father had gone to work with the railroad.

After World War II, a group of citizens in Denison formed the Eisenhower Birthplace Foundation which purchased the old house at the corner of Lamar

Figure 110. Eisenhower Birthplace State Historic Site, Denison, Texas, Photograph courtesy of Eisenhower Birthplace State Historic Site, Denison, Texas.

and Day streets, just across from the railroad tracks where Eisenhower's father had worked. The house (Figure 110) was renovated and the surrounding block became part of the Eisenhower Birthplace State Historic Site that encompasses almost ten acres of the neighborhood where Eisenhower had lived, including a number of buildings, a wooded area, a creek, a nature trail, and picnic sites.

The birth house is the centerpiece of the site. A bedroom quilt is the sole possession of the Eisenhowers on display, but the home is furnished in the style of the 1890s, the period when "Ike" was born, with numerous objects representative of the period. Interpretive exhibits relating to President Eisenhower's long life and career in public service, including a video room where visitors may view their choice of a number of historic videotapes, may be found in the visitor center located on the site.

The Foundation dissolved in 1958 and the property was turned over to the Texas Parks and Wildlife Department. In January, 2008, the property was transferred to the Texas Historical Commission, the agency that is now responsible for its operations and maintenance.

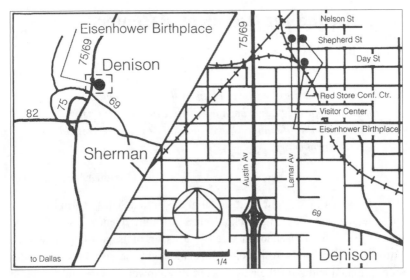

Figure 111. Location of Eisenhower Birthplace State Historic Site, Denison, Texas.

DIRECTIONS: Denison is 75 miles north of Dallas, Texas, on US 75. Take Exit 69 and follow the historical markers to the Eisenhower Birthplace (Figure 111).

PUBLIC USE: Season and hours: Tours are available Tuesday-Saturday, 10 AM-4 PM; Sunday, 1 PM-5 PM. Closed Christmas Day, New Year's Day. **Admission fee. Gift shop. For people with disabilities:** Accessible.

FOR ADDITIONAL INFORMATION: Contact: Eisenhower Birthplace State Historic Site, 609 South Lamar Avenue, Denison, Texas 75021, (903) 465-8908. **Web site:** *http://www.thc.state.tx.us/hsites/hs_eisenhower _birthplace.shtml.* **Read:** (1) Kenneth S. Davis. 1945. *Soldier of Democracy: A Biography of Dwight Eisenhower.* (2) Sherrie S. McLeRoy. 1989. "Ike's Birthplace: Our 34th President Came from Humble Beginnings." (3) Laura Black. 1990. "Texas Remembers Ike."

The Eisenhower Presidential Center

ABILENE, KANSAS

> *The proudest thing I can claim is that I am from Abilene . . . .*
> *through this world it has been my fortune or misfortune to wander*
> *at considerable distance. Never has this town been outside my*
> *heart or my memory.*

— Dwight D. Eisenhower

General of the Armies, President of the United States, world leader —
and graduate of Abilene High School, class of 1909. Abilene will never let the
memory of Dwight Eisenhower fade, proud as it is of its most famous son. To
perpetuate his memory, Abilene, in association with the Eisenhower Foundation, initiated and built the magnificent Eisenhower Presidential Center, a
five-building complex situated on twenty-two acres on the south edge of
town.

A visit to the Eisenhower Center starts at the visitor center with the
screening of a film that reviews the life of President Eisenhower. Then a self-
guided tour continues at the adjacent museum which was dedicated on Veterans' Day, 1954. Five major galleries within the museum contain items associated with Eisenhower's military and political history, including childhood
artifacts, high school memorabilia, military souvenirs, and presidential gifts
from heads of state and ordinary citizens.

Next door to the museum stands Eisenhower's boyhood home, a small
two-story frame house with an attic (Plate 12). His mother lived in the house
until her death in 1946, when her sons donated the house to the Eisenhower
Foundation. Left as it was at the time of Mrs. Eisenhower's death, it contains
original furnishings, including the upright piano the boys learned to play,
and the big double beds in which they slept.

The Dwight D. Eisenhower Presidential Library, across the park, was
established to preserve the president's papers and other related historical
material. The library is administered by the National Archives and Records
Administration. Like the other presidential libraries, it is archival and dedicated to scholarly research. In the marbled lobby an exhibit, "Where's the
Books?" describes the workings of the library. An upper gallery features
changing exhibits. President Eisenhower requested to be buried in Abilene

and his wishes were honored. President and Mrs. Eisenhower, with their infant son, Doud, are entombed in The Place of Meditation, a steepled sanctuary located at the head of the mall that centers the park. Etched above their marble sarcophagi are the memorable words spoken by General Eisenhower at London's Guildhall on July 12, 1945:

> *Humility must always be the portion of any man who receives*
> *acclaim earned in blood of his followers and sacrifices of his friends.*

DIRECTIONS: Abilene is 85 miles west of Topeka, Kansas, just off I 70. From I 70 eastbound or westbound, take Exit 275 and proceed southbound on SR 15 for 2 miles to Abilene where historical markers guide visitors to the Eisenhower Center (Figure 112).

PUBLIC USE: Season and hours: 9 AM-4:45 PM. Closed Thanksgiving Day, Christmas Day, New Year's Day. **Admission fee:** For the museum only. **Gift shop. For people with disabilities:** Fully accessible.

FOR ADDITIONAL INFORMATION: Contact: The Eisenhower Center, 200 Southeast Fourth Street, Abilene, Kansas 67410, (785) 263-6700 *or* 1-877-RINGIKE. **Web site:** *www.eisenhower.archives.gov.* **Read:** Stephen E. Ambrose. 1990. *Eisenhower: Soldier and President.*

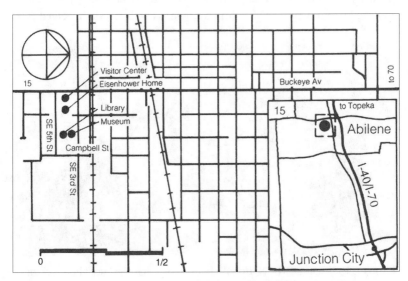

Figure 112. Location of the Eisenhower Presidential Center, Abilene, Texas.

Eisenhower National Historic Site

GETTYSBURG, PENNSYLVANIA

In 1915, Dwight David Eisenhower graduated from West Point and began his long army career at Fort Sam Houston in Texas as a second lieutenant. By 1918, he was a captain and placed in command of the army's fledgling tank corps training center at Camp Colt in Gettysburg, Pennsylvania. Frustrated over being stationed stateside while a war was being fought in Europe, he nonetheless fell in love with Gettysburg, a pretty rural town in the foothills of the Appalachians.

Thirty-three years later, General of the Armies Dwight D. Eisenhower and his wife bought a ramshackle farm and its rundown house on the outskirts of Gettysburg. It was a dream come true for the army couple who had spent a lifetime moving from one military post to another; from one rental to another, to at last find permanence and pride of ownership. They had the house partially razed and replaced it with "Mamie's Dream House," a twenty-room Georgian that was completed in 1955 (Figure 113).

The house has eight bedrooms, eight baths, a living room, dining room, kitchen, and a porch. The living room is filled with Mrs. Eisenhower's treasures, an accumulation of furniture, family pictures, and decorative objects collected over thirty-nine years of marriage, as well as gifts received from

Figure 113. Eisenhower National Historic Site, Gettysburg, Pennsylvania. Photograph courtesy of National Park Service.

friends and admirers around the world. The heart of the house, however, was the sun porch. Mrs. Eisenhower once said, "We lived on the porch," and it is easy to see why. The comfortable furniture and casual atmosphere were perfect for informal entertaining and relaxation. The view from the sun porch looks out to the east, toward the Gettysburg battlefield.

Just outside the porch is the home's most famous conversation piece — Ike's putting green and sand trap that was installed by the Professional Golfers' Association in the 1950s as a thank-you gift to America's most famous duffer.

Eisenhower National Historic Site actually consists of three farms, two of which are open to the public — the Eisenhower farm with the house, barn, guest house, and reception center — and an adjoining farm that housed Eisenhower's show cattle. The focal point was the show barn where Eisenhower took world leaders to see his prize-winning animals. At the farm, those interested in walking may take a half-mile tour that includes a visit to the cattle barns, show barn, and skeet range where an exhibit explains Eisenhower's interest in the shooting sports. The reception center houses exhibits on Eisenhower's life, work, and times, and has a book store and video display.

During the Eisenhower presidency, the Gettysburg farm was an essential retreat from the pressures of Washington and once served as the temporary White House while the president recuperated from his first heart attack. Thus it hosted many national and world leaders. Charles De Gaulle, after a visit to the Eisenhower farm, wrote,

> *Place, agreeable.*
> *Site, interesting.*
> *Host, charming.*

The Eisenhowers presented the farm to the federal government in 1967, although they remained in residence until Ike's death in 1969 and Mamie's in 1979. She had often remarked, "We had only one home — our farm."

DIRECTIONS: Gettysburg is 35 miles southwest of Harrisburg, Pennsylvania, on US 30, just west of its intersection with US 15. The Historic Site is on US 15 (Business) southwest of downtown Gettysburg. Follow the historical markers to the Gettysburg National Military Park Visitor Center (Figure 114).

PUBLIC USE: Season and hours: 9 AM-4 PM. Closed Thanksgiving Day, Christmas Day, New Year's Day. Due to the lack of on-site parking and space limitations at the Eisenhower home, visits may be made only by a shuttle bus leaving from the Gettysburg National Military Park Visitor Center. The Center opens at 8 AM and tickets may be purchased on a first-come, first-served basis for the next available tour. **Admission fee. Gift shops. For people with disabilities:** Advance arrangements should be made at the visitor center.

FOR ADDITIONAL INFORMATION: Contact: Site Manager, Eisenhower National Historic Site, 250 Eisenhower Farm Lane, Gettysburg, Pennsylvania 17325, (717) 338-9114. **Web site:** *www.nps.gov/eise.* **Read:** Dwight D. Eisenhower. 1967. *At Ease: Stories I Tell to Friends.*

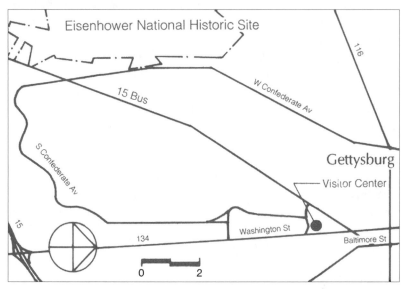

Figure 114. Location of Eisenhower National Historic Site, Gettysburg, Pennsylvania.

John Fitzgerald Kennedy

Thirty-Fifth President — 1961–1963

Born May 29, 1917, Brookline, Massachusetts
Died November 22, 1963, Dallas, Texas

> *And so, my fellow Americans, ask not what your country can do for you: ask what you can do for your country.*

> — John F. Kennedy, Inaugural address

John F. Kennedy was the first president born in the twentieth century and the youngest ever elected to the nation's highest office. Despite doubts about his lack of experience and fears of his Roman Catholicism, he prevailed to win the presidency as he captured the imagination of the nation and the world with his idealism, youthful vigor and vision. He envisioned a "New Frontier of renewal as well as change" led by a young generation brought up in a fast-paced world of instant communication and expanding global responsibility.

Just short of three years into his term, Kennedy was felled by an assassin's bullet, his dream for America unrealized. His memory, however, lives on in the hearts, minds, and actions of those left behind who are dedicated to fulfilling his dream.

> *We in this country, in this generation are, by destiny rather than choice, the watchmen on the walls of world freedom. We ask, therefore, that we may exercise our strength with wisdom and restraint, and that we may achieve in our time and for all time the*

ancient vision of "peace on earth, good will toward men." That must always be our goal...and the righteousness of our cause must always underlie our strength. As was written long ago: Except the Lord keeps the city, the watchman waketh but in vain.

— Kennedy's last written words, 1963

John Fitzgerald Kennedy National Historic Site

BROOKLINE, MASSACHUSETTS

John Kennedy was born into modest circumstances in a small frame house (Plate 13) on quiet, tree-lined Beals Street in a middle-class suburb of Boston. His father, an up-and-coming young executive, had not yet accumulated fortune, notoriety, or political influence. Joseph and Rose Kennedy had moved into the house on Beals Street in 1914, but the addition of four children made for cramped living and necessitated a move to a larger house in the same neighborhood. They resided in a house on Abbottsford Road from 1920 until 1927.

The Kennedy family re-purchased the six-room house on Beals Street in 1966. Matriarch Rose supervised restoration through recollections that reflected her memorial efforts and a nostalgic perspective that she introduced — whether consciously or not — into her recreation of what she referred to as "those happy days." The house, furnished and decorated to its earlier appearance, was donated by the family to the federal government in 1967, at which time it was designated a National Historic Site.

Four sites that are important to the early years of John F. Kennedy are within walking distance of Beals Street — the Abbotsford Road residence, Saint Aidan's Church, and the Dexter and Edward Devotions schools, the latter three attended by John and his older brother, Joseph. None of these four sites is open to the public, but many visitors enjoy the historic walk and the ambience of the friendly neighborhood that spawned and nurtured one of our most beloved presidents.

DIRECTIONS: Brookline is a suburb of Boston, Massachusetts. From Boston by car, take the Massachusetts Turnpike westbound and exit at Allston/

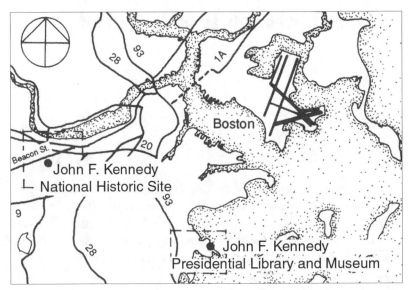

Figure 115. Location of John Fitzgerald Kennedy National Historic Site, Brookline, Massachusetts and John F. Kennedy Presidential Library and Museum, Boston, Massachusetts.

Cambridge that flows into Cambridge Street. After ¾ mile, turn left on Harvard Street and proceed over two sets of trolley tracks. Beals Street is the sixth street after the second set of tracks. Turn left on Beals to the Kennedy house. From Boston by rapid transit, take the Green Line ("C"— Cleveland Circle) train. Exit at the Coolidge Corner station (intersection of Beacon and Harvard Streets). Walk four blocks north on Harvard Street, turn right onto Beals Street and proceed ¾ block to #83 (Figure 115).

PUBLIC USE: Season and hours: Mid-May to September 30, Wednesday-Sunday, 10 AM-4:30 PM. The house is shown by ranger-led tours that leave from 10 AM-3:30 PM on the half-hour. From 3:30 PM-4:30 PM the house is open for self-guided tours which utilize hand-held audiowands with narration by matriarch Rose Kennedy. Closed major holidays. **Admission fee. Museum shop.**

FOR ADDITIONAL INFORMATION: Contact: John Fitzgerald Kennedy National Historic Site, 83 Beals Street, Brookline, Massachusetts 02446, (617) 566-7937. **Web site:** *www.nps.gov/jofi.* **Read:** (1) Arthur M. Schlesinger, Jr. 1965. *A Thousand Days: John F. Kennedy in the White House.* (2) *Victorian Homes* April, 1993.

The John F. Kennedy Hyannis Museum

HYANNIS, MASSACHUSETTS

> *I always come back to the Cape and walk the beach when I have a tough decision to make. The Cape is the one place I can think and be alone.*

— John F. Kennedy

The John F. Kennedy Hyannis Museum (Figure 116), administered by the Hyannis Area Chamber of Commerce, was founded by a private foundation, the Committee of the JFK Hyannis Museum. The museum opened in the summer of 1992 with the objective of providing visitors with an opportunity to explore and appreciate President Kennedy's deep affection for Cape Cod and the lifestyle he enjoyed there.

The exhibits, including over eighty photographs and a video, *Summer White House*, narrated by Walter Cronkite, are a reflection of the Kennedy years in Hyannis and a celebration of the individual man, his family, and his friends in the context of a place he loved. Changing exhibits have focused on the wedding of Jack and Jackie and that of daughter Caroline, as well as on

Figure 116. The John F. Kennedy Hyannis Museum, Hyannis, Massachusetts, Photograph by David Still, *The Barnstable Patriot.*

other themes. Visitor favorites are a silk-screen family tree wall showing the ancestors and descendants of Joseph P. and Rose Kennedy, and a stunning portrait of John F. Kennedy, Jr. Perhaps the most talked-about item is a maquette, "What Could've Been," that shows JFK with his arm around his adult son. The sample sculpture was considered controversial, however, and was never completed as a full-sized work of art. On the other hand, many visitors find it extremely moving.

DIRECTIONS: From US 6, "The Road to the Cape", take Exit 6 and proceed on SR 132 to Hyannis. At the Airport rotary, take the second right onto Barnstable Road to Main Street and go right (one-way) to the Museum on the left (Figure 117).

PUBLIC USE: Season and hours: Mid-April-Memorial Day, Monday-Saturday, 10 AM-4 PM; Sunday and holidays,12 M-4 PM. Memorial Day-Columbus Day, Monday-Saturday, 9 AM-5 PM; Sundays and holidays,12 M-5 PM. Columbus Day-October 31, Monday-Saturday, 10 AM-4 PM; Sundays and holidays, 12 M-4 PM. November-mid-April, Thursday-Saturday, 10 AM-4 PM; Sundays, 12 M-4 PM. **Admission fee. For people with disabilities:** Accessible.

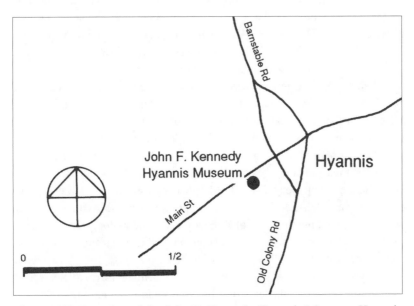

Figure 117. Location of the John F. Kennedy Hyannis Museum, Hyannis, Massachusetts.

FOR ADDITIONAL INFORMATION: Contact: John F. Kennedy Hyannis Museum, 397 Main Street, Hyannis, Massachusetts 02601, (508) 790-3077. **Web site:** *www.jfkhyannismuseum.org.* **Read:** J. Julius Fanta. 1968. *Sailing with President Kennedy, the White House Yachtsman.*

The Sixth Floor Museum at Dealey Plaza

DALLAS, TEXAS

> *This is a very fine, objective presentation. Generations will benefit. We understand where we are and who we are and where we are going only by understanding our past.*

> — Entry in Sixth Floor Memory Book

Few events in recent American history affected the nation more than the assassination of President John F. Kennedy on November 22, 1963. Morally, psychologically, and emotionally our lives changed with the death of the young and vibrant leader. Our world would never be the same. Dealey Plaza, like Ford's Theatre, Pearl Harbor, the Alamo, the Oklahoma City Federal Building, the World Trade Center, and others, will remain a place of national tragedy, ever reminding us that history is not always celebratory — that things sometimes go terribly wrong. Since that fateful day, thousands of people have traveled to Dallas to remember, to study, to look within themselves — asking questions and searching for answers.

To help fill the public need for introspection, understanding, and closure, Dallas opened The Sixth Floor Museum at Dealey Plaza (Figure 118) in 1969. The museum is located on the sixth and seventh floors of the former Texas School Book Depository Building where a sniper's nest was discovered following the shooting — a nest reproduced in the southeast corner window overlooking the route of Kennedy's ill-fated motorcade. The assassination has been placed in historical context with exhibits and audio-visual presentations examining the social climate of the early 1960s, President Kennedy's life and career, the political reasons behind his trip to Texas, and the enduring effect of his death on American society and culture.

Yet the exhibits are not macabre. Conover Hunt, the original project director, said:

Figure 118. The Sixth Floor Museum at Dealey Plaza, Dallas, Texas. Photograph by Bret St. Clair, The Sixth Floor Museum at Dealey Plaza.

> *I believe visitors come here to find something tangible, to get a sense of reality. Over and over again, they have expressed a profound regret that there was nothing here to clarify the information they'd read or to interpret what they saw . . . . There is no museum like this anywhere in the United States and, truly, there is no better place for it. The view of Dealey Plaza alone speaks volumes about a tragedy that changed the course of history. The public has a right to come here.*

Following the tragic events of September 11, 2001, the Sixth Floor Museum, at the time preparing an exhibit that focused on the history of Dealey Plaza, shifted gears to create "Loss and Renewal: Transforming Tragic Sites," an exhibit designed to address important and timely questions about commemorating tragic events. Other important exhibits followed: "Unfinished Business: Kennedy and Cuba," "Jackie Kennedy, The First Lady," "Preserving Presidential History," and "Covering Chaos," which explored the challenge faced by the reporters in Dallas at the time of Kennedy's assassination. Information about these exhibits is available on the museum's web site. Of interest is the museum's oral history collection, consisting of over 400 interviews with assassination eyewitnesses, law enforcement officials, community leaders, White House officials, and others whose firsthand accounts provide future generations with a tangible link to the past. The oral history program is ongoing.

In addition to The Sixth Floor Museum at Dealey Plaza, Dallas has honored President Kennedy with the John F. Kennedy Memorial Plaza at Main, Commerce, and Market streets. Designed by Philip Johnson, it is an impressive cenotaph ("open tomb") with high walls designed to block traffic noise for those using it as a place of meditation and quiet contemplation. The cenotaph symbolizes the belief that Kennedy's spirit cannot be contained.

DIRECTIONS: The Sixth Floor Museum at Dealey Plaza is at the northwest corner of Houston and Elm streets on the western edge of downtown Dallas. From I 35E, take the Commerce Street Exit eastbound (one-way) to the third light at Market Street and turn north. Continue to Elm Street and turn west. The museum is two lights farther, on the right (Figure 119).

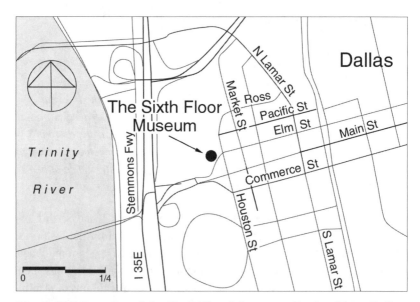

Figure 119. Location of the Sixth Floor Museum at Dealey Plaza, Dallas, Texas.

PUBLIC USE: Season and hours: 9 AM-6 PM. Closed Christmas Day. **Admission fee. Museum store. For people with disabilities:** Wheelchair accessible.

FOR ADDITIONAL INFORMATION: Contact: The Sixth Floor Museum at Dealey Plaza, 411 Elm Street, Dallas, Texas 75202-3308, (214) 747-6660. **Web site:** *www.jfk.org.* **Read:** Conover Hunt. 1989. *JFK for a New Generation.*

John F. Kennedy Presidential Library and Museum

BOSTON, MASSACHUSETTS

One man can make a difference and every man should try.

— John F. Kennedy

The John F. Kennedy Library and Museum (Figure 120) — stark, striking, imposing — stands beside the sea President Kennedy loved. The park-like surroundings and a unique view of Boston's historic skyline and harbor combine to provide a particularly dramatic setting. The interior of the library, with its huge picture windows and spacious galleries, is an aesthetic experience in perfect harmony with Kennedy's interest in the arts. The building was designed by the internationally renowned architect I. M. Pei, who captured the modernity and vision of the man the structure honors.

Like other presidential libraries, the Kennedy Library is an archival repository and research center. In addition to Kennedy's personal and presidential papers, the library houses the papers of his parents, brother Robert Kennedy, and associates such as John Kenneth Galbraith, McGeorge Bundy, and many others. It contains an extensive collection of oral history interviews and the Ernest Hemingway Collection.

The museum section, open to the public, presents the life and work of President Kennedy and the office of the president as illustrated by a combination of films, videotapes, audio recordings, photographs, letters, speeches, and other artifacts. There are twenty-one exhibits covering President Kennedy's administration, his family and his legacy from 1960 to the present. All exhibits are permanent except those in the Ceremonial Room, and they are changed every six months. These changing exhibits relate to ceremonial

Figure 120. John F. Kennedy Presidential Library and Museum, Boston, Massachusetts. Photograph courtesy of John F. Kennedy Presidential Library and Museum.

occasions at the White House and the significance of those occasions to cultural values and the arts. There are two theaters in the museum; one shows an introductory film and a special mini-theater in the exhibit area screens a film on the Cuban Missile Crisis.

The intention of the museum is to place the Kennedy story into the broad perspective of American and world history. The library's own description expresses the hope that "visitors will take from the museum a deeper appreciation of our system of government and a greater awareness of the benefits and responsibilities of living in a free society."

DIRECTIONS: By car, from the south of Boston, take I 93 (Southeast Expressway) to Dorchester, then Exit 14 to Morrissey Boulevard. Follow the historical markers to the Library. From the North and Boston, take the Southeast Expressway to Exit 15, then follow the historical markers (Figure 115). Rapid transit, take the MBTA Red Line to the JFK/UMass station where free shuttle buses transport visitors to the Library every thirty minutes between 9 AM and 5 PM.

PUBLIC USE: Season and hours: 9 AM-5 PM. Closed Thanksgiving Day, Christmas Day, New Year's Day. **Admission fee. Food service:** A cafe is open from 9 AM-4:30 PM. Picnics are allowed on the grounds. **Gift shop. For people with disabilities:** Fully accessible.

FOR ADDITIONAL INFORMATION: Contact: John F. Kennedy Presidential Library and Museum, Columbia Point, Boston, Massachusetts 02125, (617) 514-1600 (or) 1-866-JFK-1960. **Web site:** *www.jfklibrary.org.* **Read:** (1) William Davis and Christina Tree. 1980. *The Kennedy Library.* (2) Carter Wiseman. 1990. *I. M. Pei: A Profile in American Architecture,* pp. 93–119, 196–479.

Lyndon Baines Johnson

Thirty-Sixth President — 1963–1969

Born August 27, 1908, Stonewall, Texas
Died January 22, 1973, Johnson City, Texas

> *I will do my best. That is all I can do. I ask for your help, and God's.*

— Lyndon Johnson

Lyndon Johnson was the eighth vice president to succeed to the nation's highest office upon the death of a president. He was, perhaps, the best prepared, as President Kennedy had entrusted Johnson with important responsibilities and kept him informed of administration policies and problems. Before becoming vice president, Johnson enjoyed a long and effective career in congress, the last several years as Majority Leader of the senate. The nation, shocked and horrified by the Kennedy assassination, was reassured by the strong and forceful image of Johnson as he assumed office.

Johnson maintained political continuity as he pressed forward with Kennedy's New Frontier agenda and, in 1964, was rewarded when he was elected president with the highest number of popular votes ever cast. With that mandate, he moved ahead with his own agenda and achieved remarkable success in the areas of civil rights, education, and the environment. His administration was credited with passage of the Clean Air and Water Acts, the Wilderness Act, and the National Trails Act. More national parklands were set aside during Johnson's term in office than in any previous administration.

In 1968, however, Johnson's presidency bogged down in the morass of Viet Nam and he chose not to run for reelection, thus perpetuating the tradition of no vice president ever having been elected to two full terms of his own.

Lyndon B. Johnson National Historical Park and Lyndon B. Johnson State Park and Historic Site

JOHNSON CITY AND STONEWALL, TEXAS

The Lyndon B. Johnson National Historical Park (Plate 13) and the Lyndon B. Johnson State Park and Historic Site represent a unique cooperative effort between the State of Texas and the federal government to memorialize the homes, life, and legacy of a famous American. The scope of the effort reflects the bigger-than-life stature of both Johnson and the vast Texas Hill Country that he loved.

The National Historical Park, administered by the National Park Service, consists of two distinct areas, fourteen miles apart — the Johnson Settlement and LBJ Boyhood Home in Johnson City and the famous LBJ Ranch in Stonewall. The State Park and Historic Site comprises more than 700 acres immediately across the Pedernales River, adjacent to the south side of the LBJ Ranch, and features recreational facilities available for swimming, hiking, picnicking, and nature study.

A modern visitor center serving both the State Park and the LBJ Ranch section of the National Historical Park interprets the natural and cultural history of the Texas Hill County with special emphasis on German settlement in the area and the presence and legacy of LBJ. There are displays of memorabilia from Johnson's presidency plus interactive displays about the land and people that shaped him. One 1870s log cabin is attached to the center and another is located just to the west. The furnishings in both are representative of the period. The center contains a modern 200-plus-seat auditorium and an outdoor amphitheater. A nature trail winds past wildlife enclosures stocked with bison, white-tailed deer, and longhorn cattle. Always popular is the Sauer-Beckmann Living History Farm, presented as it was in the era

1915–1918, with costumed interpreters performing farm and household chores as they were done at the time LBJ was born just across the river.

National Park Service bus tours leave regularly from the visitor center to drive past the LBJ Ranch house, pause at the one-room schoolhouse where Johnson began his education, at a reconstructed birthplace house, and then stop at the Johnson family cemetery, the final resting place for the active, Texas-sized president.

At Johnson's funeral, John Connally eulogized:

> *Along the stream and under the trees he loved he will now rest. He first saw light here. He last felt life here. May he now find peace here.*

In 1913, when Lyndon was five, the family moved into a comfortable house located on Elm Street in Johnson City, fourteen miles east of Stonewall. This house remained home to the Johnsons for decades, and it was from the front porch of this house in 1937 that Lyndon announced his intent to run for the US House of Representatives. The house was designated a unit of the National Park Service in 1969 and has been restored to its appearance during the 1920s when Johnson knew it as a youth. The National Park Service visitor center for the Johnson City sites is in what was formerly the Pedernales Hospital, built during the Johnson administration. The center features exhibits and two films, one of which is a biographical look at the life of Lady Bird Johnson. The Johnson Settlement, within walking distance of the center, is a complex of restored structures that trace the evolution of the Hill Country from the days of rugged, open-range cattle kingdoms to those of dry land farming.

DIRECTIONS: Johnson City is 50 miles west of Austin, Texas. From Austin, take US 290 and proceed westbound to Johnson City (Figure 121). To the LBJ Ranch, take US 290 westbound for another 14 miles to the Lyndon B. Johnson State Park and Historic Site. Tickets for the LBJ Ranch bus tour are purchased at the State Park visitor center.

PUBLIC USE: Season and hours: *Johnson City Visitor Center:* 8:45 AM-5 PM. Guided tours of the LBJ Boyhood Home are available every half-hour. ***Stonewall Visitor Center:*** 8 AM-5 PM. Bus tours of the LBJ Ranch are conducted from 10 AM-4 PM. Reservations are required for groups of 15 or more. After-hours self-guided auto tours of portions of the ranch are available from 5 PM until sunset. ***Sauer-Beckmann Living History Farm:*** 8 AM-4:30 PM. All areas are closed Thanksgiving Day, Christmas Day, New Year's

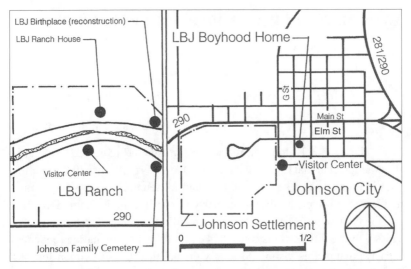

Figure 121. Location of Lyndon B. Johnson National Historical Park and Lyndon B. Johnson State Park and Historic Site at Johnson City and Stonewall, Texas.

Day. **Admission fee:** There is a charge for the bus tour. **Gift shops:** One in each visitor center. **For people with disabilities:** Accessible to those using wheelchairs. Visitor center films are close-captioned.

FOR ADDITIONAL INFORMATION: Contact: Lyndon B. Johnson National Historical Park, P.O. Box 329, Johnson City, Texas 78636, (830) 868-7128 (extension 244), *or* Lyndon B. Johnson State Park and Historic Site, Box 238, Stonewall, Texas 78671, (830) 644-2252. **Web site: National Historical Park**: *www.nps.gov/lyjo.* **State Park and Historic Site**: *www.tpwd.state.tx.us/spdest/ findadest/parks/lyndon_b_johnson/.* **Read:** (1) Robert Dallek. 1991. *Lone Star Rising.* (2) Robert Dallek. 1998. *Flawed Giant.* (3) Hal K. Rothman. 2001. *Our Heart's Home.*

Lyndon B. Johnson Library and Museum

AUSTIN, TEXAS

It's all here, the story of our time...with the bark off.

— Lyndon B. Johnson, at the dedication

The Lyndon B. Johnson Library and Museum (Figure 122), similar to the other presidential library and museum facilities built since FDR's administration, consists of separate library and museum divisions. The library, available for use primarily for scholarly research, contains some forty-five million documents related to Johnson and his presidency. The museum provides public exhibits of historical and cultural interest, including sequential displays that enable visitors to follow the political life of Lyndon Johnson from his tenure as a young congressman to his terms as President of the United States. There is a seven-eighths scale replica of the Oval Office, a

Figure 122. Lyndon B. Johnson Library and Museum, Austin, Texas. Photograph courtesy of National Park Service.

1968 presidential limousine (a Lincoln), and an exhibit interpreting Mrs. Johnson's legacy as a humanitarian, unofficial diplomat, and champion of nature. Among the most popular exhibits is "Humor of LBJ," a life-size animatronic figure of the president telling five of his short stories.

Lyndon Johnson was responsible for some of the most sweeping and far-reaching social legislation in our history, but was finally victimized by the nation's division over the conflict in faraway Viet Nam. As President Johnson remarked:

> *I hope that visitors who come here will achieve a better understanding of the presidency and that the young people who come here will get a clearer understanding of what this nation tried to do in an eventful period of history.*

DIRECTIONS: The library and museum is on the campus of the University of Texas, 1 block from I 35. Exit I 35 at 26th Street and proceed westbound to Red River Street. Go left on Red River and continue to the library (Figure 123).

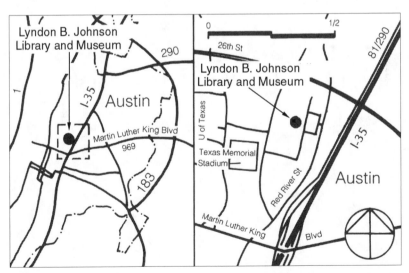

Figure 123. Location of the Lyndon B. Johnson Library and Museum, Austin, Texas.

PUBLIC USE: Season and hours: *Museum:* 9 AM-5 PM. Closed only on Christmas Day. *Library and Reading Room:* Monday-Friday, 9 AM-5 PM. Closed all federal holidays. **Gift shop. For people with disabilities:** Accessible.

FOR ADDITIONAL INFORMATION: Contact: Lyndon B. Johnson Library and Museum, 2313 Red River Street, Austin, Texas 78705, (512) 721-0200. **Web site:** *www.lbjlib.utexas.edu.* **Read:** (1) Robert A. Caro. 2002. *The Years of Lyndon Baines Johnson: Master of the Senate.*

Richard Milhous Nixon

Thirty-Seventh President — 1969–1974

Born January 9, 1913, Yorba Linda, California
Died April 22, 1994, New York, New York

> *We think that when someone near us dies, we think that when we lose an election, we think that when we suffer a defeat that all is ended. Not true. It is only a beginning, always.*

— Richard Nixon, 1974

> *I believe in the American Dream, because I have seen it come true in my own life.*

— Richard Nixon

Richard Nixon's dream of being President of the United States became a nightmare when he was forced to resign from the presidency, tainted by the scandal of Watergate, a national trauma that overshadowed the real accomplishments in domestic and world affairs by this unusual politician and statesman. Exemplifying the American dream, Nixon rose from hardship and political obscurity to earn the presidency — a journey made possible by his many positive attributes and punctuated by his sometimes pugnacious and unforgiving nature.

Richard Nixon entered politics following naval service in World War II and rose steadily in elected office. In 1952, presidential candidate Eisenhower picked United States Senator Nixon of California to be his running mate. During the ensuing campaign, Nixon was accused of having a secret expense account, but survived the attack and went on to be a dutiful and effective vice president for eight years. He was defeated in his own bid for the presidency in 1960, then lost a race for the governorship of California. Most political observers then considered Nixon a political dinosaur, but he rose from the ashes to win the Republican presidential nomination in 1968 and, subsequently, to defeat Hubert Humphrey and win the White House.

Richard Nixon's presidential successes include the initiation of a War on Cancer, the formation of the Environmental Protection Agency, the dramatic opening of relations with China, the ending of the Viet Nam War, and the negotiation of SALT I, the first nuclear arms limitation agreement concluded with the Soviet Union.

He was assured of greatness. Until Watergate.

I let the American people down. And I have to carry that burden with me for the rest of my life.

— Richard Nixon

The Richard Nixon Presidential Library and Museum

YORBA LINDA, CALIFORNIA

What you will see here, among other things, is a personal life — the influence of a strong family, of inspirational ministers. Of great teachers. You will see a political life — running for Congress, running for the Senate, running for governor, running for President three times. And you will see the life of a great nation — 77 years of it. A period in which we had unprecedented progress for the United States. And you will see great leaders — leaders who changed the world, who helped make the world what it is today.

— Richard Nixon at the dedication, 1989

282

Richard Nixon was born in 1913 in a small farmhouse that has been restored on the exact spot where it was built by his father. The house (Plate 13), part of a nine-acre complex of gardens and buildings that showcase President Nixon's personal life and political career, stands at one end of a distinctive formal "First Lady's Rose Garden," that features seasonal plantings around a 130-foot-long reflecting pool of quiet beauty. Completing the full circle of his life, President Nixon's final resting place is in the garden, only a few steps from the house in which he was born. Wife Pat lies at rest with him.

At the other end of the garden is a magnificent Main Gallery that houses archives, a motion-picture theater, an amphitheater, and 14,000 square feet of museum galleries that highlight Nixon's political career and legacy. Among the exhibits are "Road to the Presidency," which focuses on his early congressional and vice presidential campaigns, and "Structure of Peace," which tells of the president as an architect of peace and includes a piece of the Berlin Wall. "Pat Nixon: Ambassador of Goodwill" is a moving tribute to the First Lady, but perhaps the most dramatic presentation is "World Leaders," a Statuary Hall displaying ten life-size figures of international leaders of the Nixon era, including Charles DeGaulle, Winston Churchill, Konrad Adenauer, Anwar Sadat, and Golda Meir, among others. President Nixon said of them:

They are leaders who have made a difference. Not because they wished it, but because they willed it.

Through the magic of electronics, visitors to the Main Gallery are able to see and hear the former president describe his personal, governmental, and diplomatic experiences. Artifacts on display include a pistol given to the president by Elvis Presley, the telephone he used to talk with the Apollo 11 astronauts on the moon and other priceless gifts of state. A favorite exhibit is "Area 37: Richard Nixon and the History of America in Space" that features over fifty photographs, documents, and space-age artifacts including a moon rock, a full-size Apollo space suit, and the text of a speech that the president would have delivered if astronauts Armstrong and Aldrin had been stranded at Tranquility Base.

President Nixon's favorite room in the White House, the Lincoln Sitting Room, which he used for relaxation, speech writing, and contemplation, has been replicated. And every guest is fascinated by a comprehensive and honest Watergate display at which they are able to listen to White House tapes while viewing a photographic montage of the president's last day in office.

President Nixon once said:

I have insisted that the Nixon Library not be a monument to the career of one man, but a place where visitors and scholars will be able to recall the events of the time I served as President and to measure and weigh the policies my administration pursued. I hope it will be a vital place of discovery and rediscovery, of investigation and contemplation, of study, debate, and analysis.

The museum nearly doubled in size in 2004 with the dedication of the Katherine B. Loker Center on the south side of the reflecting pool which features 4100-square-feet of additional gallery space dedicated to original presentations and important traveling museum exhibitions. The centerpiece of the expansion, however, is a full-size replica of the East Room of the White House, the elegant room used for diplomatic receptions, state dinners, and other events. This East Room is an unforgettable location for conferences, lectures, weddings, and charity galas.

The most recent addition to the library is the presidential helicopter utilized by presidents Kennedy, Johnson, Nixon, and Ford that provides visitors with an opportunity to see how presidents traveled in luxury and security. President Nixon alone made more than 180 flights in this helicopter, including overseas trips with heads of state and other times with the First Family on jaunts to Camp David.

DIRECTIONS: Yorba Linda is a 45-minute drive from Los Angeles to the north, 90 minutes from San Diego to the south. From Los Angeles, drive southbound on I 5 to SR 91. Exit eastbound and proceed to SR 57. Exit northbound on SR 57 and proceed to Yorba Linda Boulevard. Exit eastbound on Yorba Linda Boulevard to the museum. From San Diego to the south, proceed north on I 5. Exit northbound on SR 57 and proceed to Yorba Linda Boulevard. Exit eastbound on Yorba Linda Boulevard to the museum (Figure 124).

PUBLIC USE: Season and hours: Monday-Saturday, 10 AM-5 PM; Sunday, 11 AM-5 PM. Closed Thanksgiving Day, Christmas Day. **Admission fee. Gift shop. For people with disabilities:** Accessible.

FOR ADDITIONAL INFORMATION: Contact: Richard Nixon Presidential Library and Museum, 18001 Yorba Linda Boulevard, Yorba Linda, California 92886, (714) 993-5075. **Web site:** *www.nixonlibrary.org.* **Read:** (1) Richard Nixon. 1978. *The Memoirs of Richard Nixon.* (2) Stephen E. Ambrose. 1987. *Nixon.* (3) Susan Spano. 1993. "Nixon Library: The Making of the Man."

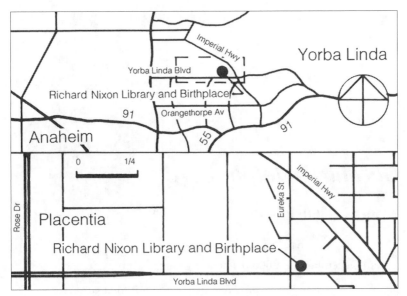

Figure 124. Location of the Richard Nixon Presidential Library and Museum in Yorba Linda, California.

Gerald Rudolph Ford

Thirty-Eighth President — 1974–1977

Born July 14, 1913, Omaha, Nebraska
Died December 26, 2006, Rancho Mirage, California

My fellow Americans, our long national nightmare is over.
Our Constitution works; our great republic is a government of
laws and not of men. Here the people rule.

— Gerald R. Ford, 1974

Gerald Ford holds a unique place in American history. He is the only person who replaced both a resigned vice president and resigned president.

Ford was born in 1913 as Leslie Lynch King, Jr., but the Kings divorced a year later and Mrs. King and her baby moved to Grand Rapids, Michigan, to live with her parents. The young mother remarried in 1917 and the lad was adopted by his stepfather and given his name, Gerald R. Ford. The young man was not aware of his early history until he was seventeen years old.

Ford's childhood was pleasant and uneventful. His biography includes a football scholarship to the University of Michigan, naval duty during World War II, and graduation from Yale Law School, after which he experienced the lumps and bumps of marriage, fatherhood, and the establishment of a law practice in Grand Rapids.

Attorney Ford gravitated to politics and was elected to congress in 1948. As he climbed the ladder of congressional seniority, leadership, and influence, he became known for his quiet, dogged, honest determination. Hence, he was a popular choice to replace disgraced Spiro T. Agnew as vice president in 1973. In that post, Ford served President Nixon with distinction.

The Watergate scandal and Nixon's dramatic resignation elevated Ford to the White House at a dark and difficult moment in America's political history. Wearied and disillusioned by the scandals and revelations of misdeeds at the highest levels of government, America welcomed the comfortable and honest Jerry Ford to the Oval Office.

Ford's administration, albeit honest to the core, was beset by an economic recession, Ford's controversial pardon of Richard Nixon, and questionable decisions on foreign policy. Ford barely edged out California Governor Ronald Reagan in a bruising battle for delegates at the Republican presidential convention in 1976, but it was a hollow victory, a precursor to Ford's narrow defeat by Jimmy Carter in the general election.

Gerald R. Ford Library

Ann Arbor, Michigan

Unlike other presidential libraries, the library and museum components of President Ford's are located in different cities. The library (Figure 125) is in Ann Arbor, on the north campus of Ford's alma mater, the University of Michigan. A handsome structure of brick and glass, the library was built by the university in 1981 with funds raised privately. The structure is staffed and operated by the National Archives and Records Administration under perpetual lease, without charge, from the University of Michigan.

Figure 125. Gerald R. Ford Library, Ann Arbor, Michigan. Photograph courtesy of Gerald R. Ford Library.

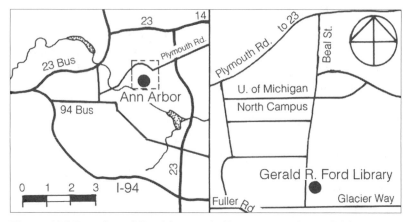

Figure 126. Location of Gerald R. Ford Library, Ann Arbor, Michigan.

The library is archival, intended as a place for collecting, preserving, and promoting public use of materials pertaining to the Ford presidency or related to public issues and events. The library houses nearly twenty million manuscript pages, many of which were moved from the White House to Ann Arbor in a convoy of nine tractor-trailer trucks immediately upon the inauguration of Jimmy Carter.

Special informative presentations and tours are available at the library to groups by advance reservation, and these may include a screening of the film *A Time to Heal,* produced by the Gerald R. Ford Foundation. In association with other organizations, the library hosts conferences and other events that focus on public policies, governmental affairs, and civic education.

DIRECTIONS: Ann Arbor is 35 miles west of Detroit. From Detroit, take I 94 westbound to US 23 and turn northbound to exit on Geddes Road that becomes Fuller Road as one passes Huron Parkway. Continue on Fuller and turn onto Beal Avenue (University of Michigan campus); continue 0.5 mile to the Library (Figure 126).

PUBLIC USE: Season and hours: Monday-Friday, 8:45 AM-4:45 PM. Closed federal holidays. **For people with disabilities:** Accessible.

FOR ADDITIONAL INFORMATION: Contact: Gerald R. Ford Library, 1000 Beal Avenue, Ann Arbor, Michigan 48109-2114, (734) 205-0555. **Web site:** *www.fordlibrarymuseum.gov.* **Read:** (1) Gerald R. Ford.1979. *A Time to Heal.* (2) Fritz Veit. 1987. *Presidential Libraries and Collections.*

Gerald R. Ford Presidential Museum

GRAND RAPIDS, MICHIGAN

The Gerald R. Ford Presidential Museum (Plate 14) is a handsome triangular building situated along the west bank of the Grand River, appropriately only a few blocks from downtown Grand Rapids, the city that Ford represented in congress for twenty-five years. The museum was dedicated in 1981 with presidents Reagan and Carter, the Prime Minister of Canada, and the President of Mexico among those in attendance. In 1997, the museum was rededicated following a five-million-dollar renovation.

Visits to the Ford Museum begin with a twenty-minute orientation film, *A Time to Heal: Gerald R. Ford's America*, and then progress to a 1970s gallery complete with disco scenes and a multi-screen tribute to the "Age of Aquarius." The Ford Museum doesn't just show history, it drops visitors into the middle of it. In the Watergate exhibit, one may see the actual burglar tools used in the break-in and a tape recorder from President Nixon's Oval Office.

The Ford Paint and Varnish Company, the business once owned by Gerald R. Ford, Sr., provides a fitting backdrop to an exhibit recalling the early life and career of the man from Grand Rapids, while a recreated Oval Office presents an audio journey, complete with a sound and light show, covering a typical day in the life of the president. The fall of Saigon is dramatized with the staircase from the American Embassy rooftop, up which fled the last evacuees when the city fell in April 1975. An interactive video projects global hot spots from the Ford years onto a world map, and a video featuring foreign policy aspects of Ford's presidency. People then enter the White House to tour eleven rooms via the latest holographic technology. Finally, patrons may participate in the 1976 Republican National Convention by giving a campaign speech with the aid of a teleprompter.

In 2003, the museum added a fascinating new exhibit, a faithful reproduction of the Cabinet Room in the White House. Visitors can sit around the Cabinet Room table and interact with video presentations of crises President Ford and his cabinet members confronted. The feature is unique among presidential libraries and the Ford Museum is justifiably proud of it.

President Ford expressed his pleasure with the museum:

The exhibits convey so much of the texture and substance of this nation's experiment in self-government.

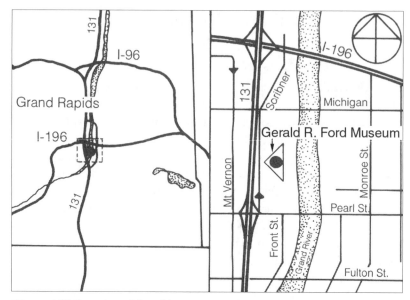

Figure 127. Location of Gerald R. Ford Presidential Museum, Grand Rapids, Michigan.

President Ford passed away in December, 2006. Following an impressive state funeral in Washington, DC, his body was transported to Grand Rapids for burial on a grassy knoll adjacent to the museum that bears his name.

DIRECTIONS: Grand Rapids is in western Michigan, 75 miles west of the state capital of Lansing. From Lansing, take I 96 to I 196; use the Ottawa Street Exit in Grand Rapids and continue southbound to Pearl Street. Turn right on Pearl Street and proceed 3 blocks to the Museum. From Kalamazoo in the south, take US 131 northbound, exiting at Pearl Street, turning right to the Museum on the left (Figure 127).

PUBLIC USE: Season and hours: 9 AM-5 PM. Closed Thanksgiving Day, Christmas Day, New Year's Day. **Admission fee. Museum shop. For people with disabilities:** Fully accessible.

FOR ADDITIONAL INFORMATION: Contact: Gerald R. Ford Presidential Museum, 303 Pearl Street NW, Grand Rapids, Michigan 49504, (616) 254-0400. **Web site:** *www.fordlibrarymuseum.gov.* **Read:** Bud Vestal. 1974. *Jerry Ford, Up Close: An Investigative Biography.*

James Earl Carter, Jr.

Thirty-Ninth President — 1977–1981

Born October 1, 1924, Plains, Georgia

My name is Jimmy Carter and I'm running for President.

— Jimmy Carter, accepting the Democratic nomination, 1976

It was a little shocking that someone we knew wanted to be President, but if Jimmy wanted to be President, why not?

— Maxine Reese, Plains resident

Buoyed by a firm belief in what experts considered to be a quixotic cause, Jimmy Carter came from nowhere to win the White House in 1976. He had no national political base, although he had been a successful governor of Georgia. What he did have was tremendous energy and absolute integrity, something the nation was seeking after the experience of Watergate.

Before Carter, only presidents Grover Cleveland and Woodrow Wilson had achieved the Oval Office with neither the benefit of previous civilian service in Washington nor the prestige of having been a commanding general. The lack of insider advantage and legislative experience proved difficult if not fatal for Carter. While he was indebted to no one, neither was congress indebted to him; his effectiveness and his popularity dwindled steadily throughout his term of office.

In spite of the difficulties, the Carter administration accomplished a number of significant goals. These included a comprehensive energy program overseen by a new Department of Energy; major educational programs led by a new Department of Education; deregulation in energy, transportation, communications, and finance; and important environmental protection legislation, including the Alaska Lands Act.

International affairs provided both the high and low points for the Carter presidency. Acting as peacemaker between the leaders of Egypt and Israel, Carter effected the Camp David Accords. His administration also accomplished the SALT II treaty with the Soviet Union, the Panama Canal treaties and the establishment of official diplomatic relations with the Peoples Republic of China. At the other end of the spectrum, Carter's presidency suffered irreparable damage when the revolutionary government of Iran seized the American embassy in Tehran and held its staff hostage for fourteen months. Jimmy Carter brought to the office business acumen, a deep religious belief, and a probity that was forged in American small-town values; none of these qualities, however, were strong enough to overcome the actions of militants half a world away.

Jimmy Carter National Historic Site

PLAINS, GEORGIA

The rural southern culture of Plains revolves around farming, church, and school — deep, lasting influences on the character of Jimmy Carter. The Jimmy Carter National Historic Site (Figure 128) was established to interpret his life and preserve the history and heritage of a small rural southern community.

Jimmy Carter was born in Wise Sanitarium — the first president born in a hospital — and grew up in the nearby community of Archery where his father was a farmer-businessman and his mother a registered nurse. He was educated in the Plains public schools and attended Georgia Southwestern College and the Georgia Institute of Technology, and, in 1946, received a degree in engineering from the United States Naval Academy. His subsequent naval tour included assignment to the staff of famed Admiral Hyman Rickover who was directing the development of the first nuclear submarine. During that assignment, Carter was promoted to lieutenant, senior grade.

When his father passed away in 1953, Lieutenant Carter resigned his commission and returned to Plains where he continued his father's fertilizer and farm equipment business. He became involved in civic affairs and served as chairman of the county school board and as first president of the Georgia Planning Association, posts that led to his election as a state senator and, later, Governor of Georgia. His accomplishments in state office eventually brought him national attention.

The Jimmy Carter National Historic Site includes the Plains railroad depot, along with Carter's boyhood home, school, and current residence, while the Plains Historic Preservation District covers most of the rest of the town. Plains High School, where Jimmy and Rosalynn Carter matriculated, has been converted to a visitor center and museum wherein the principal's office, a classroom, and three other rooms are filled with exhibits pertaining to Carter's local upbringing and presidency. The visitor center features a film narrated by Charles Kuralt — an overview of the Carter's relationship to Plains as told by friends and family. Since the Carter residence is not open to the public, the center also screens a sixteen-minute video tour of the house. The famous Seaboard Railroad Depot, the location of Carter's 1976 campaign headquarters, is open as a museum that concentrates on the 1976 presidential campaign. Jimmy Carter's Boyhood Farm Home (1928–1942), 2½ miles south of town, was recently restored to its exact appearance during the depression. The restoration includes the house, a reconstructed barn, a small farm store, a windmill, a blacksmith shop, a milk shed, a tenant house, a reconstructed privy, and seventeen acres of peanuts, cotton, corn, sugar cane, and a vegetable garden in season on what was once the family's 360-acre farm. Younger visitors are especially delighted with the four goats and a mule named Francis in residence. There are audio stations throughout the site at which visitors may listen to President Carter talk about growing up on the farm.

Self-guided driving and walking tours of Plains are popular. A tour of Plains, with its ordinary homes and friendly, industrious people, is a walk bearing witness to the true spirit and community of small-town America.

DIRECTIONS: From Atlanta, Georgia, take I 75 southbound to US 19; follow US 19 southwest to Americus and turn westbound on US 280 to Plains (Figure 129).

PUBLIC USE: Season and hours: *Plains High School Museum:* 9 AM-5 PM. *Plains Depot:* 9 AM-4:30 PM. *Jimmy Carter Boyhood Farm Home:* 10 AM-5 PM. Closed Thanksgiving Day, Christmas Day, New Year's Day. **Gift shop. For people with disabilities:** Accessible.

Figure 128. Carter Home, Jimmy Carter National Historic Site, Plains, Georgia. Photograph courtesy of National Park Service.

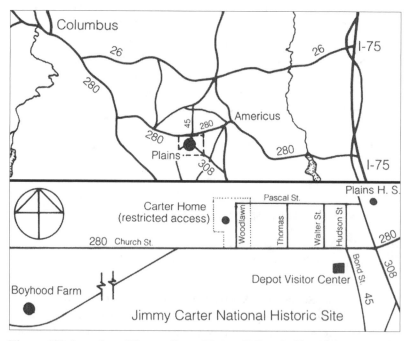

Figure 129. Location of Jimmy Carter National Historic Site, Plains, Georgia.

FOR ADDITIONAL INFORMATION: Contact: Jimmy Carter National Historic Site, 300 N. Bond Street, Plains, Georgia 31780, (229) 824-4104 *or* The Georgia Welcome Center, 1763 Highway 280 West, Plains, Georgia 31780, (229) 824-7477. **Web site:** *www.nps.gov/jica.* **Read:** (1) Jimmy Carter. 1988. *An Outdoor Journal.* (2) Jimmy Carter. 2001. *An Hour before Daylight, Memories of a Rural Boyhood.*

Carter Presidential Center

ATLANTA, GEORGIA

The Carter Presidential Center (Plate 14) is a sprawling complex of interconnected modern buildings set amidst beautifully landscaped rolling hills that afford breathtaking views of the Atlanta skyline. The Jimmy Carter Library and Museum, the most conspicuous part of the center, houses the presidential papers from the Carter administration, intended primarily for use by scholars.

A public museum within the library depicts the life and career of President Jimmy Carter. In addition to exhibits of personal and political items there are elaborate state gifts presented to the Carters during his term of office. Prominent among them are a portrait of George Washington woven into a Persian rug, a gift of the Shah of Iran; a gold evening-purse with diamonds, rubies, and green onyx, a gift from the Kingdom of Morocco; and an oil portrait of President Carter, presented by President Lopez Portillo of Mexico. "Town Hall" is an interactive video display by which modern technology allows visitors to ask President Carter questions ranging from "What did daughter Amy do all day in the White House?" to "Why did you choose Camp David as the site for the Sadat-Begin talks?" Also popular with visitors are a replicated Oval Office and a formal dinner setting from the White House.

In addition to the Jimmy Carter Library and Museum, the Carter Presidential Center houses the Carter Center, which promotes peace, democracy, and health world-wide.

DIRECTIONS: From the North or South, take I 75/85 to exit 248C, the Freedom Parkway, then follow the historical markers to the Carter Presidential Center. From the East or West, take I 20, exiting at Moreland Avenue northbound and follow Moreland Avenue northbound about 2 miles to Freedom

Parkway. Turn left on Freedom Parkway and follow the historical markers (Figure 130).

PUBLIC USE: Season and hours: *Museum:* Monday-Saturday, 9 AM-4:45 PM; Sunday, 12 M- 4:45 PM. *Library:* Monday-Friday, 8:45 AM-4:30 PM. Closed Thanksgiving Day, Christmas Day, New Year's Day. **Admission fee. Food service. Museum shop. For people with disabilities:** Accessible.

FOR ADDITIONAL INFORMATION: Contact: Carter Presidential Center, 441 Freedom Parkway, Atlanta, Georgia 30307, (404) 865-7100. **Web site:** *www.jimmycarterlibrary.gov.* **Read:** (1) Erwin C. Hargrove. 1988. *Jimmy Carter as President: Leadership and the Public Good.* (2) Donald B. Schewe. 1989. "Establishing a Presidential Library: The Jimmy Carter Experience."

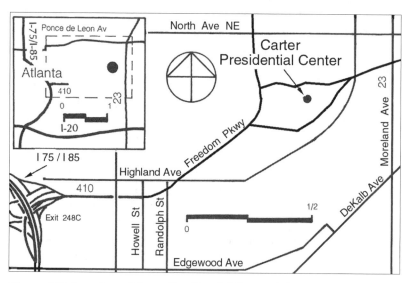

Figure 130. Location of Carter Presidential Center, Atlanta, Georgia.

Ronald Wilson Reagan

Fortieth President — 1981–1989

Born February 6, 1911, Tampico, Illinois
Died June 5, 2004, Los Angeles, California

> *When people tell me that I became President on January 20, 1981, I feel I have to correct them. You don't become President of the United States. You are given temporary custody of an institution called the presidency, which belongs to our people.*

— Ronald Reagan

Ronald Wilson Reagan was born in the homespun Illinois farming town of Tampico, the son of a strong mother and a charming rogue of a father who suffered from what Reagan later called the "Irish disease." The family moved frequently as the elder Reagan lost or changed employment, and eventually settled in Dixon, Illinois.

Reagan's boyhood in Dixon was pleasant, albeit uneventful, and his youthful exuberance and good looks made him very popular. Small-town influences and Mrs. Reagan's strength of character helped instill in Ronald solid Midwestern values. He developed an ebullient personality and charming presence that easily translated into success on radio, television, and the silver screen. It was not a great leap, then, for Reagan to transfer his winning personality to the political arena, especially in the age of television and instant communication. As president, Ronald Reagan led the nation into an era of good feeling and prosperity.

Although Reagan was elected president as a conservative Republican, his political roots were those of a New Deal Democrat and his political hero was Franklin D. Roosevelt. As early as 1952, Reagan expressed reservations about the direction of the Democratic Party, but he was reluctant to switch his affiliation due to a corporate commitment to General Electric and union activities on behalf of the Screen Actors Guild. After fulfilling those commitments, however, he switched parties in 1962. Some observers speculated that the impetus to switch was Reagan's desire to run for office — with the Democratic Party controlled by the Kennedys, the chances for immediate success lay with the Republicans. To the critics, Nancy Reagan responded, "Remember when Churchill left the Liberal Party to join the Conservatives? He said, 'Some men change their party for the sake of their principles; others their principles for the sake of the party.' Ronnie feels that way about becoming a Republican."

Reagan had little else in common with Churchill, but he did share some dramatic coincidences with his hero, Franklin Roosevelt. Without question, they were two of the most persuasive American orators of the twentieth century. Both survived assassination attempts, each was an eternal optimist and each led the United States with dignity and enthusiasm through a period of economic ennui and political misgivings. One, a privileged scion of wealth, led the nation to victory against the forces of fascism. The other, a product of the Great Depression, led the country when communism fell, the final victory in what was known as the Cold War. The two leaders differed in background and political philosophy, yet both were forceful champions for change — their lives, their similarities, and especially their differences symbolized the glory of our form of free and representative government.

Although scandal touched the Reagan presidency, his personal charisma enabled him to retain the confidence and admiration of most of the American people.

Ronald Reagan Birthplace

TAMPICO, ILLINOIS

John Reagan has been calling thirty-seven inches a yard and giving seventeen ounces for a pound this week at Pitney's store, he has been feeling so jubilant over the arrival of a ten pound boy Monday.

— *The Tampico Tornado*, February 10, 1911

Figure 131. Ronald Reagan Birthplace, Tampico, Illinois. Photograph by William G. Clotworthy.

Ronald Reagan was born in the cramped bedroom of a walk-up apartment (Figure 131) situated above a bakery on the main street of Tampico, a tiny Midwestern farming community. The apartment consisted of six small but comfortable rooms. The Reagans lived in the apartment for six years; they moved to a house when Ronald was four months old and to at least one other location in Tampico before they moved to Dixon, Illinois, in 1920.

The birthplace apartment has been restored to approximate its 1911 appearance and includes period furnishings and pictures. The lower floor, which once housed the bakery, has been reconstructed as an early 1900s bank, with the original fixtures and vault that were once utilized there. It also contains a gift shop and small museum that features a display of original Reagan movie posters.

DIRECTIONS: Tampico is 100 miles west of Chicago, 15 miles south of I 88. From I 88, take the Sterling Exit and proceed southbound on SR 40 to SR 172, then follow the historical markers to Tampico (Figure 132).

PUBLIC USE: Season and hours: April-October 31, Monday-Saturday, 10 AM-4 PM; Sunday, 1 PM-4 PM. February-March, Saturday, 10 AM-4 PM; Sunday, 1 PM-4 PM. Closed November-January (except by appointment),

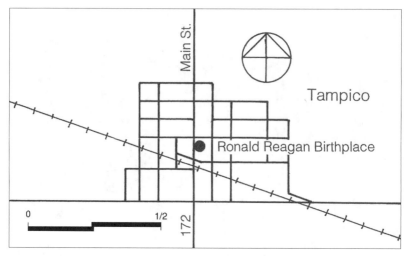

Figure 132. Location of Ronald Reagan Birthplace, Tampico, Illinois.

Easter Sunday, Mother's Day. **Gift shop. For people with disabilities:** *Gift shop and Bank:* Accessible. *Apartment:* Not accessible.

FOR ADDITIONAL INFORMATION: Contact: Ronald Reagan Birthplace, 111 South Main Street, Box 344, Tampico, Illinois 61283, (815) 438-2130 *or* (815) 438-7581. **Web site:** *www.tampicohistoricalsociety.citymax.com/ R_reagan_birthplace_museum.html.* **Read:** Lou Cannon. 1991. *President Reagan: The Role of a Lifetime.*

Ronald Reagan Boyhood Home

Dixon, Illinois

The Reagans moved to Dixon in 1920 when Ronald was nine; he spent important formative years in the lively community, which afforded plenty of activities devoted to the development of young bodies, minds, and spirits. The city library, the First Christian Church, and the YMCA all had programs designed to advance the growth of healthy, solid values.

The Reagan home (Plate 15) was a modest, two-story frame building of seven rooms — middle-class and comfortable. Ronald and his older brother,

Neil, shared one upstairs bedroom and their parents another. The third was a sewing room for Mrs. Reagan, who took in sewing to supplement income. Downstairs was a parlor, a sitting room, and a dining room, in addition to a kitchen with its Jewel gas stove and top-loading icebox. Outside was a barn where the boys raised rabbits and a large vegetable garden.

Shortly after Reagan's nomination for president in 1980, a local letter carrier noticed that the old Reagan house was for sale. He rushed to the real estate office and made a $250 down payment, an act that initiated a community fundraising drive to preserve the house. The movement was coordinated by the Ronald Reagan Home Preservation Foundation, a nonprofit organization of over one hundred volunteer citizens, many of whom continue to serve as tour guides, interpreters, and maintenance personnel.

The foundation acquired the house next door to the Reagan home and converted it into a visitor center that provides a tour of the home, souvenir ticket, ten-minute video, and a Ronald Reagan life timeline of photos, quotes, and facts.

DIRECTIONS: Dixon is 100 miles west of Chicago, just off I 80. Take the Dixon exit and follow the historical markers to the house (Figure 133).

PUBLIC USE: Season and hours: March, Saturday, 10 AM-4 PM; Sunday, 1 PM-4 PM. April-October, Monday-Saturday, 10 AM-4 PM; Sunday, 1 PM-4 PM. Closed November-February. **Gift shop. For people with disabilities:** The visitor center, next door to the house, is accessible; the house is not.

FOR ADDITIONAL INFORMATION: Contact: Ronald Reagan Boyhood Home, 816 South Hennepin Avenue, Dixon, Illinois 61021, (815) 288-5176. **Web site:** *www.ronaldreaganhome.com.* **Read:** (1) Anne Edwards. 1987. *Early Reagan.* (2) Norman E. Wymbs. 1987. *A Place to Go Back To: Ronald Reagan in Dixon, Illinois.*

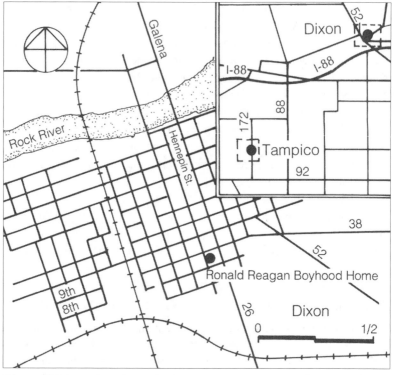

Figure 133. Location of Ronald Reagan Boyhood Home, Dixon, Illinois.

The Ronald Reagan Trail

In 1999, the Illinois General Assembly officially recognized the Ronald Reagan Trail, a self-guided driving tour that celebrates the home-town values and heritage of Ronald Reagan. To the north are his birthplace in Tampico and boyhood home in Dixon. The trail meanders southward to Eureka where he attended Eureka College. In between are cities and towns with Reagan ties: Galesburg and Monmouth where he attended elementary school before the family moved on to Henry, Walnut, Chillicothe, Dixon, and others. Tampico, Dixon, and Eureka are included in this book as major sources of information about Reagan. The others have Reagan displays as remembrances of their relationship with our fortieth president.

For Additional Information: Contact: Ronald Reagan Trail, 509 University Street, Henry, Illinois, (309) 364-3289. **Web site***: www.ronaldreagantrail.net.*

Ronald Reagan Presidential Library and Museum

SIMI VALLEY, CALIFORNIA

This land, its people, the dreams that unfold here and the freedom to bring it all together . . . . these are what makes America soar . . . up where you can see hope billowing in those freedom winds.

— Ronald Reagan

The Ronald Reagan Presidential Library and Museum (Figure 134), a Spanish mission-style complex of 153,000 square feet, stands high in the rugged mountains of southern California and commands a spectacular sweeping view of the surrounding valleys and foothills. Reagan's was the first presidential library opened under the terms of the Presidential Records Act, legislation that differentiated between presidential records, which are public property, and presidential papers, which are the personal property of the president. As is typical of all presidential libraries, this library houses all of the papers and other records related to President Reagan's presidency and makes these documents available to scholars.

A public exhibit area includes gifts from world leaders, and sequential displays recount President Reagan's personal and political history. A replicated Oval Office, accurate to the pictures on the walls and knickknacks on the president's desk, always intrigues visitors as does a section of the Berlin Wall that was presented to President Reagan by the people of Germany in 1990. Its commemorative plaque reads, ". . . for his unwavering dedication to humanitarianism and freedom over communism throughout his presidency."

The Berlin Wall section is displayed on the outside rear verandah where visitors are able to visit the simple but moving Reagan memorial gravesite with its expansive view of the mountains and valleys the president so loved. It is a fitting and proper resting place.

President Reagan often stated that he hoped one day to share Air Force One with the American people, a wish that came true when the Air Force One Pavilion opened for public visitation in 2005. The centerpiece of the pavilion is Air Force One (72-27000), the Boeing 707 used by President Reagan during his eight years in office. After almost twenty years of service for seven presidents, the 707 was retired in 2001 and flown to southern California where it was stored until the pavilion at the Reagan Library was completed.

The huge plane is displayed in a dramatic multi-storied, glass-enclosed domed pavilion, raised one-story above the floor on specially designed pedestals, giving the impression of actual flight. Visitors are raised to the plane by stairway or elevator to be treated to a tour of the craft's interior that includes a look at the president and first lady's private cabins, his office, galleys, cockpit, staff and press quarters, and the communications center.

The ground floor of the pavilion displays the helicopter used by President Johnson and several automobiles, including President Reagan's limousine, arranged in the form of a presidential motorcade. It also contains the Ronald Reagan Pub snack shop, the actual pub that President Reagan visited in Ballyporeen, Ireland, in June of 1984. The entire pub was shipped to the Library in July of 2004.

The upper floor, actually a balcony with a 270-degree view, features a montage of President Reagan's eight years of travel in the United States and abroad.

Figure 134. Ronald Reagan Presidential Library and Museum, Simi Valley, California. Photograph by Donald Clotworthy.

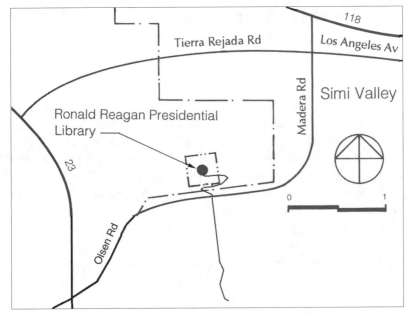

Figure 135. Location of Ronald Reagan Presidential Library and Museum, Simi Valley, California.

DIRECTIONS: From US 101 (Ventura Freeway), turn northbound onto SR 23. Exit at Olsen Road and proceed northbound for 2 miles to Presidential Drive and the entrance to the library. From Los Angeles, take I 405 (San Diego Freeway) northbound to SR 118 West. Exit at Madera Road southbound. Turn right on Madera Road and proceed 3 miles to Presidential Drive (Figure 135).

PUBLIC USE: Season and hours: 10 AM-5 PM. Closed Thanksgiving Day, Christmas Day, New Year's Day. **Admission fee. Gift shop. Food service:** There are two restaurants: Reagan's Country Café and the Ronald Reagan Pub snack shop. **For people with disabilities:** Fully accessible.

FOR ADDITIONAL INFORMATION: Contact: Ronald Reagan Presidential Library and Museum, 40 Presidential Drive, Simi Valley, California 93065, 1-800- 410-8354. **Web site:** *www.reaganlibrary.com.* **Read:** (1) Garry Wills. 1987. *Reagan's America: Innocents at Home.* (2) Ronald Reagan. 1990. *An American Life.*

The Ronald Reagan Museum at Eureka College

EUREKA, ILLINOIS

A graduate of Eureka College, class of 1932, Ronald "Dutch" Reagan majored in economics and sociology although he was once quoted to have said that he had been accused of majoring in extracurricular activities. Certainly he was a campus leader, active in sports, drama, and campus life. His humble beginnings necessitated financing his education and it is to Eureka's credit that they took a chance on the young man by granting a scholarship and finding him a campus job to pay for his meals.

He remained close to Eureka throughout his life and credited his experience there in a commencement address in 1992: "We took with us from Eureka College the strength of a spirit of fellowship, willingness to work together for common goals, and a deep faith in the word of God." Graduating in the early years of the Great Depression, those values helped propel him to a lifetime of leadership.

Eureka College has honored its most famous alumnus with the Ronald Reagan Museum at Eureka College, housed in the Donald B. Cerf Center. The

Figure 136. Peace Garden, Ronald Reagan Museum at Eureka College, Eureka, Illinois. Photograph courtesy of Eureka College Archives.

museum houses a collection of over 5,000 artifacts and photographs from his life in Dixon and at Eureka College, his Hollywood career, his terms as Governor of California and eight years as president. These include such charming items as a 1932 Eureka College yearbook, his college diploma, and many letters and speeches in his own handwriting. Altogether, the documents and other artifacts make up the largest collection of Reagan memorabilia outside the Ronald Reagan Presidential Library in Simi Valley, California.

On the museum grounds is the Ronald Reagan Peace Garden (Figure 136), dedicated on May 9, 2000, the eighteenth anniversary of President Reagan's address at Eureka in which he first proposed the START initiative. The intimate and restful garden is glorified with a bust of the late president crafted by noted sculptor Lonnie Stewart and further commemorated by a section of the Berlin Wall, presented to Eureka College by the Federated Republic of Germany.

DIRECTIONS: From I 74, eastbound or westbound, take Exit 112 (SR 117). Drive north to College Street (just past Reagan Drive) in Eureka and turn right into the campus. Parking for the museum is located on the west side of Burgess Street, between College Street and Reagan Drive (Figure 137).

PUBLIC USE: Season and hours: August 15-May 15, Monday-Friday, 9 AM-8 PM; Saturday, 10 AM-6 PM; Sunday 12 M-8 PM. May 15- August 15, Monday-Friday, 8 AM-4 PM. Open select Saturdays and Sundays. Closed holidays. **For people with disabilities:** Accessible.

FOR ADDITIONAL INFORMATION: Contact: Eureka College, 300 E. College Street, Eureka, Illinois 61530, (309) 467-6407. **Web site:** *http:// reagan.eureka.edu.*

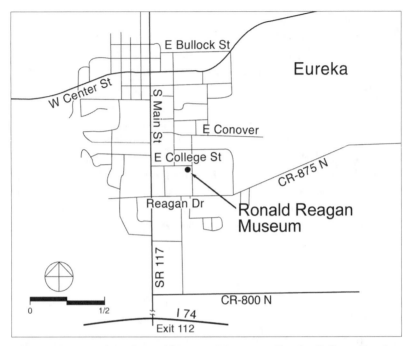

Figure 137. Location of Ronald Reagan Museum at Eureka College, Eureka, Illinois.

George Herbert Walker Bush

Forty-First President — 1989–1993

Born June 12, 1924, Milton, Massachusetts

America is never wholly herself unless she is engaged in high moral principle. We have such a purpose today. It is to make kinder the face of the nation and gentler the face of the world.

— George Bush, Inaugural address

The public career of George Bush brings to mind the tradition of the nation's first leaders, those men of substance and wealth who believed in public service as a way of life and accepted responsibility to their fellow citizens as a matter of natural course. George Bush, scion of an aristocratic New England family, was educated at Phillips Andover Academy and Yale University, where he earned Phi Beta Kappa honors in economics. His college career was interrupted by service in World War II, wherein he served as the Navy's youngest commissioned pilot and flew fifty-eight combat missions in the Pacific Theater.

After the war, he eschewed his father's investment banking business and opted to enter the risk-filled oil business in Texas. He briefly represented a Texas district in congress, but was unsuccessful in two campaigns for election to the United States Senate. His solid Republican credentials, however, earned him an appointment as Ambassador to the United Nations, and he was later named Chairman of the Republican National Committee. He also served as head of the United States liaison office in China and as Director of the Central Intelligence Agency.

In 1980, Bush contested Ronald Reagan for the Republican presidential nomination but was defeated in the primary contest. He accepted Reagan's offer of the vice presidency, a post he held for eight years with ability and dedication. He ran for president in 1988 and handily defeated Democratic challenger Michael Dukakis.

The Bush presidency was marked by wild swings of success and failure. In 1990, Bush promulgated Operation Desert Storm, a military operation to rescue the Kingdom of Kuwait from subjugation by its neighbor, Iraq. Bush cobbled together an international coalition under the aegis of the United States. The military operation was brilliantly conceived and fought, an unqualified diplomatic and military success.

Bush's domestic policies, on the other hand, were unsuccessful. The nation was in a deep recession and seemed unable to recover from its economic decline. The president attempted to persuade the voters that his policies were sound, but he was defeated for reelection by Bill Clinton in 1992.

In 2001, George Bush joined John Adams as the only two presidents whose sons have also become President of the United States.

George Bush Presidential Library and Museum

COLLEGE STATION, TEXAS

The George Bush Presidential Library and Museum complex (Plate 15), located on the campus of Texas A&M University, is one of the twelve presidential libraries administered by the National Archives and Records Administration and the third located on a college campus. As with other such presidential facilities, it consists of a library/archives building filled with millions of papers and documents, hundreds of hours of video footage, and thousands of rolls of film pertaining to George Bush's vice presidential and presidential years. The archives are restricted to use by archivists and researchers.

The museum building, which is open to the public, is a magnificent 21,000-square-foot edifice where visitors enter a majestic fifty-foot-high rotunda constructed of Texas limestone, marble, and granite. After viewing a brief orientation film on the life and times of the former president, a self-guided tour takes visitors past exhibits that feature many facets and experiences of Bush's life and career, including The Family, The Man, World War II, Yale and Marriage, Public Service, Vice Presidential and Presidential Years, Cold War/Berlin Wall, Domestic Policy, Barbara Bush, Head of State Gifts, George Bush Outdoorsman, Camp David Office, Operation Desert Storm, Air Force One, and Gifts from the People. The most popular exhibits are precise replicas of the president's offices at Camp David and aboard Air Force One. An Avenger Torpedo Bomber hanging from the ceiling is the type flown by Ensign George Bush in World War II. It and a slab of the Berlin Wall are moving reminders of the scope of service performed by the devoted public servant honored here.

In the spring of 2002, the museum dedicated the Barbara Bush Botanical Garden, a four-acre panoply of antique roses located to the rear of the museum. Over the years, the garden will be expanded to more than one hundred acres of colorful flowers indigenous to the area.

The core exhibits of the George Bush Presidential Library and Museum recently have been renovated. All of the original technology in the museum was dated and has now been brought into line with contemporary technologies such as flat panel LCD displays and smaller content delivery systems. Many of the most popular exhibits remain — the TBM Avenger airplane, the section of the Berlin Wall, and the Gulf War exhibit. The Air Force One office has been replaced by a replica of the White House situation room that features an interactive presentation on the decisions leading up to the first Gulf War. The museum also added a replica of the Oval Office where visitors can actually sit in "the seat of power."

DIRECTIONS: College Station is in southeastern Texas about 80 miles northwest of Houston. From Houston, take I 45 northbound to Conroe and turn left on SR 105 to Navasota, turning right on SR 6 to Bryan/College Station (Business 6). At the second light (FM 2818), turn left and proceed 4 miles to George Bush Drive. Turn right and proceed 0.25 mile to the entrance on the left. From Dallas, take I 45 southbound to Madisonville, then SR 21 westbound to College Station. Continue to FM 2818 and turn left. Proceed 6 miles to George Bush Drive and turn left for 0.25 mile to the entrance on the left (Figure 138).

PUBLIC USE: Season and hours: Monday-Saturday, 9:30 AM-5 PM; Sunday, 12 M-5 PM. Closed Thanksgiving Day, Christmas Day, New Year's Day. **Admission fee. Gift shop. For people with disabilities:** Fully accessible, with wheelchairs available.

FOR ADDITIONAL INFORMATION: Contact: George Bush Presidential Library and Museum, 1000 George Bush Drive West, College Station, Texas 77845, (979) 691-4000. **Web site:** *http://bushlibrary.tamu.edu.* **Read:** (1) Nicholas King. 1980. *George Bush: A Biography.* (2) Fitzhugh Green. 1989. *George Bush: An Intimate Portrait.*

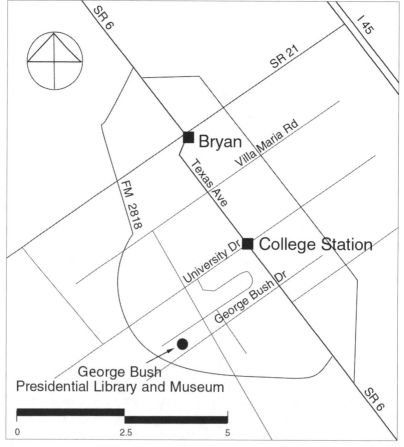

Figure 138. Location of George Bush Presidential Library and Museum, College Station, Texas.

William Jefferson Clinton

Forty-Second President — 1993–2001

Born August 19, 1946, Hope, Arkansas

All I am or ever will be came from Hope.

— Bill Clinton

Bill Clinton was born in the small town of Hope, Arkansas, as William Jefferson Blythe, III, three months after his father was killed in an automobile accident. Bill and his mother, Virginia Cassidy Blythe, lived with her parents, Eldridge and Edith Cassidy, until Mrs. Blythe married Roger Clinton in 1950.

In 1953, when Bill was seven, the Clintons moved to Hot Springs, Arkansas, hoping for a more secure financial situation, but family life was not easy. Stepfather Roger loved his family, but was a cyclic alcoholic and subject to frequent rages. Through the family turmoil, Bill became exceptionally responsible at school, church, and home. Half-brother Roger, born in 1956, once remarked, "My brother took over the leadership role in our family when he was just a kid." During this time Bill's last name was changed to Clinton so that he and his younger half-brother would have the same surname.

Adversity powered ambition, and Bill Clinton progressed to an exemplary career. He received a Bachelor's degree from Georgetown University, then studied at Oxford University as a Rhodes Scholar from 1968 to 1970 before earning a law degree from Yale University. He returned home to teach at the University of Arkansas Law School, to initiate a private law practice in Little Rock, and to run for public office. In his first attempt to win a congressional post, he was defeated by a popular sitting congressman, but two years later he was elected Arkansas's Attorney General, then elected Governor in 1978. At thirty-four he lost his re-election bid, which earned him the dubious distinction of being the youngest ex-governor in American history. "The people sent me a message," he later remarked, "and I learned my lesson."

He learned it well. In 1982, the still-youthful Clinton swept back into the Little Rock statehouse where he served five terms. His successes in office included balanced budgets, a scandal-free and efficient administration, and an innovative, albeit controversial, program to upgrade the state's weak educational system.

To the surprise of many political experts, Clinton eschewed an attempt for the presidency in 1988, but ran an almost perfect primary campaign four years later to win the Democratic nomination. He went on to defeat Republican George Bush and Independent Ross Perot in a rancorous general election.

President Bill Clinton, who reigned over a strong economy during a generally peaceful period, was assured a place of historical greatness until the fallout from personal peccadilloes stained his presidency. A concurrent investigation into alleged malfeasance while Governor of Arkansas resulted in impeachment charges against the president for perjury and obstruction of justice. After more than a year of national agony, the United States Senate found him not guilty of "high crimes and misdemeanors," but the fact that he was the first elected president to be impeached sullied his character and reputation.

President Bill Clinton's 1st Home Museum

Hope, Arkansas

I owe so much to my childhood in Hope.

— Bill Clinton

Hope, a vibrant small town with an economy based on the agriculture that surrounded it, was once — and still is — fondly known as the "home of the world's largest watermelons." Now, however, it also is renowned as the birthplace and childhood home of President Bill Clinton. In response to its new-found popularity, a nonprofit foundation was formed with the purpose of purchasing, restoring, and renovating the house where little William Jefferson

Blythe had lived with his widowed mother and grandparents for five years. This 2½-story American foursquare house (Figure 139) was acquired in 1994 by the Clinton Birthplace Foundation, restored, and placed on the National Register of Historic Places in 1996 — at which time it was recognized as:

> *The single property most significantly and exclusively associated with Clinton's humble beginnings, the inner strength he learned from his mother and the dedication to purpose that has sustained him throughout his distinguished political career.*

When the Home Museum was dedicated in 1997, President Clinton remarked:

> *I still remember that my grandfather was the first person who taught me by his example to treat all people, without regard to their race, the same. And also, without regard to their income, because he gave food to people without regard to whether they had a dime in their pockets.*

A separate Museum Exhibit Center located adjacent to the home contains extensive photographic exhibits of President Clinton's life, from his birth in Hope to his tenure in the White House. Elsewhere in Hope are a number of other places associated with President Clinton's early years.

In the tradition of restored presidential homes, Bill Clinton's is of historic importance. Hope should be proud of the civic effort expended in restoring the home in order to inform the public about the childhood of President Clinton and the personality of a progressively traditional southern town.

DIRECTIONS: Exit I 30 at Exit 30 southbound onto SR 278 B (Hervey Street), travel 1.4 miles to the museum, located immediately south of the railroad underpass. Parking and entrance are behind the museum off of 2nd Street (Figure 140).

PUBLIC USE: Season and hours: Monday-Saturday, 9:30 AM-5:30 PM. **Admission fee. Gift shop. For people with disabilities:** The first floor of the house and the museum exhibit are accessible.

FOR ADDITIONAL INFORMATION: Contact: Clinton Birthplace Foundation, Inc., Box 1925, Hope, Arkansas 71801-1925, (870) 777-4455. *clintonbirthplace@sbcglobal.net.* **Web site:** *www.clintonbirthplace.com.* **Read:** (1) Virginia Cassidy Clinton Kelley, 1994: *Leading with My Heart.* (2) Bill Clinton, 2004. *My Life.*

Figure 139. President Bill Clinton's 1st Home Museum, Hope, Arkansas. Wanda J. Powell, official Clinton Birthplace photographer; courtesy of The Clinton Birthplace Foundation.

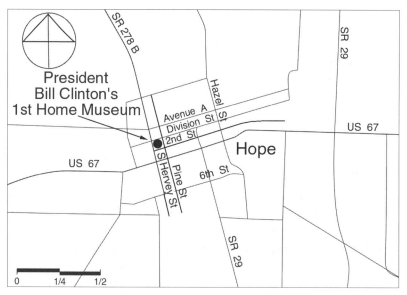

Figure 140. Location of President Bill Clinton's 1st Home Museum, Hope, Arkansas.

Clinton House Museum

FAYETTEVILLE, ARKANSAS

In the mid-1970s, unmarried and living separately, Bill Clinton and Hillary Rodham were teaching at the law school of the University of Arkansas in Fayetteville. Driving around town, Hillary had evinced interest in a modest house near the campus, which Bill bought secretly and said, "Remember the house you liked so much? Well, I just bought it and now you have to marry me because I can't live there alone." On October 11, 1975, they married in the living room of that house before a gathering of family and close friends.

The Clinton home, now owned by the University and managed by the City of Fayetteville, opened for public visitation in 2005. (Figure 141). It is an unpretentious, one-bedroom, 1800-square-foot house epitomizing "cozy,"

Figure 141. Clinton House Museum, Fayetteville, Arkansas. Photograph courtesy of Clinton House Museum.

perfect for a young couple embarking on their professional careers in law and politics. The building has a warm, dark stone façade and the inside contains elements such as an alcove fireplace and a small breakfast nook.

As a museum, the house contains photographs, displays, and memorabilia from Bill Clinton's early political career, numerous mementos of his eight years as president, and "on-loan" pieces from the official Clinton Presidential Library collection. By a large window in the living room is a replica of Hillary's wedding dress and a nearby display case contains pictures of the wedding and the Clintons' marriage license. All of the rooms are representative of a young couple starting out in life without much furniture. In the living room, for example, they had only a couple of canvas director's chairs and little else.

The bedroom is utilized as a media room, where fascinating commercials Bill Clinton used during his congressional and attorney general campaigns in the 1970s are shown.

DIRECTIONS: From I 540 northbound, take Exit 62 (Arkansas SR 60/180) eastbound to Arkansas State Route 112 northbound. After going ¼ mile on SR 112, turn right onto Leroy Pond Drive and go another ¼ mile until it dead ends at California Drive. Turn left onto California and proceed to #930 (Figure 142).

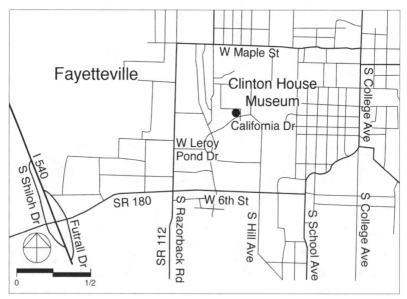

Figure 142. Location of Clinton House Museum, Fayetteville, Arkansas.

PUBLIC USE: Season and hours: Monday-Saturday, 8:30 AM-4:30 PM. **Admission fee. Gift shop. For people with disabilities:** Not accessible.

FOR ADDITIONAL INFORMATION: Contact: Museum Director, Clinton House Museum, 930 California Drive, Fayetteville, Arkansas 72701, (877) BIL-NHIL (245-6445). **Web site:** *www.clintonhousemuseum.com.* **Read:** (1) Roger Morris. 1996. *Partners in Power: The Clintons and Their America.* (2) Christopher Andersen. 1999. *Bill and Hillary: The Marriage.*

The Clinton Presidential Center

LITTLE ROCK, ARKANSAS

On November 18, 2004, former President Bill Clinton joined President George W. Bush and former presidents George H. W. Bush and Jimmy Carter in ceremonies to dedicate the William J. Clinton Presidential Center and Park in Little Rock, Arkansas (Plate 16).

The $165-million complex, built on a thirty-acre riverfront tract, is one phase of a significant redevelopment and revitalization program in downtown Little Rock. The centerpiece is the striking, unusual, state-of-the-art Clinton Library and Museum, its form a glass bridge that symbolizes President Clinton's theme of "Building a Bridge to the Twenty-First Century."

As *Newsweek* described the building, "Like Clinton himself, the library is larger than life: bold and dramatic. Yet, as he wanted, it is also people-friendly and light. It campaigns hard for your vote of 'Wow!' The long glass box cantilevers ninety feet to the edge of the Arkansas River . . . its structure — the supports that slice through the building — is honestly revealed, and the details are crisp and elegant. An outer glass screen shades the main glass wall, creating an airy verandah in the best Southern tradition. The inside is filled with light and has expansive views of the river and the city."

The Library/Museum is the largest in size (20,000 square feet) of the twelve libraries in the Presidential Library System operated by the National Archives and Records Administration. The holdings consist of 76.8 million pages of paper documents, 1.85 million photographs and over 75,000 museum artifacts. Presidential libraries are both repositories of documents that serve scholars and museums that feature exhibits, conduct special events and sponsor educational programs. The Clinton Museum contains twenty-three thematic alcoves with permanent and changing exhibits that utilize documents, photographs, videos, and interactive stations examining the Clinton administration and showcasing life in the White House. There are replicas of the Oval Office and the Cabinet Room, a multi-purpose Great Hall that seats 350 theatre-style, classrooms, and a smaller eighty-seat theater.

Surrounding the main building is an impressive park, its centerpiece building the University of Arkansas Clinton School of Public Service, the only university in the nation that offers a Master of Public Service (MPS) degree. It is located in a restored passenger train depot. The park also contains a pavilion, a grass amphitheater, and walking/bicycle trails. Future plans call for the 1899 railroad bridge that crosses the Arkansas River to be converted to a pedestrian walkway.

DIRECTIONS: Take Exit 141A off I 30 in downtown Little Rock's River Market district. The Exit splits. Loop to the right down to the stop sign on 2nd

Figure 143. Location of Clinton Presidential Center, Little Rock, Arkansas.

Street. Turn left, then left again on Ferry Street to another stop sign. Turn right on President Clinton Avenue and proceed to the Clinton Presidential Center (Figure 143).

PUBLIC USE: Season and hours: Monday-Saturday, 9 AM-5 PM; Sunday, 1 PM-5 PM. Closed Thanksgiving Day, Christmas Day, New Year's Day. **Admission fee. Museum shop:** Located in a separate building across I 30 at 610 President Clinton Avenue. **Food service**: On-site full-service indoor-outdoor café. **For people with disabilities**: Accessible.

FOR ADDITIONAL INFORMATION: Contact: The Clinton Presidential Center, 1200 President Clinton Avenue, Little Rock, Arkansas 72201, (501) 374-4242. **Web site**: *www.clintonfoundation.org* and *www.clintonschool.uasys.edu.*

George Walker Bush

Forty-Third President — 2001–

Born July 6, 1946, New Haven, Connecticut

George W. Bush was born in New Haven, Connecticut, where his father was completing his education at Yale University. After graduation, the elder Bush took a job in the oil business and moved his family to Odessa, Texas, and then on to a series of other oil towns in Texas and California before settling permanently in Midland, Texas. George W. Bush described Midland as "a town of embedded values with a heavy dose of individualism and fairly healthy disrespect for government." When asked by a reporter whether his own skepticism about the role of government was a product of conservative Midland attitudes, he paused before saying, "I think there's a parallel there, I do." After young George graduated from Midland schools, he matriculated at Andover, Yale, and the Harvard Business School.

He followed in his father's footsteps and returned to Texas in the early 1970s as an independent oil man. The younger Bush became an entrepreneur, and eventually married a quiet but strong-willed librarian named Laura Welch. Moving on to a life in politics, George successfully ran for Governor of Texas and while in his second term, ran for the presidency.

In January, 2001, George W. Bush joined John Quincy Adams as only the second president to follow his father into the presidency. But there are other parallels to these two men. Each was involved in a disputed election, each was the scion of a distinguished political family that believed in public service as an inherent privilege and right, and the presidency of each followed a period of national prosperity. However, the similarities end when it comes to personality. John Quincy Adams was brilliant but dour, a rather unfriendly man who did not suffer fools gladly. George W. Bush, on the other hand, is a gregarious and ebullient Texan with a positive attitude who promised to bring a spirit of cooperation and unity to Washington.

President George W. Bush is a delegator who runs the White House like a well-managed business enterprise. Seriously tested after only nine months in office by the terrorist attacks in New York and Virginia, Bush responded to the threat decisively and, in doing so, clearly demonstrated his leadership abilities. His dream for America is contained somewhere in the view of childhood friend Joe O'Neill of Midland:

> *I think his political philosophy comes completely from the philosophy of the independent oil man. His homage to his parents, his respect for his elders, his respect for tradition, his belief in religion, his opposition to abortion — that's the philosophy he grew up with here.*

In 2004, President Bush was reelected, although the campaign was bitter, divisive, and rancorous. The president had engineered an invasion of Iraq intending to overthrow the despotic regime of Saddam Hussein, a campaign that was successful. Unfortunately, brokering a lasting peace in Iraq proved difficult as militants initiated a deadly campaign of guerrilla warfare that resulted in the deaths of many innocent civilians as well as American and international forces of occupation. The frustration of the American people with the war, combined with disagreement over abortion rights, social security reform, immigration, foreign affairs, the war on terrorism, congressional relations, and budgetary problems, promised that the president's second term would be difficult.

George W. Bush Childhood Home

MIDLAND, TEXAS

A plain and unimposing house in Midland, Texas, was the home of two special people, each of whom would one day become President of the United States. From 1952 to 1956, however, it was merely the home of young oilman George Bush, wife Barbara, sons George and Jeb, and daughter Robin (Plate 16).

In 2006, Midland opened the little house on West Ohio Avenue as the George Bush Childhood Home, its mission being to represent the character of the state, the town, and the people who lived there, and to be a place where visitors may learn of the world in which this very special family lived and began its journey to achieve the American dream.

The house has been restored to the era of the 1950s when the Bush family was in residence. There are no Bush artifacts in the house, but Mrs. Jenna Welch, Laura Bush's mother, contributed a 1950s GE refrigerator. A visitor center and museum are in the planning stages although no date is set for completion.

DIRECTIONS: From I 20 eastbound or westbound in Midland, take SR 349 (Rankin Highway) north to Illinois Avenue. Turn left (westbound) onto Illinois Avenue, then right (north) onto North G Street and go one block to West Ohio Avenue. The Bush home is at 1412 West Ohio Avenue (Figure 144).

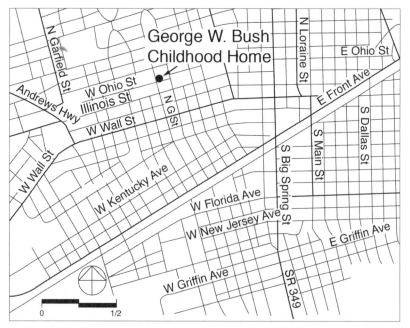

Figure 144. Location of George W. Bush Childhood Home, Midland, Texas.

PUBLIC USE: Season and hours: Tuesday-Saturday, 10 AM-5 PM; Sunday, 2 PM-5 PM. Closed Thanksgiving Day, Christmas Day, New Year's Day. **Admission fee. Gift shop. For people with disabilities:** Accessible.

FOR ADDITIONAL INFORMATION: Contact: George W. Bush Childhood Home, Box 8586, Midland, Texas 79708. (432)-685-1112). **Web site:** *www.bushchildhoodhome.org.* **Read:** George W. Bush. 2001. *A Charge to Keep: My Journey to the White House.*

The White House

WASHINGTON, DC

One of the enduring symbols of our government is the White House (Figure 145), home and office to our presidents since 1800. George Washington initiated and approved its design but never lived there. Washington was inaugurated in New York City, capital of the new United States before it was moved to Philadelphia and finally to Washington, DC. The executive office and mansion in New York was a three-story brick building at 3 Cherry Street, close to what is now the Manhattan foot of the Brooklyn Bridge. The private home of Robert Morris in Philadelphia, used as the temporary executive residence, was similar in design to the New York house. It was on High Street near Independence Hall. Unfortunately, neither of those early presidential homes has been saved.

In 1790, congress passed the Residency Act that authorized a house for congress and a house for the president as part of a "Grand Columbian Federal City" to be built "at some place on the Potomac between the mouth of the Eastern branch and the Conococheague." Thus was the District of Columbia conceived.

Major Pierre L'Enfant was commissioned to design the major government buildings, but was dismissed in 1792 when the design of the President's House was opened to an architectural competition that was won by Irish-born James Hoban, who based his winning entry on the Dublin home of the Duke of Leinster. The cornerstone was laid in 1792 by George Washington, but eight years passed before President John Adams moved into the still-unfinished house. Despite such inconveniences as inadequate firewood and lack of running water, Mrs. Adams somehow managed to make six rooms livable.

Figure 145. The White House, Washington, DC. Photograph courtesy of National Park Service.

Thomas Jefferson was the next occupant. Working with the designer Benjamin Latrobe, he effected many changes and improvements, as might be expected from an architectural tinkerer. The west colonnade facing the Rose Garden is a legacy of Jefferson's presidency. During the design competition years earlier, Jefferson had championed a red brick façade. If he had prevailed, we might be referring to the White House as the Brick House or the Red House — proving, perhaps, that Thomas Jefferson was fallible, after all. Instead, the house was made of stone; whitewashed in 1798, the nickname

"The White House" followed, even before it was torched by the British during the War of 1812. Most of the outer walls were preserved and the stone covered with white paint when the house was finally rebuilt. The appellation "White House" did not become the official name of the structure until the presidency of Theodore Roosevelt.

From Thomas Jefferson on, presidents have redecorated, personalized, restored, or expanded the White House, some more dramatically than others, but each leaving an imprint. Julia Gardiner Tyler used her own money to spruce up the house after Andrew Jackson's friends had left it tarnished. During Andrew Johnson's term, his daughter and hostess, Martha Patterson, supervised its refurbishing from post-Civil War shambles. President Taft, who desired more office space, installed the Oval Office. Rutherford B. Hayes, a man of wealth and good taste, redecorated extensively, but with an eye to enhancing tradition rather than eliminating it. On the other hand, Chester A. Arthur got rid of much of the house's historic furniture and hired Louis Comfort Tiffany to furnish the house in lavish Victorian style. With Franklin Roosevelt's presidency, the White House received an indoor swimming pool, wheelchair ramp, and its East and West wings.

The grounds of the White House, too, have undergone changes. The original sixty acres have grown smaller and more private while extensive conservatories have given way to smaller, decorative gardens.

Late in the 1940s, an engineering study discovered that the White House was structurally unsound — literally falling down — and a major renovation was initiated. Thus the White House arrived at its present form during the term of Harry Truman.

Seat of government, home to presidents, center of the free world — all have been used to describe the White House, the house that hosts more tourists than any other and the house that all Americans view with respect. Men battle to move into it but sometimes discover that living there may be less than rewarding. Harry Truman called it a "glamorous prison." Gerald Ford said that it was "the best public housing I've ever seen," and Mary Lincoln referred to it as "that white sepulcher." Most of its residents have decried the lack of privacy, one exception being Barbara Bush, who noted, ". . . and about those tourists . . . . We love them. George and I often walk the dogs down to the gate to chat with the people who come to see this beautiful place."

The White House has been home to newlyweds and old married folks, widowers, and one bachelor. Proposals, marriages, births, and christenings have taken place under its roof. It has known the experiences of Teddy Roosevelt's children roller-skating across the floor, the pillow fights of the Garfield boys, and the courtship of Lynda Johnson in the third-floor solarium. In short, the White House is little different from homes all across the nation, for it is the home — temporary and less private, perhaps — of a genuine American family. Home, too, to the dreams, aspirations, and faith of an entire nation of people. It is the president's home. And ours.

The White House is open to the public for tours, although some areas, such as the Oval Office and the family living quarters, are not accessible. Tours begin in the East Wing and proceed by the Library and the Vermeil Room, then up the staircase to the State Floor, where visitors may see the East Room, the Green Room, the Blue Room, the Red Room, the State Dining Room, and the Entrance Hall.

DIRECTIONS: The White House is on Pennsylvania Avenue, between 15th and 16th Streets. It is easily reached via the Metro subway system. It is a 3-block walk from the Farragut North, McPherson Square, and Metro Center stations, all stops on the Blue and Orange lines. Metro Center is also served by the Red Line (Figure 15).

PUBLIC USE: Season and hours: Tours of the White House are available for groups of ten or more people. Requests must be submitted through one's Member of Congress and are accepted up to six months in advance. These self-guided tours are available from 7:30 AM to 12:30 PM, Tuesday through Saturday (excluding federal holidays), and are scheduled on a first-come, first-served basis approximately one month in advance of the requested date. Visitors are encouraged to submit requests as early as possible since a limited number of tours are available. All tours are enhanced by visiting the recently opened White House Visitor Center at the southeast corner of 15th Street and "E" before or after their tour. The center, maintained by the National Park Service, is open seven days a week from 7:30 AM to 4 PM and features information on many aspects of the White House, including furnishings, first families and social events, plus a descriptive video. **Gift shop. For people with disabilities:** Fully accessible.

FOR ADDITIONAL INFORMATION: Contact: The White House, 1600 Pennsylvania Avenue, Washington, DC 20500. **Tour information:** (202) 456-7041. **Web site:** *www.whitehouse.gov.* **Read:** (1) William Seale. 1986. *The President's House: A History.* (2) William Seale. 1992. *The White House: The History of an American Idea.*

Section III

Additional Information about Presidential Sites

Birthplaces of the Presidents

George Washington: Popes Creek Plantation, Virginia. Open to the public.

John Adams: Braintree (now Quincy), Massachusetts. Open to the public.

Thomas Jefferson: Goochland County, Virginia. Historical marker.

James Madison: Port Conway, Virginia. Historical marker.

James Monroe: Westmoreland County, Virginia. Historical marker.

John Quincy Adams: Braintree (now Quincy), Massachusetts. Open to the public.

Andrew Jackson: The Waxhaws, South Carolina. Historical marker.

Martin Van Buren: Kinderhook, New York. Historical marker.

William Henry Harrison: Charles City, Virginia. Open to the public.

John Tyler: Charles City, Virginia. Historical marker.

James K. Polk: Pineville, North Carolina. Open to the public.

Zachary Taylor: Montebello, Virginia. Historical marker.

Millard Fillmore: Locke, New York. Historical marker.

Franklin Pierce: Hillsborough, New Hampshire. Open to the public.

James Buchanan: Cove Gap, Pennsylvania. Historical marker.

Abraham Lincoln: Hardin (now Larue) County, Kentucky. Open to the public.

Andrew Johnson: Raleigh, North Carolina. Open to the public.

Ulysses S. Grant: Point Pleasant, Ohio. Open to the public.

Rutherford B. Hayes: Delaware, Ohio. Historical marker.

James A. Garfield: Orange Township (now Moreland Hills), Ohio. Historical marker.

Chester A. Arthur: Fairfield, Vermont. Open to the public.

Grover Cleveland: Caldwell, New Jersey. Open to the public.

Benjamin Harrison: North Bend, Ohio. Historical marker.

William McKinley: Niles, Ohio. Historical marker.

Theodore Roosevelt: New York, New York. Open to the public.

William Howard Taft: Cincinnati, Ohio. Open to the public.

Woodrow Wilson: Staunton, Virginia. Open to the public.

Warren G. Harding: Blooming Grove, Ohio. Historical marker.

Calvin Coolidge: Plymouth Notch, Vermont. Open to the public.

Herbert Hoover: West Branch, Iowa. Open to the public.

Franklin D. Roosevelt: Hyde Park, New York. Open to the public.

Harry S Truman: Lamar, Missouri. Open to the public.

Dwight D. Eisenhower: Denison, Texas. Open to the public.

John F. Kennedy: Brookline, Massachusetts. Open to the public.

Lyndon B. Johnson: Stonewall, Texas. Open to the public.

Richard M. Nixon: Yorba Linda, California. Open to the public.

Gerald R. Ford: Omaha, Nebraska. Historical park.

Jimmy Carter: Plains, Georgia. Hospital. Not open to the public.

Ronald Reagan: Tampico, Illinois. Open to the public.

George H. W. Bush: Milton, Massachusetts. Private home. Not open to the public.

William J. Clinton: Hope, Arkansas. Historical marker.

George W. Bush: New Haven, Connecticut. Hospital. Not open to the public.

Burial Sites of the Presidents

George Washington: Mount Vernon, Virginia

John Adams: United First Parish Church, Quincy, Massachusetts

Thomas Jefferson: Monticello, Charlottesville, Virginia

James Madison: Montpelier, Montpelier, Virginia

James Monroe: Hollywood Cemetery, Richmond, Virginia

John Quincy Adams: United First Parish Church, Quincy, Massachusetts

Andrew Jackson: The Hermitage, Nashville, Tennessee

Martin Van Buren: Kinderhook Cemetery, Kinderhook, New York

William Henry Harrison: William Henry Harrison Memorial State Park, North Bend, Ohio

John Tyler: Hollywood Cemetery, Richmond, Virginia

James K. Polk: State Capitol Grounds, Nashville, Tennessee

Zachary Taylor: Family Graveyard, Louisville, Kentucky

Millard Fillmore: Forest Lawn Cemetery, Buffalo, New York

Franklin Pierce: Old North Cemetery, Concord, New Hampshire

James Buchanan: Woodward Hill Cemetery, Lancaster, Pennsylvania

Abraham Lincoln: Oak Ridge Cemetery, Springfield, Illinois

Andrew Johnson: Andrew Johnson National Cemetery, Greeneville, Tennessee

Ulysses S. Grant: Grant's Tomb, New York, New York

Rutherford B. Hayes: Hayes Presidential Center, Fremont, Ohio

James A. Garfield: Lakeview Cemetery, Cleveland, Ohio

Chester A. Arthur: Rural Cemetery, Albany, New York

Grover Cleveland: Old Princeton Cemetery, Princeton, New Jersey

Benjamin Harrison: Crown Hill Cemetery, Indianapolis, Indiana

William McKinley: McKinley Memorial, Canton, Ohio

Theodore Roosevelt: Young Memorial Cemetery, Oyster Bay, New York

William Howard Taft: Arlington National Cemetery, Arlington, Virginia

Woodrow Wilson: National Cathedral, Washington, DC

Warren G. Harding: Harding Memorial, Marion, Ohio

Calvin Coolidge: Plymouth Cemetery, Plymouth, Vermont

Herbert Hoover: Herbert Hoover National Historic Site, West Branch, Iowa

Franklin D. Roosevelt: The Rose Garden, Home of Franklin D. Roosevelt National Historic Site, Hyde Park, New York

Harry S Truman: Truman Presidential Museum and Library, Independence, Missouri

Dwight D. Eisenhower: "Place of Meditation," Eisenhower Center, Abilene, Kansas

John F. Kennedy: Arlington National Cemetery, Arlington, Virginia

Lyndon B. Johnson: Johnson State and National Historical Parks, Stonewall, Texas

Richard M. Nixon: Richard Nixon Presidential Library and Museum, Yorba Linda, California

Gerald R. Ford: Gerald R. Ford Presidential Museum, Grand Rapids, Michigan

Ronald Reagan: Ronald Reagan Presidential Library and Museum, Simi Valley, California

Foundations and Associations

There are a number of nonprofit foundations and other organizations devoted to the study of the presidents, the perpetuation of their heritage, the celebration of their accomplishments, or the maintenance of their homes, libraries, and museums. These are membership groups that welcome newcomers whose contributions and membership fees may be tax-deductible. Almost all issue informative publications and conduct a variety of educational programs.

The American Architectural
Foundation
The Octagon Museum
1799 New York Avenue, NW
Washington, DC 20006
(202) 626-7318
Web site:
www.archfoundation.com

The Colonial Williamsburg
Foundation
Box 1776
Williamsburg, Virginia 23187
(800) HISTORY
Web site:
www.colonialwilliamsburg.org

National Parks Conservation
Association
1300 19th Street, NW, Suite 300
Washington, DC 20036
(800) 628-7275
Web site: *www.npca.org*

National Park Foundation
11 Dupont Circle, NW
Washington, DC 20036
(202) 238-4200
Web site:
www.nationalparks.org/npf

National Park Trust
415 2nd Street, NW, Suite 210
Washington, DC 20002
(202) 548-0595
Web site: *www.parktrust.org*

The National Trust for Historic
Preservation
1785 Massachusetts Avenue, NW
Washington, DC 20036
(202) 588-6000
Web site: *www.nthp.org*

Friends of Mount Vernon
c/o Mount Vernon Ladies'
Association
Mount Vernon, Virginia 22121
(703) 780-2000
Web site:
www.mountvernon.org

Adams Memorial Society
Adams National Historic Site
1250 Hancock Street
Quincy, Massachusetts 02269
(617) 773-1177
Web site: *www.nps.gov/adam*

Thomas Jefferson Memorial
Foundation
Monticello
Box 316
Charlottesville, Virginia 22902
(804) 977-7380
Web site: *www.monticello.org*

Friends of Thomas Jefferson's
Poplar Forest
Box 419
Forest, Virginia 24551-0419
(434) 525-1806
Web site: *www.poplarforest.org*

Montpelier Foundation
Montpelier
11407 Constitution Highway
Montpelier Station, Virginia
22957
(540) 672-2728
Web site: *www.montpelier.org*

James Madison Memorial
Foundation
129 Caroline Street
Orange, Virginia 22960
(540) 672-1776
Web site:
www.jamesmadisonmuseum.org

Friends of Ash Lawn-Highland
1000 James Monroe Parkway
Charlottesville, Virginia 22902
(434) 293-9539
Web site:
www.ashlawnhighland.org

James Monroe Foundation
908 ½ Charles Street
Fredericksburg, Virginia 22401
(804) 231-1827
Web site:
www.monroefoundation.org

Friends of the Hermitage
Ladies' Hermitage Association
4580 Rachels Lane
Hermitage, Tennessee 37076-
1334
(615) 889-2941
Web site:
www.thehermitage.com

Friends of Lindenwald
1013 Old Post Road
Kinderhook, New York 12106
(518) 758-9689
Web site: *www.nps.gov/mava*

James K. Polk Memorial
Association
Box 741
Columbia, Tennessee 38402
(931) 388-2354
Web site: *www.jameskpolk.com*

The Pierce Brigade
Box 425
Concord, New Hampshire 03301
(603) 225-4555
Web site: *ww.piercemanse.org/*
about/pierce_brigade.htm

The James Buchanan Foundation
1120 Marietta Avenue
Lancaster, Pennsylvania 17603
(717) 392-8721
Web site: *www.wheatland.org*

New Salem Lincoln League
Box 272
Petersburg, Illinois 62675
(217) 632-4000
Web site:
*www.lincolnsnewsalem.com/
league.html*

The Lincoln Memorial Association
The Lincoln Shrine
125 W. Vine Street
Redlands, California 92373
(909) 798-7632
Web site:
www.lincolnshrine.org

Abraham Lincoln Association
1 Old State Capitol Plaza
Springfield, Illinois 62701
(866) 865-8500
Web site: *www.abrahamlincoln
association.org/contact.htm*

**Friends of the Abraham Lincoln
Library and Museum**
Lincoln Memorial University
Harrogate, Tennessee 37752
(423) 869-6235
Web site: *www.lmunet.edu/
museum*

**The Friends of the Ulysses S. Grant
Cottage**
Box 990
Saratoga Springs, New York !2866
(518) 587-8277
Web site:
www.nysparks.state.ny.us

The Ulysses S. Grant Association
Morris Library
Southern Illinois University
Carbondale, Illinois 62901
(618) 453-2773
Web site: *www.lib.siu.edu/
projects/usgrant*

**Rutherford B. Hayes Presidential
Center**
Spiegel Grove
Fremont, Ohio 43420
(800) 998-7737
Web site: *www.rbhayes.org*

**Western Reserve Historical Society
(Lawnfield)**
10825 East Boulevard
Cleveland, Ohio 44106
(216) 721-5722
Web site: *www.wrhs.org*

**President Benjamin Harrison
Foundation**
1230 North Delaware Street
Indianapolis, Indiana 46202
(317) 631-1888
Web site:
www.presidentbenjaminharrison.org

**Wm McKinley Presidential Library
and Museum**
Stark County Historical Society
800 McKinley Monument Drive
NW
Canton, Ohio 44708
(330) 455-7043
Web site:
www.mckinleymuseum.org

Theodore Roosevelt Association
Box 719
Oyster Bay, New York 11771
(516) 921-6319
Web site:
www.theodoreroosevelt.org

Edith and Theodore Roosevelt Pine Knot Foundation
Box 213
Keene, Virginia 22946
(434) 286-6106
Web site: *www.pineknot.org*

Friends of the William Howard Taft Birthplace
2038 Auburn Avenue
Cincinnati, Ohio 45219-3050
(513) 684-3262
Web site: *www.nps.gov/wiho*

Friends of Wilson House
2340 S Street, NW
Washington, DC 20008
(202) 387-4062
Web site:
www.woodrowwilsonhouse.org

Historic Augusta, Inc.
Woodrow Wilson Boyhood Home
111 10th Street, Box 37
Augusta, Georgia 30903
(706) 724-0436

Historic Columbia Foundation
Wilson Family Home
1601 Richland Street
Columbia, South Carolina 29201
(803) 252-7742
Web site:
www.historiccolumbia.org

The Woodrow Wilson Birthplace Foundation
18–24 Coalter Street
Staunton, Virginia 24402
(540) 885-0897
Web site:
www.woodrowwilson.org

Calvin Coolidge Memorial Foundation, Inc.
P. O. Box 97
Plymouth, Vermont 05056
(802) 672-3389
Web site: *www.calvin-coolidge.org*

Herbert Hoover Presidential Library Association
Box 696
West Branch, Iowa 52358-0696
(319) 643-5327
Web site: *www.nps.gov/heho*

Franklin and Eleanor Roosevelt Institute
4079 Albany Post Road
Hyde Park, New York 12538
(845) 486-1150
Web site: *www.feri.org*

Harry S. Truman Institute
US Hwy 24 and Delaware Street
Independence, Missouri 64050
(816) 833-1400
Web site:
www.trumanlibrary.org

Eisenhower Foundation
The Eisenhower Center
200 Southeast Fourth Street
Abilene, Kansas 67410
(785) 263-4751
Web site:
www.eisenhower.utexas.edu

The John F. Kennedy Presidential Library Foundation
Columbia Point
Boston, Massachusetts 02125
(617) 514-1600
Web site: *www.jfklibrary.org*

LBJ Foundation
LBJ Library and Museum
2313 Red River Street
Austin, Texas 78705
(512) 916-5137
Web site: *www.lbjlib.utexas.edu*

The Nixon Library Associates' Club
Richard Nixon Presidential Library and Museum
18001 Yorba Linda Boulevard
Yorba Linda, California 92886
(714) 993-5075
Web site: *www.nixonlibrary.org*

The Gerald Ford Foundation
Gerald R. Ford Library
1000 Beal Avenue
Ann Arbor, Michigan 48109
(734) 741-2218
Web site: *www.ford.utexas.edu*

Carter Presidential Center
441 Freedom Parkway
Atlanta, Georgia 30307
(404) 331-3942
Web site:
www.jimmycarterlibrary.org

The Ronald Reagan Foundation
Reagan Presidential Library and
    Museum
40 Presidential Drive
Simi Valley, California 93065
(805) 522-8444
Web site:
www.reagan.utexas.edu

Ronald Reagan Home Preservation Foundation
816 South Hennepin Avenue
Dixon, Illinois 61021
(815) 288-3404
Web site: *www.dixonil.com*

George Bush Presidential Library Foundation
1000 George Bush Drive West
College Station, Texas 77845
(979) 260-9552
Web site: *http:// bushlibrary.tamu.edu*

William J. Clinton Presidential Foundation
1200 President Clinton Avenue
Little Rock, Arkansas 72201
(501) 370-8000
Web site:
www.clintonpresidentalcenter.com

George W. Bush Childhood Home, Inc.
Box 8586
Midland, Texas 79708
(432) 685-1112
Web site:
www.bushchildhoodhome.org

Bibliography

Ackerman, Ken. 2003. *Dark Horse*. New York: Avalon Publishing Group.

Ambrose, Stephen E. 1987. *Nixon*. 3 volumes. New York: Simon and Schuster.

_____. 1990. *Eisenhower: Soldier and President*. New York: Simon and Schuster.

Ammon, Harry. 1991. *James Monroe: The Quest for National Identity*. Charlottesville: University Press of Virginia.

Andersen, Christopher. 1999. *Bill and Hillary: The Marriage*. New York. William Morrow and Co.

Anderson, Judith Icke. 1981. *William Howard Taft: An Intimate History*. New York: Norton.

Anonymous. 1990. "McKinley Birthplace Memorial." *Ohio Libraries* July/August: 12.

Anthony, Carl Sferrazza, ed. 2003. *The National First Ladies' Library and the Importance of First Lady History*. Canton: The National First Ladies' Library.

Antiques Magazine. 1989. (The issue for February is devoted to Mount Vernon.)

Antiques Magazine. 1993. (The issue for July is devoted to Jefferson, Monticello, and Poplar Forest.)

Ash Lawn-Highland. 1999. *Ash Lawn-Highland: A Guide*. Williamsburg: The College of William and Mary.

Bartlett's Familiar Quotations. 15th ed. 1980. Boston: Little, Brown.

Bauer, K. Jack. 1985. *Zachary Taylor: Soldier, Planter, Statesman of the Old Southwest*. Baton Rouge and London: Louisiana State University Press.

Beale, Marie. 1954. *Decatur House and its Inhabitants*. Washington, DC: National Trust for Historic Preservation.

Bergere, Richard, and Thea Bergere. 1962. *Homes of the Presidents*. New York: Dodd, Mead.

Bergeron, Paul H. 1987. *The Presidency of James K. Polk*. Topeka: University Press of Kansas.

Betts, Edwin M., and Hazelhurst Bolton Perkins. 1986. *Thomas Jefferson's Flower Garden at Monticello*. 3rd ed. Charlottesville: Monticello.

Black, Laura. 1990. "Texas Remembers Ike." *Texas Highways Magazine* October: 16.

Boas, Norman S. 1983. *The Pierce-Aiken Papers.* Stonington: Seaport Autographs.

Boller, Paul F., Jr. 1988. *Presidential Wives.* New York: Oxford University Press.

Bowling, Kenneth R. 1988. *Creating the Federal City, 1774–1800: Potomac Fever.* Washington, DC: AIA Press.

Bragdon, Henry. 1967. *Woodrow Wilson: The Academic Years.* Cambridge: Belknap Press of Harvard University Press.

Brant, Irving. 1942–1962. *James Madison.* 6 volumes. Indianapolis: Bobbs-Merrill.

Brinkley, Douglas. 1999. *The Unfinished Presidency: Jimmy Carter's Journey Beyond the White House.* New York: Viking Penguin.

Brooks, Chester L., and Ray H. Matison. 1983. *Theodore Roosevelt and the Dakota Badlands.* Medora: Theodore Roosevelt Nature and History Association.

Brown, Katherine L. 1991. *The Woodrow Wilson Birthplace.* 2nd edition. Staunton: Woodrow Wilson Birthplace Foundation, Inc.

Brownstein, Elizabeth. 2005. *Lincoln's Other White House.* New York: John Wiley & Sons.

Bullock, Helen Duprey. 1967. *Decatur House.* Washington, DC: National Trust for Historic Preservation.

Burgess, Larry. 1981. *The Lincoln Memorial Shrine Genesis: Prelude to the Golden Jubilee.* Redlands: Lincoln Memorial Shrine.

_____. 1982. *The Lincoln Memorial Shrine Golden Jubilee: History Looking to the Future.* Redlands: Lincoln Memorial Shrine.

Burner, David. 1979. *Herbert Hoover: A Public Life.* New York: Alfred A. Knopf.

Bush, George W. 2001. *A Charge to Keep: My Journey to the White House.* New York: HarperTrade Books.

Butler, Joseph G. 1924. *Life of William McKinley and History of the National McKinley Birthplace Memorial.* Self published.

Cahalan, Sally Smith. 1988. *James Buchanan's Wheatland.* Lancaster: The James Buchanan Foundation.

_____. 1989. *At Home with James Buchanan.* Pennsylvania: Science Press.

Calhoun, Charles W. 2005. *Benjamin Harrison.* American Presidents Series, Arthur M. Schlesinger, Jr., General Editor. New York: Time-Life Books, Henry Holt.

Campbell, Thomas A., Jr. 1979. "The U. S. Grant Home State Historic Site." *Historic Illinois* 1 (5: February): 1–4.

Cannon, Lou. 1991. *President Reagan: The Role of a Lifetime.* New York: Simon and Schuster.

Carls, Glen E., and Gwendolyn A. Gardner. 1986. *Cultural Landscape Report, Lyndon B. Johnson National Historical Park.* College Station: Texas A&M University.

Caro, Robert A. 2002. *The Years of Lyndon Baines Johnson: Master of the Senate.* New York: Knopf.

Carson, Barbara G. 1990. *Ambitious Appetites.* Washington, DC: AIA Press.

Carter, Jimmy. 1975. *Why Not the Best?* Nashville: Broadman Press.

_____. 1988. *An Outdoor Journal.* New York: Bantam Books.

_____. 1992. *Turning Point.* New York: Times Books, Division of Random House.

_____. 2001. *An Hour Before Daylight; Memories of a Rural Boyhood.* New York: Simon and Schuster.

Chambers, Allen S., Jr. 1933. *Poplar Forest and Thomas Jefferson.* Lynchburg: The Corporation for Jefferson's Poplar Forest.

Chitwood, O. P. 1990. *John Tyler: Champion of the Old South.* Newton: American Political Biography Press.

Clinton, Bill. 2004. *My Life.* New York: Knopf.

Christianson, A. M. 1955. "The Roosevelt Cabin." *North Dakota History* 22 (July): 117–119.

Cleaves, Freeman. 1990. *Old Tippecanoe: William Henry Harrison and His Times.* Newton: American Political Biography Press.

Cole, Donald. 2004. *Martin Van Buren and the American Political System.* Princeton: Princeton University Press.

Cook, Don. 1995. *The Long Fuse: How England Lost the American Colonies, 1760–1785.* New York: The Atlantic Monthly Press.

Cooke, Alistair. 1973. *Alistair Cooke's America.* New York: Alfred A. Knopf.

Coolidge, Calvin. 1929. *The Autobiography of Calvin Coolidge.* New York: Cosmopolitan Book Corporation.

Coski, John. 1989. *The Army of the Potomac at Berkeley Plantation: The Harrison's Landing Occupation of 1862.* Self published.

Curtis, Jane, Will Curtis, and Frank Lieberman. 1985. *Return to These Hills: Calvin Coolidge in Vermont.* Woodstock: Lieberman Books.

Cutler, Wayne, ed. 1986. *North for Union: John Appleton's Journal of a Tour to New England made by President Polk in June and July, 1847.* Nashville: Vanderbilt University Press.

Dallek, Robert. 1991. *Lone Star Rising.* New York: Oxford University Press.

_____. 1998. *Flawed Giant.* New York: Oxford University Press.

Daniels, Jonathan. 1950. *The Man of Independence.* Philadelphia: J. B. Lippincott Company.

Davenport, Don. 1991. *In Lincoln's Footsteps: A Historical Guide to the Lincoln Sites in Illinois, Indiana, and Kentucky.* Madison: Prairie Oak Press.

Davis, Kenneth S. 1945. *Soldier of Democracy: A Biography of Dwight Eisenhower.* Garden City: Doubleday.

Davis, William, and Christina Tree. 1980. *The Kennedy Library.* Exton: Schiffer Publishing Co.

De Costa, Beverly, ed. 1971. *Historic Houses of America.* New York: Forbes Custom Publishing.

Durant, John, and Alice Durant. 1978. *Pictorial History of American Presidents.* New York: A. S. Barnes and Company.

DeGregorio, William A. 1984. *The Complete Book of US Presidents.* New York: Dembner Books.

Dermody, Larry. 1992. "Fire and Ice: Col. Madison's Ironworks, 1762 to 1801." The Society for Historical Archaeology 1992 meetings, January, Kingston, Jamaica. (Manuscript on file in the research center, Montpelier.)

Donald, David Herbert. 1996. *Lincoln.* New York: Simon and Schuster, Inc.

Dowdey, Clifford. 1957. *The Great Plantation.* Charles City: Berkeley Plantation.

Downes, Randolph. 1970. *The Rise of Warren Gamaliel Harding, 1865–1920.* Columbus: Ohio State University Press.

Edwards, Anne. 1987. *Early Reagan.* New York: Morrow.

Eisenhower, Dwight D. 1967. *At Ease: Stories I Tell to Friends.* New York: Doubleday.

Elder, Betty D. 1980. *A Special House.* Columbia: James K. Polk Memorial Association.

Fanta, J. Julius. 1968. *Sailing with President Kennedy, the White House Yachtsman.* New York: Sea Lore.

Ferrell, Robert. 1991. *Harry S. Truman: His Life on the Family Farms.* Worland: High Plains Publishing Company.

_____. 1998. *The Strange Deaths of President Harding.* Columbia: University of Missouri Press.

Freeman, Douglas Southall. 1948–1952. *George Washington.* 6 volumes. New York: Charles Scribner's Sons. (Volume 7 edited posthumously by J. A. Carroll and M. W. Ashworth.)

Ford, Gerald R. 1979. *A Time to Heal.* New York: Harper and Row.

Gable, John A. 1977. *Sagamore Hill: A Historic Guide.* Oyster Bay: Theodore Roosevelt Association.

Gallagher, Hugh Gregory. 1985. *FDR's Splendid Deception.* New York: Dodd, Mead.

Gara, Larry. 1991. *The Presidency of Franklin Pierce.* Lawrence: University Press of Kansas.

Gardiner, Stephen. 1983. *Inside Architecture.* Englewood Cliffs: Prentice-Hall, Inc.

Garrett, Wendell, ed. 1998. *George Washington's Mount Vernon.* New York: Montacelli Press.

Geselbracht, Raymond H. 1991. *Guide to Historical Materials in the Harry S. Truman Library.* Independence: Harry S. Truman Library.

Gleason, David K. 1989. *Virginia Plantation Homes.* Baton Rouge: Louisiana State University Press.

Goodwin, Doris Kearns. 2005. *Team of Rivals: The Political Genius of Abraham Lincoln.* New York: Simon and Schuster.

Grant, Julia Dent. 1975. *The Personal Memoirs of Julia Dent Grant.* New York: Putnam.

Grant, U. S. 1885. *Personal Memoirs of U. S. Grant.* 2 volumes. New York: Charles L. Webster and Company.

Green, Fitzhugh. 1989. *George Bush: An Intimate Portrait.* New York: Hippocrene Books.

Green, J. R. 1997. *Calvin Coolidge's Plymouth, Vermont.* Dover: Arcadia Publishing.

Greer, Emily A. 1984. *First Lady: The Life of Lucy Webb Hayes.* Fremont: Kent State University Press and the Rutherford B. Hayes Presidential Center.

Haas, Irvin. 1991. *Historic Homes of the American Presidents.* 2nd revised edition. New York: Dover Publications.

Hagedorn, Hermann. 1953. *A Guide to Sagamore Hill.* New York: Theodore Roosevelt Association.

_____. 1954. *The Roosevelt Family of Sagamore Hill.* New York: The Macmillan Company.

_____. 1987. *Roosevelt in the Badlands.* Medora: Theodore Roosevelt Nature and History Association.

Hamby, Alonzo. 1995. *Man of the People.* New York: Oxford University Press.

Hamke, Loretha. 1985. *All about William Henry Harrison.* 2nd edition. Vincennes: Grouseland.

Harbaugh, William. 1993. *The Theodore Roosevelts' Retreat in Southern Albemarle: Pine Knot 1905–1908.* Charlottesville: Albemarle County Historical Society, Inc.

Hargrove, Edwin C. 1988. *Jimmy Carter as President: Leadership and Public Good.* Baton Rouge: Louisiana State University Press.

Harris, John, and Jill Lever. 1979. *Illustrated Glossary of Architecture, 850–1830.* New York: Faber and Faber, Inc.

Harris, Wilhelmina S. 1983. *A Family's Legacy to America.* Washington, DC: National Park Service.

Hatch, Charles E. 1979. *Popes Creek Plantation.* Washingtons Birthplace: Wakefield Memorial Association.

Heald, Edward T. 1992. *The Condensed Biography of William McKinley.* Canton: Stark County Historical Society.

Hecht, Marie B. 1972. *John Quincy Adams.* New York: The Macmillan Company.

Heckscher, August. 1985. "Historic Houses: Campobello." *Architectural Digest.* March: 220-228.

_____. 1991. *Woodrow Wilson.* New York: Simon and Schuster.

Holzer, Harold, and Mark E. Neely, Jr. 1960. *The Lincoln Family Album.* New York: Doubleday.

Hoogenboom, Ari. 1988. *The Presidency of Rutherford B. Hayes.* Lawrence: University Press of Kansas.

_____. 1995. *Rutherford B. Hayes: Warrior and President.* Lawrence: University Press of Kansas.

Hoover, Herbert. 1931. *A Boyhood in Iowa.* New York: Aventine Press.

_____1951–1952. *The Memoirs of Herbert Hoover.* 3 volumes. New York: Macmillan

Horn, Joan. 2002. *Thomas Jefferson's Poplar Forest; A Private Place.* Lynchburg: Thomas Jefferson's Poplar Forest.

Horn, Stanley. 1976. *The Hermitage.* Nashville: Ladies' Hermitage Association.

Hosler, Joseph. 1992. "A Shrine in the Golden State." *Civil War Times* 31 (2: May): 20–24, 64.

Howe, George Frederick. 1934. *Chester A. Arthur: A Quarter Century of Machine Politics.* New York: Dodd, Mead.

Hudson, Patricia L. 1990. "Old Hickory's House." *Americana* 17 (6): 32–38.

Hunt, Conover. 1989. *JFK for a New Generation.* Dallas: SMU Press and the Sixth Floor Museum.

Information Please Almanac. 1992. Boston: Houghton Mifflin.

Jones, Cranston. 1962. *Homes of the American Presidents.* New York: McGraw-Hill.

Katz, Herbert, and Marjorie Katz. 1965. *Museums, USA: A History and Guide.* New York: Doubleday.

Kelley, Virginia C. C., with James Morgan. 1994. *Leading with My Heart.* New York: Simon and Schuster.

Kenney, Christopher. 2006. *The McKinley Monument: A Tribute to a Fallen President*. Charleston: History Press.

Kern, Ellyn R. 1962. *Where the American Presidents Lived*. Indianapolis: Cottontail Publications.

Ketcham, Ralph. 1990. *James Madison: A Biography.* Charlottesville: University Press of Virginia.

King, Nicolas. 1980. *George Bush: A Biography.* New York: Dodd, Mead.

Klein, Jonas. 2000. *Franklin and Eleanor and the Legacy of Campobello*. New York: Paul S. Eriksson.

Klein, Philip Shriver. 1962. *President James Buchanan.* Lancaster: The James Buchanan Foundation.

_____1967. "Bachelor Father — James Buchanan as a Family Man." *Western Pennsylvania Historical Magazine* 50 (July): 199–224.

_____2003. *The Story of Wheatland*. Lancaster: Art Printing Company of Lancaster, Inc.

Kochman, Rachel. 1990. *President's Birthplaces, Homes and Burial Places.* 7th revised edition. Osage: Osage Publications.

Kruh, David, and Louis Kruh. 1992. *Presidential Landmarks.* New York: Hippocrene Books.

Krusen, Jessie T. 1976. *Tuckahoe Plantation.* Richmond: Whittet and Shepperson.

Kunhardt, Dorothy Meserve, and Philip Kunhardt, Jr. 1985. *Twenty Days.* New Hollywood: Newcastle Publishing Co.

Langston-Harrison, Lee. 1992. *Images of a President: Portraits of James Monroe.* Fredericksburg: The James Monroe Museum.

Lash, Joseph P. 1971. *Eleanor and Franklin.* New York: Norton.

Lawing, Hugh. 1962. "Andrew Johnson National Historic Site." *Tennessee Historical Quarterly* 20: 103–109.

Leech, Margaret. 1941. *Reveille in Washington.* New York: Harper and Row.

Leepson, Marc. 2001. *Saving Monticello: The Levy Family's Epic Quest to Rescue the House that Jefferson Built.* New York: Free Press.

The Lincoln Newsletter. Lincoln: Lincoln College Museum.

McLeRoy, Sherrie S. 1989. "Ike's Birthplace: Our 34th President Came from Humble Beginnings." *Texas Parks and Wildlife Magazine* 47 (1:January): 34–37.

Malone, Dumas. 1948–1981. *Jefferson and His Time.* 6 volumes. Boston: Little, Brown.

Marchman, Watt P. 1988. *The Story of a President: Rutherford B. Hayes and Spiegel Grove.* Fremont: Rutherford B. Hayes Presidential Center.

Mares, Franklin D., and Richard Cheek. 1993. *Springwood*. Hyde Park: Hyde Park Historical Association.

McAlester, Virginia, and Lee McAlester. 1984. *A Field Guide to American Homes*. New York: Alfred A. Knopf.

McCoy, Donald R. 1967. *Calvin Coolidge: The Quiet President*. New York: Macmillan.

McCullough, David. 1992. *Brave Companions*. New York: Prentice-Hall.

_____. 1992. *Truman*. New York: Simon and Schuster.

_____. 2001. *John Adams*. New York: Simon and Schuster.

_____. 2005. *1776*. New York. Simon and Schuster.

McElroy, Richard L. 1996. *William McKinley and Our America*. Canton: Stark County Historical Society.

McFeely, William S. 1981. *Grant: A Biography*. New York: Norton.

McKee, Larry. 1992. "Reinterpreting the Construction History of the Service Area of the Hermitage Mansion." Pp. 161–176 in *Text-Aided Archaeology*, ed. Barbara J. Little. Boca Raton, Ann Arbor, London: CRC Press, Inc.

McLaughlin, Jack. 1988. *Jefferson and Monticello: The Biography of a Builder*. New York: Henry Holt.

Merk, Frederick. 1971. *Fruits of Propaganda in the Tyler Administration*. Cambridge: Harvard University Press.

Miller, Ann L. 1990. "Historic Structure Report — Montpelier, Orange County, Virginia: Phase II: Documentary Evidence Regarding the Montpelier House 1723–1983." (Manuscript on file in the research center, Montpelier.)

Miller, Walter, and Bill Gaetner. 1994. *Lincoln Lived Here*. Williamsburg: Bicast Publishing Company.

Minutaglio, Bill. 1999. *First Son: George W. Bush and the Bush Family Dynasty*. New York: Crown.

Monroe, James. 1959. *The Autobiography of James Monroe*. Syracuse: Syracuse University Press.

Morgan, H. Wayne. 1963. *William McKinley and His America*. Syracuse: Syracuse University Press.

Morgan, Ted. 1968. *FDR: A Biography*. New York: Simon and Schuster.

Moritz, Charles, ed. 1988. *Current Biography Yearbook*. New York: H. W. Wilson Company.

Morris, Edmund. 1979. *The Rise of Theodore Roosevelt*. New York: Coward, McCann and Geoghegan.

_____. 2001. *Theodore Rex*. New York: Random House.

Morris, Roger. 1996. *Partners in Power: The Clintons and Their America.* New York: Henry Holt.

Morris, Sylvia Jukes. 1980. *Edith Kermit Roosevelt, Portrait of a First Lady.* New York: Penguin.

Murray, Robert K. 1969. *The Harding Era.* Minneapolis: University of Minnesota Press.

Nagel, Paul. 1983. *Descent from Glory: Four Generations of the John Adams Family.* New York: Oxford University Press.

_____. 1991. *Ford's Theatre and the House Where Lincoln Died* (brochure). Washington, DC: National Park Service.

National Park Service, Department of the Interior. 1985. *The Complete Guide to America's National Parks (1884–1985).* New York: Viking Press.

Nichols, Roy. 1958. *Franklin Pierce: Young Hickory of the Granite Hills.* Philadelphia: University of Pennsylvania Press.

Nisenson, Samuel, and Alfred Parker. 1931. *Minute Biographies.* New York: Grosset and Dunlap.

Niven, John. 1983. *Martin Van Buren, The Romantic Age of American Politics.* New York: Oxford University Press.

Nixon, Richard. 1979. *The Memoirs of Richard Nixon.* New York: Grosset and Dunlap.

_____. 1990. *Richard Nixon in the Arena: A Memoir of Victory, Defeat, and Renewal.* New York: Simon and Schuster.

O'Connell, Kim A. 2008. "New directions for the old retreat." *Preservation* 60 (1): 26–31.

Official Museum Directory. 1989. New York: Macmillan.

Owens, Kenneth N. 1963. *Galena, Grant and the Fortunes of War: A History of Galena, Illinois during the Civil War.* DeKalb: Northern Illinois University in cooperation with the Galena Historical Society.

Parks, Arva Moore. 1991. *Harry Truman and the Little White House in Key West.* Miami: Centennial Press.

Peskin, Allan. 1978. *Garfield.* Kent: The Kent State University Press.

Petz, Weldon. 1973. *In the Presence of Lincoln.* Harrogate: Lincoln Memorial University Press.

Phillips, Steven J. 1989. *Old House Dictionary.* Lakewood: American Source Book.

Pinsker, Matthew. 2003. *Lincoln's Sanctuary: Abraham Lincoln and the Soldiers' Home.* New York: Oxford University Press.

Pitkin, Thomas M. 1973. *The Captain Departs: Ulysses S. Grant's Last Campaign.* Carbondale: Southern Illinois University Press.

Pratt, Dorothy, and Richard Pratt. 1956. *A Guide to Early American Homes, North.* New York: McGraw-Hill.

_____. 1956. *A Guide to Early American Homes, South.* New York: McGraw-Hill.

Preston, Daniel. 2000. *The Presidency of James Monroe.* Charlottesville: Ash Lawn-Highland.

_____. 2001. *The Life of James Monroe.* Charlottesville: Ash Lawn-Highland.

Pringle, Henry Fowles. 1939. *The Life and Times of William Howard Taft.* New York: Farrar and Rinehart.

Rayback, Robert J. 1959. *Millard Fillmore.* Buffalo: Buffalo Historical Society.

Reagan, Ronald. 1990. *An American Life.* New York: Simon and Schuster.

Reeves, Thomas. 1975. *Gentleman Boss: The Life of Chester Alan Arthur.* New York: Alfred A. Knopf.

Remini, Robert. 1998. *Andrew Jackson.* 3 volumes. Baltimore: Johns Hopkins University Press.

Rideout, Orlando V. 1989. *Building the Octagon.* Washington, DC: AIA Press.

Roberts, Bruce. 1990. *Plantation Homes of the James River.* Chapel Hill: University of North Carolina Press.

Roosevelt, Theodore. 1913. *The Autobiography of Theodore Roosevelt.* New York: Scribner's.

Ross, Ishbel. 1964. *An American Family: The Tafts.* Cleveland: World Publishing.

Rothman, Hal K. 2001. *Our Heart's Home.* College Station: Texas A&M University Press.

Rouse, Parke, Jr., and Susan Burtch. 1980. *Berkeley Plantation and Hundred.* Williamsburg: Williamsburg Publishing Company.

Sale, Edith. 1927. *Interiors of Virginia Houses of Colonial Times.* Richmond: Wm. Byrd Press.

Scarry, Robert. 1993. *Millard Fillmore: Thirteenth President of the United States.* Moravia: Self published.

Schewe, Donald B. 1989. "Establishing a Presidential Library: The Jimmy Carter Experience." *Prologue* Summer: 101, 125–133.

Schlesinger, Arthur M., Jr. 1953. *The Age of Jackson.* Boston: Little, Brown.

_____. 1965. *A Thousand Days: John F. Kennedy in the White House.* Cambridge: Houghton Mifflin.